More Praise for
GOD OF THE RODEO

"*God of the Rodeo* is an eloquent and moving book that takes us into the nooks and crannies of one of America's most brutal prisons. Bergner's perception and documentation of the convict mentality is acute and compassionate at once, and he wrestles no-holds-barred with a warden who wants everyone to believe, not just in God, but in the warden, too, as beneficent patriarch. If you want to know what it's like inside, read this book."

KIM WOZENCRAFT, author of *Rush*

"If you've ever thought that parts of contemporary America closely resemble the Old South, *God of the Rodeo* gives new proof. Daniel Bergner pulls back the barbed-wired curtain on Angola, Louisiana's farm-prison on the Mississippi, to reveal a place much like the slave plantations of old. Here is a stunted world presided over by Warden Burl Cain, a modern master who is half evangelist, half despot. Under his watch, prison life ebbs away in a cycle of futile work, self-improvement, and fleeting salvation."

EDWARD BALL, author of *Slaves in the Family*

"This is a book about much more than riding broncos. It is about some of the people caught up in one of the fastest growing enterprises in America: the prison-industrial complex; the traffic in human lives. And it tells the story of a master manipulator, Warden Burl Cain, whose pious posturing Bergner boldly unmasks. It is a courageous and important work."

RICHARD STRATTON,
former editor and publisher of *Prison Life* magazine

"In *God of the Rodeo*, Daniel Bergner brilliantly leads us through one of the darkest corners of the American landscape—the storied and notorious Louisiana prison known as Angola. It is a moving, unforgettable journey."

DAVID M. OSHINSKY,
author of *"Worse than Slavery": Parchman Farm and the Ordeal of Jim Crow Justice* and Professor of History at Rutgers University

GOD

OF THE

RODEO

THE SEARCH FOR HOPE, FAITH,

AND A SIX-SECOND RIDE IN

LOUISIANA'S ANGOLA PRISON

DANIEL BERGNER

Crown Publishers, Inc.
NEW YORK

Parts of this book originally appeared, in somewhat different form, in *Harper's* magazine.

Copyright © 1998 by Daniel Bergner

Published by Crown Publishers, Inc., 201 East 50th Street, New York, New York 10022. Member of the Crown Publishing Group.

Random House, Inc. New York, Toronto, London, Sydney, Auckland
www.randomhouse.com

CROWN and colophon are trademarks of Crown Publishers, Inc.

Printed in the United States of America

Design by LYNNE AMFT

Library of Congress Cataloging-in-Publication Data

Bergner, Daniel.
God of the rodeo: the search for hope, faith, and a six-second ride in Louisiana's Angola Prison / Daniel Bergner.—1st ed.
1. Louisiana State Penitentiary. 2. Prisoners—Recreation—Louisiana. 3. Rodeos—Louisiana. I. Title.
HV9475.L22L635 1998
365'.66—dc21   98-18485

ISBN 0-609-60105-9

10 9 8 7 6 5 4 3 2 1

First Edition

FOR NANCY

O N E

WHEN HE HAD FINISHED WORK—BUILDING FENCE
or penning cattle or castrating bull calves with a knife supplied by his
boss on the prison farm—Johnny Brooks lingered in the saddle shed.
The small cinder-block building is near the heart of Angola,
Louisiana's maximum-security state penitentiary. Alone there,
Brooks placed his saddle on a wooden rack in the middle of the
room, leapt into it, and imagined himself riding in the inmate rodeo
coming up in October. He prepared himself. The afternoon he first
showed me what he did, the shed's corrugated metal door was half
shut. The air in the unlit room had a dusky, textured quality, almost
like the weave of a fabric. He floated on it, the fabric. To vault himself into the saddle, which rested at chest height, he did not use a stir-
rup. Nor, it seemed, did he bend his knees. He merely flicked his
ankles to rise well above the leather, and for an instant he was frozen
there, suspended above it, legs spread in perfect symmetry and spine
impeccably upright.

 That morning, in early September, I had watched him train a colt
in a tight, fenced ring. Brooks stood at the center and taught the
young quarter horse to cut, to switch directions fast, on command,
so that eventually it could work the cattle. "Get around there," he

demanded. "Get around; get around." And warned, "Better behave yourself." The colt kept half an eye on Brooks always. Brooks's voice was quiet, but the horse had no desire to feel the whip he carried. And though floggings were a thing long past at Angola, Brooks maintained his own sidelong glance on his boss, one of the "freemen" who ran the range crew, leaning against the fence. The sleeves of Brooks's T-shirt looked taut as rubber bands around his muscles, which were thick as tree roots. His boss was short, heavy, more like a softening stump. "Give me handle," he said, and Brooks answered, "Yassuh," and "Yassuh" was much of what I heard him say during the first weeks I knew him, whether in response to me or to prison employees. He kept his shoulders stooped. His head hung slightly. Often his eyes were lowered. He had, at times, an unrestrained, affecting smile that included his eyes, though he was missing three bottom teeth and the upper ones didn't look so healthy. He was a caricature, an illusion from another era, humble black servant, Stepin Fetchit.

"Yassuh," he replied after finishing with the colt, when another of the freemen called, "Mr. Jimmy wants his truck washed." He jogged over, caught the keys that were tossed his way, and hustled off to soap, scrub, rinse, and dry.

But later, inside the saddle shed, his shoulders were straight and his speech gained authority. The air seemed not only textured but, like the air over all of Angola's vast grounds, laden, palpably heavier than the atmosphere outside the gates. Five thousand men were incarcerated there. Eighty-five percent had killed or raped or robbed with violence. About eight in ten were sentenced either to life without parole or to so many years they might as well have been. (Louisiana had good claim to the toughest sentencing laws in the nation. It was one of only three states where all lifers were "natural lifers"—the governor's clemency offered the only way out. Other states with a natural life sentence used it sparingly.) Brooks, here for beating a woman to death during a robbery twenty-two years ago, was no longer floating above his saddle. He sat on the brown leather. Yet his new posture and voice, and his eyes that were suddenly direct and animated, defied more than his submissiveness; they defied Angola's excess gravity.

In the previous year's rodeo a gold-tinted bull had knocked him unconscious. Hurtling, the 1,600 pound animal snapped Brooks's neck back then forward, slamming his head into the knobby rock of muscle between the bull's shoulders. Now Brooks envisioned drawing the same bull, reminded himself to stay out of its "territory," not to let his weight fall too far back. Or he would lose all control and the whiplashing would start.

He schooled himself, in the hush of the room, to slice the air with the elbow of his free arm, the way the pros on TV did, for balance against the bull's spin. He taught himself to spur constantly against that spin, a plea—as much as a command—for an end to centrifugal force. The bull rope would be tied around his right hand. He imagined how hard he wanted the rope pulled by the inmate helping him in the chute. "It should feel like the tire of a truck pinning me there, Mr. Dan," he said. "When I get done it should feel like my hand been inside a vise."

To fix his eyes only on the bull's left shoulder, never on its head— he trained himself about that, too. The head was a temptation but would trick you; the animal always went where the shoulder did. And he tried to anticipate the sensation when the chute gate opened and the bull exploded. Fear would blacken his mind, make him deaf to every sound. There would be no conscious control from then on. There would be only the reactions he tried to drill into himself here, daydreaming.

Besides last year's injury, Brooks had, after his first ride in his first rodeo more than a decade ago, been kicked in the back by the bull that threw him. He had then watched another convict thrown immediately in front of the chute. The bull found the man on the ground and shook him between its horns, cracking his spine—the man was left a quadriplegic, living in the Department of Corrections' version of a nursing home. A few years later, Brooks had broken his arm, and the year before last the flesh just below his eye had been sliced open by a bull's horn. Rodeo anywhere is a dangerous sport, bull riding its most extreme event. The prison staff who oversaw Brooks on the range crew, and who organized Angola's rodeo, were quick to remind me of this. Brooks's medical history would be about the gentlest on the pro tour. But many pros enter two rodeos in a weekend, ride several bulls every week, hundreds in a year. Each year Brooks mounted exactly four. His odds were not gentle at all.

They were not meant to be. The inmate rodeo, a thirty-two-year-old tradition that year, 1996, was held every Sunday in October and was billed by the prison as "The Wildest Show in the South." The public was invited through Angola's gates, lured by write-ups in the fun section of the local paper promising untrained convicts "thrown every which way." The men could not practice. Many, unlike Brooks and a few others who worked with horses as part of their prison jobs, had never so much as ridden a pony at a childhood street fair. They were not given the protective vests the pros wear to save themselves from shattered ribs and punctured lungs when the bronco kicks or the bull stomps down. Broken shoulders or wrists or ribs occurred daily. One past rider, petrified on his horse in a slapstick event called "Buddy Pick-Up," had died of a heart attack. Hours before the rodeo started, to be sure of getting in, the fans would line their cars along the shoulder of the road leading to Angola; there was rarely enough room for everyone in the prison's old 5,000-seat arena. Weeks before, the convicts signed up to compete in the spectacle—and signed a release absolving the prison of all liability—then begged their way into the featured events.

And yes, Brooks knew what the public came for. "Some of them, sure," he said when I asked about rooting for broken bodies. But not all. "And if you give them something good…" He spoke more of technique, of the bull's "pivot point," of a "suicide tie" for his right hand, of locking his right elbow, of watching J. W. Hart and Tuff Hedeman and Ted Nuce on ESPN, "studying them tight, tight." Then he talked again of the spectators, who cheered loudly for the best performances. He had heard it. He knew they did. And he recalled the day a rodeo clown—hired from the pro circuit to draw the bulls away from fallen riders—hugged him, lifted him off his feet in congratulations after a beautifully executed ride. "He liked what I done," Brooks remembered, his eyes completely at odds with the understatement of his words, "and he just picked me up like this."

Ten years ago Littell Harris was mixing a cocktail of his own feces at Angola's Camp J. This October, on the rodeo's opening day, he sat in the convict section of the bleachers. He had a profusion of dread locks, vines spilling in every direction, and a thick beard that hid much of his face. The hair was an aberration at the prison. His harsh eyes, with their faintly Asian slant, were almost his only visible feature. By early spring, being one of Angola's lucky few, he would have served his fifteen years for armed robbery. Under laws increasingly severe, more recent Louisiana armed robbers would spend the rest of their lives in the penitentiary. But for Littell, a few more months and he was gone.

The cocktail was accomplished like this: Littell lined the steel toilet at the back of his cell with newspaper. He shit onto the paper. Then he crouched down, with his back to the bars, and mashed and stirred the stool in a cup of water; at the right consistency he would pour the liquid into a drinking bottle with a squirt top. He could stir in private because Camp J, where Angola's worst disciplinary cases were sent, had single-man cells on only one side of a narrow concrete hall. The nearest guard sat at the end of the corridor, outside a barred gate. Because of cocktails like Littell's, the guard preferred not to venture down that hall.

In this case the mix was meant for another inmate. When that man got his tier time, to shower and to walk along the seventy-foot-long corridor, Littell would douse him. A self-proclaimed "Camp J warrior," he did battle in this way with three or four men on the tier. He no longer remembered why. That was just how it was: something had been said; "draft" in cigarettes had gone unpaid; someone came from the wrong town, the wrong part of the state. "They shitted me down"; Littell did the same. Or they each found ways, makeshift and intricate, to reconfigure and extend the electrical circuits behind their ceiling light fixtures; by running a wire into their toilets they boiled water for flinging. Or they added Ben-Gay to the scalding water, creating what was quaintly called "a stinger." It worked on the eyes like acid.

So Littell stirred his feces. "I'm sitting there," he recalled when we talked alone, "and I'm doing this disgusting ass shit, and it's like I had an out-of-body experience, man, it's like I could see myself from the back, squatting down, playing with these fucking turds, mashing this fucking turd up, souping it up, and I'm watching myself, and I said, Man, that's a fucking shame, fucking disgusting animal savage that I've turned into. Savage. And I'm looking at myself, and I started thinking, I don't know nothing, I don't read, I'm caught up in this bullshit. I knew then that I had to turn around....From that day on I tried to enlighten myself. But I still went and did what I had to do. Because I don't want to be no fucking victim."

There was plenty that Littell still "had to do." He had finished his most recent stint at J and on other disciplinary cellblocks only months before he sat in the rodeo stands—with about two hundred other convict spectators, separated from the public by a simple rail—and less than half a year before his scheduled freedom. If nothing major happened, no prison murder or stabbing to warrant new state charges against him, he would go more or less directly from savagery back into the world.

For the first time, he watched the rodeo's opening procession. At his back the Main Prison sprawled. It housed half of Angola's inmates. The outermost of its tall, razor-wired fences surrounded the stadium. In the distance were maroon-and-yellow guard towers, endless fields, the levees that lined the Mississippi, the lake the river had left behind, the outcamps that held the rest of the convicts. "Louisiana State Penitentiary. L.S.P. Last Slave Plantation," Littell said. Below him the Rough Riders, the mounted inmate drill team, galloped into the arena. In red bandannas and black straw cowboy hats, they veered in tenuous patterns—their practice had been scarcely more extensive than that of the rodeo competitors—and finally lined up along the red, white and blue rodeo fence. They settled their horses. They bowed their heads for the chaplain's prayer.

Waving in the breeze above their heads were the flags they carried: the state's, the country's, the penitentiary's, and, in this prison whose inmate population was 77 percent black, whose guards were two-thirds white, and whose administration couldn't have been more pale, the Confederacy's. There were two of those flags, with the blue X and the thirteen stars and the red background, one carried by a black man. The crowd was virtually all white. "Do you see this?" Littell leaned toward the inmate beside him. "That fucking idiot." The next man down the bleachers answered, "It ain't nothing but a piece of cloth." And the prayer began.

The chaplain gave thanks to the warden, thanks to God. He asked Jesus to bless this rodeo and to bless all the riders with protection. "Heavenly Father, you have favored us with this day and with the hope and beauty of this Creation....Bless all of us with an appreciation of the joy of living." Littell wasn't feeling too joyful. He stared hard—without pleasure—at any attractive woman he found in the stands, his main purpose for being here. But as the chaplain's words seeped in, he figured he did have something to be thankful for. At least he knew what he should about that flag. At least he wasn't like the men around him, illiterate. At least he'd educated himself. Nat Turner, Frederick Douglass, Malcolm X, he'd read about them all since that moment on Camp J. "And at least I'm getting ready to take my GED," he said. "I'm getting ready to establish myself."

At least he was getting out of here.

So he tried to enjoy himself, ignore the guards barking down into the convict section, "Caps off! Get your hoods off!" as the loud-speaker introduced "the greatest song ever written," ignore his own thoughts about pride and nationhood as the inmate band played the national anthem. A young horsewoman, sent by the car dealership that sponsored the rodeo, rode around the arena bearing the American flag through the day's drizzle, the rhythmic sloshing of hooves on the wet turf audible beneath the band, a slow and strange percussion. Littell tried to concentrate on the woman's body in her blue spangled jumpsuit.

The black guys hurt him the most, but the whites—who made up about half the rodeo's participants—sickened him, too. They were all willing to price their lives at zero. They were all willing to turn them-selves into a joke. "Waiting in Department of Corrections bucking chute number one, serving *lllllife…*" he heard the mounted emcee (like the clowns, hired from the pro circuit) announce the six riders in the first event. "Waiting in Department of Corrections bucking chute number two, serving *LLLLLIFE…*"

"*LLLLLIFE,*" the emcee bellowed. "*LLLLLIFE! LLLLLIFE!! LLLLLIFE!!!!!*"

All chutes opened at once, and six convicts on six bulls churned into the arena. This was the "Bust-Out," a special feature of Angola's rodeo. The name was a play on "escape," the event designed for futility. It was hard enough for an untrained man to avoid injury when riding a bull alone in the ring; with five other animals and five other hapless contestants all bounding and tumbling at one end of the arena, the risks multiplied. Johnny Brooks wanted to score points early. He wanted Angola's all-around cowboy belt buckle when the month was over (the all-around champion's only prize, though first place in each riding event would bring fifty dollars). Wearing elaborate suede chaps in turquoise and black, a matching vest, a black felt hat studded with moons and stars, all commissioned from a convict who did his tooling in a prison hobby shop, Johnny Brooks spurred frantically and kept from keeling as his bull twisted and leapt off all four hooves. But he couldn't control where the animal went amid the chaos, not at the last instant, when another inmate, a rodeo veteran and past belt buckle winner, sailed sideways. Brooks's bull trampled across the man's back, injuring him badly enough to keep him out of the rest of the month's competition. Thrown in the process, Brooks scored no points at all.

Soon a small wooden table was carried out to the center of the ring. It was time for "Convict Poker," a new event that year, another special feature, the inspiration of the range-crew bosses. The table was painted bright red. Four folding chairs were placed around it, and four inmates jogged out to occupy those chairs. Johnny Brooks was one. There were no cards involved. The men would merely sit as though playing poker. The emcee boomed, "Brrrrring on the dealer!" and in one of the chutes, an inmate delivered an electric prod to a 2,000 pound black bull with perfectly sweeping, perfectly pointed white horns. The animal bolted into the arena. The last man sitting would win one hundred dollars.

The trouble was that bulls aren't attracted to stationary targets. And the men were stationary, palms flat and fingers spread on the table, never turning to check on the animal as it circled behind their backs, knowing that if the three minute whistle blew with more than one convict left, the one who had moved least, who had kept his trembling under control, whose fingers hadn't so much as twitched, would win. The crowd—all those fans who'd waited for hours along the shoulder of the road to buy their eight dollar tickets; the prison staff; the inmates in their section of the bleachers; the few members of the media in their ramshackle press box; me—wasn't going to get its payoff.

So the clown, usually a figure of protection, started taunting. He tossed his floppy hat into the bull's face. Imitating a bull on the verge of attack, he stooped down, snorting, and scraped the dirt with his hands. He grabbed Brooks's cowboy hat and waved it behind Brooks's shoulder blades. He climbed up on the table, made a racket with his feet, ready to jump over the inmates' heads to safety as the bull charged.

It didn't. It only convinced one man to leave his seat with a side-caress of horn, and ambled off to a distance of four or five yards. The clown picked up the vacated metal chair. He lifted it over his head and hurled it into the bull's snout. It clattered against the horns, and still the men did not shift. At last the animal processed the message, drove forward to deliver on the promise of its size, on the promise of those gorgeously sweeping and immaculately pointed horns which slammed, by one convict's pure good fortune, into the minimal back of his folding chair instead of into his kidney. The man was now down, the bull ready to spear or stomp. But at that moment Johnny Brooks lost his nerve or gained his sanity, leapt out of his seat, and began sprinting for the fence. The bull caught motion in the corner of its eye. Fleeing across the arena, Brooks stayed five feet, two feet, twelve inches ahead of the horns. Arms and legs pumping, and back arching away from his own death, he looked like a cartoon character in comic escape. As if a firecracker had been lit under his ass, he scrambled up the rails of the fence.

"How did you enjoy the Convict Poker, ladies and gentlemen?"

the emcee asked. There was some applause. And laughter. I'm sure some of the reaction to the event was electrified, exhilarated, the thrill of watching men in terror made forgivable because the men were murderers. I'm sure some of it was racist *(See that nigger move)*, some disappointed (that there had been no goring), and some uneasy (with that very same disappointment). I'm sure nearly everyone, including me, felt some measure of each of these things. But I know as well that many people were not laughing, were too bewildered or stunned by what they had seen, even if they'd heard about the new event named Convict Poker and it was exactly why they had come. Angola's stadium is an intimate place. There are no faraway seats. And just outside the arena inmates sold Cokes and hot dogs and cotton candy. They sold what they made in the hobby shops—key chains and purses, dollhouses and oil paintings. Some were allowed to deal directly with the customers, others called out from a fenced bullpen while prison employees stood with the craftwork. The spectators had bought these handmade things. There had been brief transactions, the briefest of dialogues. The convicts at the center of the ring had become men, only men, to at least a degree.

Or perhaps this was only a wishful, sentimental perception on my part. Since September I had begun to know the inmates. *I* felt a confusion of reactions, electricity and revulsion and disappointment and discomfort and, as Johnny Brooks took flight, a tinge of racism: certainly it was easier for me to watch—and be curious and analytic about—a black man in danger and fear and abasement, precisely because he had that adjective next to him, black, was slightly less close to being me. Perhaps my sense of the crowd was only projection. I spoke with few of the public. Perhaps I should limit myself to saying that the crowd, overall, was quieter than I thought it would be. Quieter than two concessions across from the Cokes and cotton candy suggested. At one, fans paid a dollar to get themselves locked inside a freestanding jail cell and have an inmate snap a Polaroid through the bars. At the other, for the same price, a convict took their pictures while they stuck their heads up from a wooden body with a cut-out neck, the body painted with a prisoner's old-fashioned striped jumpsuit and adorned with a ball and chain on each ankle.

The bull riding came second to last. Here was an event that replicated the pro tour. The rider had to stay on for eight seconds to score points; the better his form, the more points he would receive. Here was the chance for Johnny Brooks to prove himself, to rise above the helplessness and degradation of contests like the Bust-Out and Convict Poker, where pure luck and sheer craziness played such overwhelming roles, the chance for this forty-year-old man, who would most likely never leave Angola, to prevail on skill and reveal his grace. He could show himself no different from J. W. Hart and Tuff Hedeman and Ted Nuce, the stars of the pro circuit, whose rides were hailed weekly by the ESPN announcer not only as demonstrations of talent but as testaments to integrity and good values. He could be those figures. And he could be, in front of the public, what he was at least part of the time in his job at Angola, a cowboy.

From a railing above the chute, he moved to climb onto the animal. With a cord tied against its belly and near its balls to add hostility, the bull tried to hurdle the wall. It braced its forelegs over the top. Quickly, before he fell backward inside the chute that was just big enough for the bull, Brooks levered himself off. "Get down there," someone prodded at the animal. Brooks tried again, set himself. The bull jostled, slammed its head into the wooden slats, drove Brooks's knees into the boards. The hide of the back was loose, sliding, and Brooks struggled to get his balance. Under the excess skin the bull's muscles contracted and rose—a fast series of giant ripples shuddering along its spine.

A convict pulled the bull rope tight as Brooks had dreamed. His palm faced upward, and the pressure of the rope across it dug the back of his hand inches into the hide. "Ready?" the inmate manning the gate called. "Ready?" The answer was the most minimal nod, the brim of the studded hat moving almost imperceptibly. The gate was tugged open, the man who'd helped with the rope cried, "Outside!" And so Brooks was. Outside. The bull thrashed and spun out of the chute, and Brooks was out under the gaze of the crowd, his mind shut down and Angola gone from it.

Three seconds later he was on his knees in the mud.

A parade of failed rides came after: one first-time contestant sent airborne immediately; a gray-haired sixty-two-year-old bank robber launched into a twisting, Olympic-style dive. Finally a convict named Carey Lasseigne, who went by Buckkey and whose bushy blond mustache and weathered skin made him look like he would do well—made him look, at least, like a typical cowboy—decided to grab the bull rope with two hands. This would have disqualified him in professional rodeo, but here, because not one other man had lasted the required time, a mere completed ride would earn him points. Which was all he wanted. He wasn't after quite the same kind of glory as Johnny Brooks.

Lately his son, Chris, refused to visit him more than once or twice each year. The boy was almost seventeen. He had been two when Buckkey began his life sentence for murder, for killing an acquaintance just one year older than his son was now, shooting him in the back of the head while he pleaded for his life. If Buckkey could win the all-around prize, that silver-plated buckle reading "All-Around Cowboy," if he could send it to Chris for his seventeenth birthday at the end of the month, he felt that Chris, his only child, might come soon.

The first time Buckkey had tried for this present, the bull had rammed and pinned him repeatedly against one of the wooden gates. He received 142 stitches to his scalp and later went into seizure on the shower floor. Two years ago he had broken his left hand; before the following weekend he had cracked open the cast and taken it off so he could ride.

Today was the day, this was the year. He needed those points. He didn't care about style. He just clung to the bull. And when the whistle blew announcing eight seconds, he was three Sundays away from that gift.

In the afternoon's finale, the "Guts & Glory," a red chip worth one hundred dollars was strung between a bull's horns. This was yet another inmate rodeo tradition. Thirty convicts poured into the ring on foot, then tried to pluck the chip without being trampled or gored.

And I was still searching for what I had glimpsed with Johnny Brooks in the saddle shed—possibilities of exaltation, hints of triumphant skill, of tremendous self-control in men who'd wound up here because they'd had little self-control at all. I sought such visions of redemption, even as I knew that the perversity of the rodeo was thoroughly at odds with what I hoped to see. Promise hung in the air above the grandstands, extraordinary promise. If these men could rise within a spectacle so troubling, and within a prison atmosphere crushingly weighted with dead victims and families destroyed and convicts put permanently away...if these men could somehow flourish...My search was surely marked by a self-indulgent need for a soothing parable within circumstances so dispiriting. But I couldn't help wishing. And my desire would keep me at Angola long after the end of rodeo month. It would carry me deep inside the prison. It would take me to levels much more abject than those of the rodeo. And it would leave me knowing men whom no amount of distance— and Angola is far, far out there—can banish from my mind.

But for now, as the Guts & Glory began, my eyes turned to Terry Hawkins, serving his life sentence for murdering his boss in an argument sparked by a demand that Terry work late on his stepdaughter's birthday. Already his participation in the rodeo was a bad joke: The job had been in a slaughterhouse; he had hacked into his employer's head and neck with a meat-ax. But Terry didn't see any strangeness or irony in his continued association with cattle. The Guts & Glory was his event. He planned to use his own well-tested strategy to beat the animal and snatch the chip: Goad the bull into charging, run away in an arc tighter than the bull could turn, and reach back behind his own shoulder to snag the prize. He had won the event several times in past years. "Terry's learnt the know-how," other inmates had told me with vicarious pride. "Watch him."

He had seemed, when we first met a month earlier, scarcely more than a teenager, though I knew he was in his mid-thirties. Six-two or -three, athletic, restless, he smiled both nervously and with bravado, slouched in a chair and jiggled his knees, appeared as naive and self-certain as the star of any high school team. A thin scar crossed his dark brown skin between his eyebrows, the remnant of his bachelor party years ago. He said his victories in the Guts & Glory were the best accomplishments of his life. I asked if that included the years before Angola. It did. I asked if he could imagine anything better in the future. He said no. I laid out a scenario, however far-fetched, in which he gained his freedom; could he imagine any better accomplishment then? No.... He showed me his cot, where he had written across the sheet and pillowcase, in large, crude red letters, "BULL-FIGHTER." He told me, "I'm going to look for you in the stands. I'm going to toss you that chip when I get it," and, ridiculing myself both because this man was a murderer and because the contest was a gladiator show, I fantasized myself a part of his triumph, his happiness, a part of something that would be—however briefly, however sadly, however terribly—wonderful.

Now an immense brown bull trotted into the ring. Wearing his good-luck red wristbands and tattered, red-ribbed T-shirt, Terry waited at the far end. He watched the commotion of other attempts. One man, rammed at the legs, was unable to stand or even drag himself away, and lay in the mud while the horns prodded at his shins. Others climbed the fence as the bull lowered its neck and came at them. Terry studied the animal's moves. Then he emerged from the crowd, or rather the other men backed away. He feinted, froze, wavered off-balance, weight too far forward in the process of taunting. Paralyzed, he leaned five feet from the horns. But he steadied himself and lunged forward again, baiting, luring the bull, sprinting away along the sharpest curve. He reached behind. He was struck by the muzzle, caught between the horns. Terry flew ten or twelve feet into the air. He landed—the only wonderful thing—*between* the horns again, was vaulted and flipped onto his back. He came down once more on the animal's forehead, was propelled upward yet again, floating and spinning, and for several seconds this went on, seconds I could count—one one-thousand, two one-thousand, three one-thousand—his body for moments beyond gravity, suspended in midair, flopping and spineless: everything about his existence, the preservation of his life, utterly beyond his control.

T W O □

THE PREVIOUS YEAR, HIS FIRST AS WARDEN OF Angola, Burl Cain had chosen to enter the rodeo arena in the closest thing he could find to a chariot. It was a wooden cart, lacquered and polished, with big white-spoked wheels, pulled by his inmate-tended team of Percheron horses. He circled the arena between the performance of the Rough Riders and the chaplain's prayer. The Percherons were huge—a head taller and a thousand pounds heavier than the average horse. Their chests were broad and deeply muscled, the base of their necks looked as thick as oil drums, and across their black coats they wore harnesses studded with chrome medallions. Browbands and collars and backstraps all glistened.

"Ladies and gentlemen," the emcee announced, "Angola's warden, Mr. Burl Cain!" The convict band gave a drum roll and a splash of electric organ. "He's just arrived eight months ago from Dixon Correctional, and he's the man in charge now. And, ladies and gentlemen, those are prize-winning Percherons from the Perche region in the country of France. Brought the knights into battle back in the Middle Ages. And Burl Cain's got 'em now. One of his Percherons was rated *the* number one stallion at the National Western Livestock show in Denver, Colorado. *Warden Burl Cain!*"

About five foot seven, round, with full white hair swept across his forehead, Cain had waved to the rodeo crowd.

In September of 1996, a month before this year's event, I had met him for the first time. Our introduction came at the end of a week I had spent at the prison, preparing what I'd thought would be only a magazine article about the inmate riders. "So you want to talk about the barbarism of the rodeo," he said before hello, before we shook hands, when I was shown into his office. He smiled. His candor more than counterbalanced the pictures I'd seen and descriptions I'd heard of his grand entrance. Leaning back at the head of his long, polished conference table, he acknowledged that barbarism was a factor.

"Look," he explained, "the rodeo, to us, is kind of like making a good cake." He wore a white shirt unbuttoned at the collar, and a colorful, unknotted tie draped around his shoulders like a minister's stole. Now he sat forward, interlacing his pale, chubby fingers on the gleaming wood. "And so there's all the ingredients in it. Some of the ingredients by themselves wouldn't be fit to eat. But you put them all together and you have a nice cake."

A nice cake? I had seen the rodeo once, as a spectator, several years before. In the Buddy Pick-Up a careening rider's forehead had connected, at full gallop, with a metal post. I had learned that the man was carted off to the prison medical center, then shackled and shipped out to a hospital in Baton Rouge, where his head was rebuilt with a steel plate.

But I had heard nice things about Burl Cain. And the highest praise had come from those I expected to be his natural enemies, the state's capital-defense attorneys. As warden, Cain carried out the executions. He stood in the chamber and gave the signal for the lethal injection. But he had made great changes for the men on death row. Given them regular contact visits with their families, something Angola had allowed only once each year and most prisons in the country seldom if ever permit. (At those others, the men awaiting execution see their visitors through Plexiglas or glimpse them through perforated steel.) And offered them literacy classes. Literacy classes! For what? They were going to die! Cain insisted on their humanity, focused on the fact that they were living now. And he hoped to save them. Though they were free to read what they wished, he hoped they would read the Bible. He hoped they found faith. Cain's own religious beliefs bred his compassion—and his deep misgivings about the death penalty. "I don't know what God would have said if He'd been in that room," a local reporter recalled him muttering, visibly shaken, after his first execution. At his second and most recent, as the convict lay strapped to the gurney and the technician struggled to find a vein, Cain had held the condemned man's hand.

"I didn't come to the rodeo for about eight years," he went on, his head almost bowed over his folded hands, "because I saw a man stomped and paralyzed. And that grieved me greatly, and I wouldn't come back. I don't want to see the inmates hurt. I don't want to see the blood and I don't want to see the guts. But the rodeo raises thousands of dollars for the Inmate Welfare Fund. And the rodeo is good for morale, for those riders, for everyone involved. The rodeo brings lifeblood into this prison."

So it was a necessary cake. The tickets, I knew, supplied much of the Inmate Welfare Fund's account. And though the participants rarely mentioned this as a reason for signing up, the Fund helped pay for the GED program and the inmate-run magazine, the *Angolite,* for TVs and sports equipment, for security on the rare trip out for a family funeral if the convict could get permission—things the state wouldn't appropriate money for, that made an entire life in Angola bearable and possibly transformative.

And he was right about morale. The riders, the concessionaires, the inmate artisans, all looked forward to the rodeo. As for lifeblood, maybe the occasion was, in a sense, sacramental. The men offered up their bodies, and in return the public came to see them, acknowledged their existence. For the rest of the year Angola was nowhere, isolated in its own corner of the state, the nearest tiny town thirty miles away. The rodeo was a rite of grace, of barely perceptible reconciliation between the inmates and society.

Even the convicts who ran the *Angolite,* self-educated and sardonic men, had said something to affirm this. They were, mostly, harshly critical of the rodeo. One editor had told me, "Most of Angola's inmates suffer from Attention Deficit Disorder," by way of explaining the men's willingness to be broken as long as they were noticed. "And whenever someone's paid attention to them, it's been to beat them up in one way or another." A second editor had added, with laughing resignation, "One thing God gave all of us: a man's allowed to choose his own path to hell," meaning not that signing up for the rodeo was a sin, but that the whole spectacle was a goddamned shame. Yet they'd said that if it were up to them, the rodeo would continue. "It brings the public here. They lay eyes on us."

Certainly nothing else would bring them. No one was going to drive hours for an inmate basketball game.

Cain's light blue eyes, when they weren't lowered toward his solemn, prayerful hands, were leveled on me. He talked of wanting society to see the inmates as people, "not as some devil with a fork and a tail," of wishing the public would gain some common sense about sentencing, see it in terms of economics if not morality, tell their legislators to "cut these life no parole sentences and give a man the chance to get out, the chance for a hearing, once he's at least forty and has served twenty years." He spoke of the need for maintaining hope among the inmates, and of his effort to do so despite the lottery-like odds of a governor's pardon. He tried to make life meaningful even here. He was fostering the GED program, nurturing a club that built toys for charity, an inmate CPR team that traveled outside the prison to give classes in local schools, a Toastmasters public-speaking club, the Forgotten Voices, that had just been honored by Toastmasters International. He talked of the work on the range crew, of men like Johnny Brooks learning to rope and tag, to palpate cattle for pregnancy, and to birth baby calves. And he talked about religion, about the absolute forgiveness he extended, according to the Gospels, to every inmate as they entered the world of Angola, about the new clergy he'd added to the staff, about saving souls. "The first meeting I had when I came here to Angola, the first meeting I called on the first day, was with the chaplains. I told them that they are shepherds and that they feed sheep. And these inmates are our sheep. God put them in my charge and I'm responsible for them, just like they're my children."

But Cain had started out after college teaching agronomy in a rural high school. Wasn't the running of prisons, I asked, an improbable career path?

"I'm a weird warden," he grinned. "I don't care."

As early as that initial conversation, I knew that I had to come back to Angola not only for the rodeo and not only for a magazine article, but for something much larger. Johnny Brooks's agility and preparation in the saddle shed, his floating and self-schooling; the *Angolite* editor saying "They lay eyes on us"; the redemptive found where it was least expected—the rodeo fit with a grand and unlikely promise Warden Cain held out: that Angola was, as he put it, "a positive prison." Its inmates would die incarcerated, yet it was a place where, under Cain's leadership, men made themselves better human beings. Society might think, They can't get out, they have nothing to lose, no reason to improve. Still, they had improvement itself, self-elevation, to gain. They had their humanity. "Our cake is good," Cain said of the penitentiary. I needed to find out if it could be true.

Unbeckoned, as Cain and I continued talking, an inmate set a can of Dr Pepper beside the warden, on one of the coasters already placed at regular intervals around the conference table. The inmate had

made no sound coming in across the green pile carpeting, nor in resting the can on the simple cork disk rimmed with black plastic. Earlier during the week, I had noticed the man, along with another
convict, dusting the warden's office. I had seen this first thing every
morning, before Cain arrived, when I checked in at the administration building. Silently the pair of dusters, in state-issued jeans and
work shirts, passed their spotless rags over the picture frames and fax
machine, the blades of the ceiling fan and the leather seat of the
warden's desk chair. All was as clean as the dark wood of the table,
which reflected Cain's face.

He sipped his Dr Pepper, spoke in his faintly scratchy, Southern-
accented voice, and a few minutes later another man came in from
behind my shoulder, unheard, and set something down before Cain.
This was an assistant warden, and his offering, a knife, was laid on
the glossy surface as gently as the drink. The weapon had a crude
cylindrical handle and a rough eight-inch blade. The shakedown
crew had just caught someone trying to take it onto the Main
Yard.

"Yes," Cain told me, gesturing with the shank to demonstrate
what it could do, "we find these. This is a phenomenal prison, but
it's not a perfect prison. And we shouldn't have been talking about
all those good things before we talked about security. Those clubs,
that church, you can't have any of that before security. I wish they'd
have taken you to that ditch-bank deal the other day."

The call for help had come in over the truck's radio while I'd
been touring the grounds. "Out of control, it's out of control," the
dispatcher's voice had gone on for minutes, giving the location. I'd
asked my guide to take me there, but he had demurred, unsure the
warden would want me as witness. Two inmates, it turned out, were
battling each other with ditch-bank blades, sharp-edged hoes with
six-foot handles. They were out with a farm line, mounted guard
over them. The guard fired into the air; the inmates ignored it,
swung at each other's faces. He fired a second time up at the sky.

One prisoner chopped into the other's scalp. Cain drove into the field as the fight finally came under control. "I told that freeman," he recalled for me, " 'There's no such thing as a second warning shot.' I told him, in front of all those free folks and all those inmates, 'Next time, shoot both of 'em.' I wanted them all to know it. I wish they'd have let you see it."

Later I found out that Littell Harris—dreadlocked, bearded, recently released from Camp J—had been in that farm line. He told a different, or perhaps more complete, account of what had been said. The guard had protested to Cain that other inmates were trying to break up the fight. If he fired down at the two men, he risked hitting one of the others. "I don't care who it is," Cain answered. "Kill some of 'em, open fire, that'll stop 'em."

I didn't know whether to believe Littell's version. I still don't know. It didn't matter terribly to me either way. If Cain had said those words, he didn't mean them literally. And I was taken with the paradoxes of the warden, his talk of forgiveness and enforcement, his quoting from the New Testament and, two hours into our long first meeting, from a book called *Leadership Secrets of Attila the Hun,* which his teenage son had given him. " 'Leaders must expect continued improvement in their Huns.' "

Was he concerned by the contradiction, Jesus and vanquishing general? "I have to be both." He picked up the shank again. "No convict can improve himself if he's worried about this going through his back."

And almost all the inmates had spoken well of him, even though I'd maneuvered so staff were out of earshot. They'd told me how he'd debated on TV against the New Orleans D.A., arguing for the release of elderly, infirm prisoners, and for a second chance for changed men. The *Angolite* had written, "Cain is as much concerned with events outside the prison as he is with internal problems. He is aware that prisoner bashing is the vogue, and that anyone who argues on prisoners' behalf will be ridiculed by posturing politicians," and then the magazine had detailed the courageous TV appearance and a series of radio and newspaper interviews Cain had done. He was on their side.

Of the legislators and past Angola wardens who, he told me, didn't like him, the charioteer said, "It's there in the Bible. No one likes a prophet close to home."

A second Dr Pepper was delivered as soon as he'd drained the first. He declared of five thousand men, five thousand murderers and rapists and armed robbers, "I am their daddy." He referred back to Attila the Hun and said, "All people aren't born leaders of men. It's an honor to be one." And while his excesses kept me off balance, the fact was his domain was amazingly peaceful. Besides a momentary shoving match, the confiscated knife and the fight on the radio were the closest I'd come to any violence, to any hint of violence, during the week I'd spent seeing every part of Angola. Everything was clean. Every inmate was polite. Even when I factored in their need to impress the visiting writer, the civility was remarkable. This was a world of the worst criminals, a fallen world, brought to order.

The striking tranquillity at Angola—confirmed by the ACLU's National Prison Project and Louisiana's own watchdogs—could not be credited to Warden Cain alone. Twenty-one years ago conditions had been so anarchic and murderous a federal judge had ruled that the prison "shocked the conscience" and breached the Eighth Amendment's guarantee against cruel and unusual punishment. Reform had begun then. Reform—but the reclamation of men was Cain's own standard. In an era when rehabilitation was a concept for fools, he said urgently, "This penitentiary is about changing lives." To men who had followed the most immediate needs of the self, he taught the self-abnegation of religion. Spirit over flesh. God over ego. The warden aimed not merely at warehousing inmates safely, but at rebuilding them, at redeeming them, whether in terms of his Southern Baptist belief or in religious terms more broad

("Love thy neighbor...") or simply in the sense of learning to live in some valuable way, without the impulses that lead to destroying others, to self-destruction.

"Wouldn't you like to run this prison?" Cain asked me.

I laughed but felt: Yes, I would like the chance to bring so much good into being.

He had to leave for a meeting in Baton Rouge. He asked me to ride with him in his car so we could keep talking. He would have his press secretary follow us and drive me back. His press secretary and I had laid out a different itinerary. I looked toward her. "He's never made that kind of invitation before," she said. Cain seemed to sense what I did, an affinity between a Baptist-Cracker-Warden and a Journalist-Yankee-Jew.

What would become my year at Angola began, effectively, then, though two months would pass before I asked the warden formally for such long-term access to his prison. Already I imagined what the growing affection between us could bring: the latitude to get to know the inmates, to follow them through their daily lives without a staff escort—a rare chance, wardens of maximum-security penitentiaries being notorious for excluding the press, or for directing carefully what little was seen and heard. Privacy would be crucial to answering the first question that would drive my year: Could Warden Cain really change lives? I needed the inmates' honesty. And to answer the second, I needed their intimacy. Given their endless sentences, what exactly were these men living for?

Once, I had been through a federal trial of a large-scale drug dealer who received, upon conviction, a mandatory term of life without parole. My wife was the prosecutor. Though I had rooted for her victory and didn't feel much for the defendant (who stared at her arrogantly throughout the trial and who'd already squandered his second chances), the sentence, however inevitable once the verdict came in, shallowed my lungs and thinned the blood in my legs and made me want to cry out in panic. How could that man exist—even contemplate existing—for the rest of his life in prison? I would kill myself, I thought reflexively.

With the most infrequent exceptions, Angola's inmates did not kill themselves. Each year, scarcely a handful tried. And now, with the warden's trust, I might understand.

Out of nothing, out of less than nothing, out of a place where men declared themselves by spraying each other with feces, what kinds of lives could the inmates build and why did they bother? With so few who would ever leave, Angola should have been a pure Hobbesian universe, where sheer animalism ruled. If it was something significantly more, what a miracle that would be. To observe it would bring me more than understanding, it would bring comfort. That even when all the artifice of society, all we erect to blind ourselves to our deepest beings—that animalistic core—was stripped away, there was still something higher, something striving. To witness this would be to know—palpably—that what we call the human spirit was something more than a pretty veil obscuring a darker awareness.

And if I could find enough that was positive at Angola, whether in its barbaric rodeo or within the prison's caves of cinder block, I could feel in the improbable goodness a hint that there was, as the true believers say, a reason for everything and that all the world was guided in a mysterious, beneficent direction. Ridiculous as it may sound, I sensed that at the prison I might find affirmation for my own tenuous faith in God.

So I got into the warden's car. He pulled out past the the penitentiary sign that bore his name. We discussed Biblical passages and Angola's bloody history. We ranged back to the nineteenth century and convict-leasing, and returned to the present, while he drove eighty down the winding state highway inmates call the Snake Road, the only way to and from the prison.

■

My chances of finding reassurance and affirmation at Angola were much increased by Warden Cain's determination to elicit the good in his men. And switching between Jesus and Attila the Hun, he himself was an example of the elevated within the Hobbesian. But there may have been yet another reason for my attraction to him. I cannot be sure it was a reason at all, and if it was, I cannot guess its importance, great or small. While Cain spoke of himself as the inmates' father, he became, in a certain way, my own.

My real father had spent his working life as a public health official. In tiny, rational ways he tried to improve upon human fallibility. His legacies were a study leading to child guards in the windows of New York City, and a more efficient Emergency Medical Service in Seattle. Undoubtedly, indirectly, his work had saved lives. Yet I had always been somewhat disappointed in it. There was something lacking in his pragmatic career, in his reasonableness that was so unshakable—and in his scorn for all things religious. Warden Cain was his opposite. Warden Cain wrestled with human fallibility on a giant scale, embodied in the those convicts. He believed in miracles and meant to carry one out. He had preached to his inmates, most of whom lived in open dorms of sixty-four men, "You are your brother's keeper. Your bed is your house, the aisle is the street, and two beds down is two houses down. That dorm is your neighborhood, and this is your community."

And meanwhile the convict club called the Toy Shop would give away 2,500 handmade wooden trucks and push-along grasshoppers through Head Start and Louisiana's State School for the Deaf this Christmas! And the CPR team was even teaching policemen! Cain was the most unlikely healer, the most unlikely savior, a man whose very existence—warden inspiring respect and redemption in his inmates—defied my father's rationalism.

Just outside Baton Rouge, Cain pulled into a McDonald's. When I looked confused, he explained that he had to talk business with a friend there before going on to his meeting with the state's Civil Service Commission, to which he had been elected the sole employee representative. "I love McDonald's," he said with exuberance, pushing himself out of the car. "Those fries are killing me!"

Then, as his press secretary trailed us inside, he handed her a ten-dollar bill. "You all treat yourselves." It was the only meal of mine he ever paid for, and if it was a bribe for favorable writing it was the smallest one I've ever heard of. The moment was strange. He ordered and went off to talk business in a Formica booth, while we, the press secretary twenty-four years old and me nearing forty, took our trays to our own corner of the restaurant, as though to the children's table.

Before Cain and I separated, I mentioned something Johnny Brooks had told me: that he'd given Cain the buckle he'd won for all-around runner-up in last year's rodeo.

"That's right. That's a cherished gift. I couldn't win it. I couldn't win it in all my life. I keep it in my other office up at the Ranch House. He walked up to me and told me, 'Warden, I want you to have this buckle. I want you to have this from me.' It was all he had. I know that. I just told him thank you. He just wanted me to have it, and that felt really great."

Cain's metamorphosis from high school agronomy teacher to warden was odd but not unique. Early in the century one man went straight from running a Baton Rouge hardware company to running Angola. A more recent predecessor had started his career selling fertilizer for Allied Chemical; a customer introduced him to the secretary of corrections, who appointed him to manage the business end of penitentiary farming; he rose directly to warden from there. For Cain, more solid personal connections had played a role. His brother was a long-entrenched state senator. Edwin Edwards, governor until recently, was a longtime associate. Cain, too, was made head of agribusiness for the Department of Corrections; then, after running Dixon Correctional Institute, a smaller prison in the state, for thirteen years, he became Warden of Angola.

His rule extended over the prison's 18,000 acres, grounds larger than the island of Manhattan. And those grounds were lovely. Coming through the gate you drove down a corridor of trees, oak and cypress and crab apple. Farther on, in season, the dark pink blossoms of crape myrtle lined the road, and, year-round, flowers bloomed in neat beds beside the white slats of corral fences, flowers that seemed impossibly large and vibrant, bright yellow balls twice the size of a fist and purple spears long as hay grass. Then came the tall magnolias, budding white.

The road arrived at Main Prison, but it was easy to look away from the barbed wire, at the fields. Long ago the flooding of the Mississippi left behind a sediment that made this low-lying acreage among the most fertile in the South. The darker, heavier earth of the surrounding areas was good; the alluvial soil of Angola was superb. Lift both in your hands and you could feel the difference in weight. It was easier to till. Gaze around and you could see what its minerals gave rise to. Okra and corn, eggplant and peppers, snap beans and tomatoes, and soy plants that started wispy and grew swiftly broad, so that within weeks their leaves merged into an endless cloud of green three feet off the ground, seemingly thick enough to walk on. And there was cotton, chest-high, in resilient, spiny rows running toward the levee.

After the crops the graze land went for miles. Almost three thousand cattle fed in fields sprayed yellow with wildflowers. One hundred horses worked the prison, and a herd of mustangs owned its separate pasture. The tall, pitched banks of the levees held back a rushing bend in the Mississippi, which bordered the prison on three sides, but there was plenty of water on the grounds. Every road seemed to hit some shore of Lake Killarney, giving the constant chance to glimpse blue herons taking off in ungainly, graceful flight. In front of Camp F, where prisoners with the best records had unofficial freedoms, inmates fished for perch under the delicate leaves of pecan trees, and, in the fall, gathered up the thousands of pecans to shell and eat.

Throughout Angola's idyll the convicts lived in several fenced compounds, Main Prison and the outcamps. Barbed concertina wire, the coils piled three high, lined the tops and bottoms of the chain-link fences. Guard towers stood at the edges of the exercise yards. Cinder-block buildings, most of them one-story, most built in the 1950s, housed all the inmates. They contained the cavernous dorms, where the cots, with their inch-thick mattresses, stood two feet apart, and where each inmate lived out of two state-issued locker boxes, about 18 by 18 by 24 inches. The noise of huge industrial fans (there to reduce the risk of tuberculosis), and of the industrial-sounding steel toilets (partitionless and utterly exposed to the dorm—the men squatted in public), and of a single shared TV blaring above the fans and the flushing, and of a manual typewriter pecking out a convict's seventy-second writ, all of it echoing off the cinder block, was relentless and difficult to talk over. Steam wafted nonstop from the showers, thickening the already hot, humid air, stagnant in the many places the fans didn't reach. The fluorescent lights, too, were constant, lowered only to a security level blue after ten at night.

Inmates convicted, in "D.B. court" by Angola's disciplinary boards, of violations committed within the prison—sex offenses, drug offenses, violence, vandalism, or repeated disrespect—were removed from the dorms and put in cells, sentenced for months and kept for years if their attitudes didn't change. The Camp J cellblocks received no natural light. Ancient bulbs barely lit surfaces of chipped, gray-painted cement. Behind their recessed bars the convicts felt no circulating air. None. The fan down by the guard missed them entirely. In their white boxer shorts they lay, through most of the day and night, in fetal positions on the cement, for a slight evasion of heat in spring, summer, early fall. As for their occasional movement, Littell's cocktail warfare was relatively undisturbing. Dark, linear scars—fifteen or twenty of them—streaked the torso of one inmate I talked with. He had slashed himself with a razor blade. Shaving was then forbidden him. When shaving was allowed again, he had resumed. He hopped to the bars to speak with me, having recently tried to cut his foot off, to saw with a razor through the bone.

Once, as I accompanied the Camp J chaplain on his rounds, he warned that we might find a particular inmate posing nude for no one, flexing his muscles at the bars, his own excrement smeared over arms and chest.

About 1,500 inmates, at any given time, were kept in cells, under lockdown ranging in severity from Camp J to the prison's many "working cellblocks," from which the convicts were let out for daily labor and recreation. The rest of the 3,500 inmates were divided into two classes, trusties and big-stripes. The 700 trusties had earned, through years with minimal infractions, the privilege of jobs as orderlies in the administration building or as ranchers on the range crew, as clerks or keepers of the chase dogs that went out on escapes, or as "counsel substitutes," the inmate paralegals who argued for defendants in the D.B. courts. The trusties could move unsupervised outside the fences of their compounds.

Angola's perimeter had no fence at all. But the current of the Mississippi was strong, and the Tunica Hills, that bordered the prison's fourth side, were almost thick as jungle with vines and snakes. On the other side of all that it was a long way to anywhere. And many of the inmates believed it was even farther than it was. They spoke of a twenty-mile buffer zone before you even reached the end of prison property. No such zone existed. But the immensity of Angola's actual land was enough to bend the mind and slow the breath. It had a subduing effect. It seemed unbeatable. There were

only two or three attempted escapes each year. There had never been
a riot, and no guard had been killed since a small and isolated racial
protest had left one officer murdered and another badly burned a
quarter century ago.

The majority of big-stripes (called by the old name, though
everyone at Angola now wore jeans with a white T-shirt or blue work
shirt) were marched a mile or so from their compounds each week-
day at dawn in double-file lines. They were ordered to pick crops or,
with those long-handled hoes, to clear weeds from ditches. Or they
might be brought to the hilly terrain behind the prison cemetery—
where unclaimed bodies were buried by the inmate grave-digging
crew beneath the simplest white crosses—and told to mow the grass
with those same unwieldy tools.

Mounted, armed guards watched the work from above and at
least five yards away, guns never being allowed too near the prisoners. Other officers, "pushers," stood among each crew to be sure the
rows of okra or cotton were picked clean, that the hand-mowed grass
was left lawn-mower even. Often, though, there wasn't enough work
to go around, and the pushers merely kept the hoes swiping at air.
The big-stripes earned a salary of four cents per hour. (Some of the
trusties made as much as twenty.) The prices in the prison commissary were about the same as on a supermarket's shelves. Half of
every convict's earnings were set aside by the state into mandatory
inmate savings accounts. Given the inmates' odds of leaving, it was
unclear to everyone I asked, convict and staff alike, what rainy day
they were saving for.

After work, they were marched home.

Home: where Terry Hawkins, specialist in the Guts & Glory, made
their dinner. Before the rodeo he had graduated out of the fields to
the position of fry cook. It was better than being A.D.H.D. (A Dude

with a Hoe and a Ditch)—after stirring fried rice or flipping hotcakes on a stove ten feet long, he could grill hamburgers, bag them, and stuff them down his pants to sell in the dorm. Sometimes he snuck out with fried chicken under his shirt and cuts of cheese in his socks. Payment came in cigarettes, the prison's currency. Later he would stand outside the canteen, and trade a few packs for shampoo or soap or deodorant, or "zoo-zoos"—snacks of candy bars or sardines. He knew which guards would allow the stealing, the selling. He made sure to send them plates of fried chicken.

Cigarettes from food sales also kept him in needle and thread from the commissary. Since coming to Angola eleven years ago, he had discovered a talent for sewing. Built powerfully enough that he didn't worry about the effeminate connotations, he did occasional business as a seamster, fashioning sweat pants from worn-out state-issued sweat shirts. He charged two packs per job. Hunched on his cot, he cut along a pattern he'd drawn onto a stray manila file folder. The ribbing of the sweat shirt became the waist of the pants, the arms became the lower half of the legs, and the elastic from an old pair of boxer shorts became the waistband string.

Besides the new job in the kitchen, Terry's life had recently changed in another way. An inmate named Rev, shaved head a light brown and voice light in emphasis, had begun cropping up at his side. One morning after the first rodeo Sunday, on Terry's way out of the classification office, he heard the man asking, "You still think-ing?" Miss Mary, the classification officer, the person assigned to inmate needs and referrals, was a fan of *The Young and the Restless*. Terry had just stopped by her office to fill her in on episodes she'd missed. He was devoted to the soap, one of Angola's most-watched programs. He had told Miss Mary the latest doings of Cassie and Grace and his own favorite, Victor, who for years had claimed every woman on the show. Miss Mary, soft and motherly, speculated on Victor's next prey. They laughed, Terry didn't stay long. He was like the ne'er-do-well student proud to be bantering with the guidance counselor, and meanwhile, in the back of his mind, angling for any advantage he could get. And then, in the hall: "You still thinking? You still thinking?"

He heard the easy, insistent voice again as he sat on his cot that evening, digging in his locker box for his photo album. It was made from a decrepit textbook, *An Anthology of American Literature,* bartered for this purpose. The pages inside were covered with pictures he'd taped on: his thirteen-year-old daughter, Jamonica, and his pregnant sixteen-year-old stepdaughter, Quiana, the two of them standing in a visiting room, wall mural behind them. The painting showed a stream and low, luminous shafts of light streaking outward from the landscape to envelop whoever posed there. That visit had been months and months ago. Most of Angola's inmates received none at all. He knew he was lucky. He turned the anthology pages and stared at a snapshot of his mother, mailed sometime in the past few years, since he'd last seen her. Smiling on her birthday, she stood in a kitchen doorway under a sign that read, "Not Older, Better." And Rev strolled by his cot, saying, "You're a good dude, you ought to take that chance."

"I'm thinking on it."

"Still? Still thinking?"

One night after the second Sunday, Terry lay back mulling strategy for the next weekend's Guts & Glory. Last Sunday he'd barely been able to chase the prize; his ribs, battered during the first Sunday's attempt, wouldn't let him move. For the second straight week, no one had taken the chip. He didn't know if his ribs were broken. It didn't matter and wasn't worth finding out. If the X rays came back positive, he wouldn't take duty status for time off work—that would bar him from the rodeo. Next Sunday he would grab that chip. The payoff was progressive, now worth three hundred. He would send money to his grandmother-in-law, Ora, whom he considered his mother, though he'd been divorced after his sentencing. And he would buy some things for himself. After last Sunday the clown had told him, "You got to just stand there and take the hit, Bullfighter, that's the only way you're going to get it." So he would give up his special technique of sprinting away in a narrow curve; he would let the bull knock him down and run him over, hope the muzzle struck and not the horn. He would win.

And then Rev walked by, told him, "You're a good person."

Among the impediments to Terry's believing this were his own recollections. Mr. Denver Tarter, his boss at the slaughterhouse, had asked him to work late on Quiana's birthday, to clean out the meat locker; Mr. Denver Tarter had called him a "black son-of-a-bitch" when he refused; Terry had, as he remembered it, "started F-ing at him" and feinted a blow without any intention of following through; Mr. Denver Tarter had swung at him with the meat-ax that Terry then knocked from his hands and used against his employer. It was hard to know whether the self defense part of Terry's story was true. There had been no witnesses. Whether it was true or not, it didn't change the way Terry felt. Mr. Denver Tarter had always treated him and his family well, stocking their freezers every Friday with sirloins and pork chops, ground meat and T-bones; Mr. Denver Tarter, he told me, hadn't been a racist, had plenty of black friends in town, had only called him a "black son-of-a-bitch" out of aggravation and the Wild Turkey he'd been drinking that day; Terry had grabbed the ax off the floor and struck his boss in the head with the handle, and then—"before I knew it"—flipped the weapon around and swung it into his boss over and over with the sharp end. "I just whacked all the way out," he said. "I can't remember all where I hit him at, but I know I hit him too many times."

By the end of it, Mr. Denver Tarter lay on his back in the hall outside the butcher room—the place where Terry scalded the pigs in a tank and shot the cows and hoisted them up and put their heads in a rack to decapitate them and stuck a knife in their hearts to bleed them and skinned them and gutted them and sawed them in half—and Mr. Denver Tarter's short, thinning brown hair was soaked in blood and there was a gash all the way through his windpipe. He was gasping, wheezing, blood spattering from the hole in his throat. His eyes were wide open. Terry bent over him, gazing at the blue uniform shirt with "Mr. Tarter," just that, stitched in red scripted letters on the breast, at the heavy face, at the hand raised weakly toward him, reaching out to him. A question droned through Terry's mind, "How did all of a sudden this happen? How did all of a sudden this happen?" He stared for a long, long moment before walking out of the building, raspy breath behind him.

Even after eleven years Terry's brain hadn't found a safe place for this scene; the memory spilled forward often from the files. If the images—and the sound of that breathing—weren't enough to convince him that Rev was mistaken, there was the fact that he'd spent time in another state prison on a robbery charge; he'd had his warnings before the murder. And at Angola, he'd been sentenced repeatedly to J and other cellblocks. He'd fought and fought, broken a man's jaw and cheekbone, blackened a guard's eye.

And perhaps it wouldn't be reading in too much to say that the circumstances of Terry's upbringing didn't make it any easier for him to hear Rev's words, that his childhood hadn't left him buoyant with self-worth. Once, I visited Ora, the old woman he adored and called his mama. I turned off a main road of large, well-kept homes within wide-open Louisiana farm country, and drove up a rutted lane. Before and after a family move to California, Terry had spent his childhood here. The dead-end street was an enclave of tiny houses, dilapidated or entirely abandoned, porches caving and paint long gone, and of structures that can only be called shacks. Until recently, Terry's real mother had lived in one of the abandoned houses. I found Ora in a two-room shack. Her clothes hung from nails in the walls. The furniture consisted solely of a bed and two torn vinyl kitchen chairs. She spoke proudly of the way Terry had carried in water for her to drink and bathe in, before he went to Angola. Running water had come later. She recalled various children, most of them family and most doing relatively well, who had grown up on this lane. She also mentioned one grandson, two nephews, and one cousin all in prison. One of Terry's brothers was in Angola for attempted murder.

But gradually Terry started listening to Rev, partly because Rev made him think of Ora. Her explanation for Terry's crimes was that "his mama wasn't religious people" and "didn't knock the stink out of him when he was doing some nasty cussin'." Now, every phone call, she told him to "get off into that Bible and ask the Lord to clean your filthy heart and mouth." Maybe it was that simple. Rev, too, made it seem so. "Man, straighten up," Rev said, and analyzed all of Terry's troubles, at Angola and before: "You just got hanging with the wrong crowd." Though his prison record had improved over the past two years, Terry wasn't so sure. Just a few weeks ago, a kitchen guard had rebuffed a suggestion—"You don't tell me what to do"— and left him trembling. Enraged. Lips literally shivering. Mind racing so fast he had no mind at all. Too much like when he'd turned the ax around and used the blade again and again and again.

Yet he *hadn't* gone after the guard, had *only* trembled, then cleaned the ovens as he'd been told. And at last he gave in to Rev's lobbying. He held hands in the circle and prayed.

Rev's group of ten or twelve met every day inside the vegetable cooler. Before their shifts stirring mammoth vats of gravy with utensils the size of spades, or frying eight hundred fish cakes, the inmates shut the door, kept the light off, took in the refrigeration and the view of the fields through the one small window. Then, surrounded by a huge potato peeler, a row of sinks, and shelves filled with okra and eggplant, they clasped hands and bowed heads. There was a man in squarish, state-issued eyeglasses, another with "Man of God" tooled

into his tan belt, a convict who'd just dashed in from the weight pile
and whose T-shirt was drenched.

Each in turn, some barely murmuring a line and others going on
for minutes, they asked for things all-encompassing, things specific.
"Lord, let us decrease that You may increase....I'm praying for them
to make me a clerk, Lord....Touch us with the faith to accept everything as Your will....I need You to stop that trickeration today, glory
hallelujah....Help us to put on the whole armor of God, O Lord, to
wrestle with the flesh, O Lord, we are flesh, O Lord, make us spirit,
O Lord, make us better than we are, O Lord, shield us in the armor
of faith, O Lord, bar that devil by Your armor, O Lord, and let us
remind ourselves that even while the world wants to see us fall, O
Lord, we got a host of witnesses up there wanting us to stand up, O
Lord....We thank you, in the name of Jesus, we thank you for bringing us Brother Terry this day...."

Terry said little, but joined them before every shift that week.
Then, on the third Saturday in October, he hesitated, put them off,
told them no, and finally followed them to church that evening in
what was known as the camp's visiting "shed," though it was simply
a large room in the cinder-block complex. The Faith City International ministry had been coming to Angola every month for eight
years. Rev had been helping with their services since the beginning
as part of their "praise team." Faith City happened not to be one of
the new religious groups taking their message to the prison since
Warden Cain had put out word for visiting preachers, since he had
brought full-scale revivals to Angola, since he had declared, "This
prison is open for religion." But Terry could decide to attend church
at the last minute, rather than having to submit his name in advance
for the "call-out" sheet, because Cain wanted his inmates to worship.

Was that why Terry went that night? So some captain who knew
the warden might see him filing in? So his name would appear on
some list of the faithful he imagined Cain compiling? Was that why
he had joined Rev's circle in the first place?

To reach the service he left his dorm through the steel door, turned down the outdoor Walk, passed through a series of checkpoints with gates that could be slammed and locked in emergency. He lined up along a fence, still two massive barred portals from the front of the camp, and waited until a guard let everyone through another checkpoint into the shed. Inside, black plastic chairs, their backs stenciled faintly I.W.F. for the Inmate Welfare Fund that had purchased them, were aligned in precise rows, the brown laminate tables pushed to one wall. A Coke machine (for use by visitors only; the inmates could not have money), a Pac-Man machine, and a mural—this one a seascape with dolphins, a killer whale, a three-masted ship and a sky of puffy clouds—were the church's side chapels. The pulpit was a dingy white wood, a small cross raised on its face.

Rev and the rest of the praise team, work shirts ironed and pens clipped businesslike to breast pockets, sat up front. Terry wasn't going to get himself trapped up there. He took a chair in the middle of a row about two-thirds back. An inmate tuned an electric guitar, another checked the keyboard's amp. Terry stared down at the crease in his jeans. He always slipped a pack to the laundry man to get his clothes pressed, but tonight's jeans were special, his own, the pair he'd ordered from a catalog as opposed to state-issue. Below the crease were white leather Converse high-tops, again distinct from the no-brand state sneakers he wore in the kitchen. This was the outfit he put on for his rare visitors. And he'd had time, as he gravitated toward coming here, to have his close-cropped hair trimmed by the camp barber.

Many of the convicts around him were just as meticulously dressed. Levi's or Lee blue jeans—subtly (or dramatically within the narrow confines of permitted dress) the men made this night different. And Sister Jackie, the leader of Faith City, encouraged the distinction. "They should feel they are going to a normal church," she told me later. That evening she wore a black skirt and jacket, the jacket adorned with large gold buttons and, descending from the shoulders, a multi-layered arrangement of gold chiffon. Forty or fifty convicts waited for her to begin. I asked if she ever worried about their motives, that they might be trying to impress the warden, or dreaming of impressing the pardon board should they ever come before it. She said no. She did not worry. She hardly thought about it. "People in the regular world use church and God for all kinds of reasons—it's the same in the penitentiary. But I would say most of the inmates I see from the pulpit are sincere. At that moment. How they are affected afterwards, how deeply the experience changes them, that isn't my place to judge."

Terry watched this heavy, pretty woman, with perfect teeth and flawless brown skin and short, waved hair and gold plumage at her shoulders, say hello to the praise team and anyone else who waited his turn. She gave them each a long hug.

"Hallelujah!" she cried, taking the pulpit. "Won't you praise the Lord tonight?" She shut her eyes. "We welcome you, Lord, we glorify you, Lord, we magnify you, Lord, we love you, Lord, everybody stand and give the Lord a wave, a wave offering tonight…." And most everybody did, stretching both arms toward the rough stucco ceiling and swaying, though five or six at the back remained in their seats and chatted, enjoying the air-conditioning, and two sipped coffee and joked in open amusement. A lone guard sat near the entryway, toying with his clipboard. "I bind every spirit of condemnation in Jesus' name!" Sister Jackie declared. Terry swayed dutifully, rigidly.

She beckoned another Faith City minister, a squat woman in floral, to a second microphone. Sister Jackie asked the musicians to step up and some of the praise team to join her, and Sister Jackie led the singing:

We're going up to the high places
We're going up to the high places

We're going up to the high places
And tear the devil's kingdom down!

It seemed her voice wrapped from the end of the chorus around again to the beginning without a breath. The sound was big as a soloist's in a fine gospel choir, and it made the plastic chairs, the yellowing ceiling, the dingy pulpit into joyful things. The praise team clapped, dancing almost in unison like back-up singers, yet also on the brink of disarray, chaos. One of them, a wispy inmate no older than nineteen, broke into a stationary hop every time she swept into the chorus again.

Run, children, run
This is the time to believe

She surged into a new, even faster hymn, hardly pausing for the organ's crescendo, and two convicts did what the lyrics instructed—ran around the room, circling the congregation, lap after lap until the words changed.

Dance, children, dance
This is the time to believe

The wispy boy rattled a tambourine, and hopped and kicked and whirled with the abandon of Hasidim at a wedding. The runners switched to skipping in place. Off in a corner, eyes closed, one man gestured at the ceiling, furling and unfurling his fingers, apparently talking to God.

Sing, children, sing

Very quietly, Terry did.

Sister Jackie did one last hymn, this one slow and a capella,

Anointing fall on me
Touch my hands, my mouth, my heart
Anointing fall on me
Fill my life, Lord, every part

and steered the congregation toward prayer, everyone soon muttering separate words and she shouting over them, "In Jesus' name I
take authority over Satan's power....O yes yes yes yes *yes*....O work
with me tonight, work with me....We know not how to pray but...
we enter in by the blood...." Terry tried mumbling praise to God
along with the man beside him, but just as in the vegetable cooler, he
didn't feel comfortable saying much. "O wonderful," the inmates
spoke around him, "O praise Jesus, O I know you hear me, Lord, O
wonderful wonderful wonderful wonderful." And then, led by Sister
Jackie, whose tilted throat glistened with sweat and whose mouth
produced "O yadareeba yasheeda. O badatimba kimba o shey," they
began speaking in tongues. "Abinda binda binda binda binda," skidded from one man's lips. It went on and on, she sliding back and
forth between language, "Come into our presence, O Lord," and
these other calls, "O yadareeba," while some inmates stayed deep in
their strange sounds, and others didn't speak but clapped randomly,
loudly, without rhythm. A few turned blindly to the walls, palms
lifted as though to feel their own shadows.

Now and then the anarchy of syllables fell into a lull, and during
onc softening a man two rows ahead of Terry, a man with his body
doubled over and his face buried in the crook of his arm, could be
heard murmuring, "Shastada koondo koondolo po li ri ri koondo
koondo koondolo." The voice pleaded, dwindled, whimpered and all
but sniveled, before it went on begging for something it could name
only in these nonwords. "O li ri ri ri ri." The syllables became more

and more broken. They became only exhalations struggling to form consonants, like the sound of someone struggling to explain himself after he's burst into sobbing. But the effort was minor, surrendering. It ended not in any explanation but in exhausted gratitude: "O thank you, thank you, Jesus, thank you thank you thank you thank you thank you."

Terry kept his head bowed and kept quiet. He studied the crease in his jeans. He didn't feel qualified to be a part of this. He knew the Spirit was supposed to lead him to the right words, the right sounds, and he didn't feel any Spirit entering into him.

"Some of you," Sister Jackie emerged into preaching, "are in some dead situations. Dead, dead, dead. And it's worse than that. You're in a cave. And that's not all. There's a stone at the front of that cave, a rock, a boulder you can't move, and it's laying there on your heart and blocking the exit from that pit, and it's crushing you, it won't let you breathe, and there's nothing you can do about it, because you're dead, you're not living, you're *entombed!* And all you have to do," her voice thinned, as though she were a kindergarten teacher directing children in their first collage, "is say, 'I believe.' That's all. 'I believe.' That's the only price for getting that rock rolled away. That's the only price you have to pay for Jesus' love. 'I believe.' How many of you are in that tomb? How many of you are without Jesus? How many of you will let Jesus take your pain? How many of you will speak that faith, 'Jesus died for me'? It's so simple. 'Jesus died for me.' We're *all* sinners. How many of you will accept the free gift of his love? How many of you will take what's offered to everyone and barred to nobody. Nobody. It's so *cheap.* You don't even need to make four cents an hour! You just pay with your anguish. Should I make it sound a little bit harder? Should I raise the price and cut back supply? Get everyone rushing up here then. How many of you are ready? How many of you are ready to come up here tonight and be saved?"

Five men went. They lined before her. The praise team stood at their backs, hands spread in the air a few inches from their shoulder blades, to catch them in case their knees buckled. "For the wages of sin is death," she recited, and asked the congregation to repeat. "But God showed his love for us while we were yet sinners.

"Do you hear that?" she broke off to ask. "We *all* fell when the Spirit left Adam in that garden. We *all* sank into our tombs…."

Terry was not among the five. He felt he was not qualified.

Next, she wandered down the center aisle. The electric organ stabbed out instrumental hymns, making the room itself bend with longing. "Someone," she said, "is having circulation trouble tonight. I don't know what kind of trouble, but it's somewhere, I can feel it, where the circulation flows. Someone—"

A hand went up. She heard the details, laid her palm on the inmate's kidney. "I speak the mind of Christ. I call out infirmity in Jesus' name. God wants to strengthen you, yes, that's it, that's it, yes…."

Someone else suffered with "reoccurring thoughts, so many reoccurring thoughts you can't even depressurate things"; she asked who that person was, curved her fingers over his forehead. "In the name of Jesus I stay your thoughts!" And someone ailed with one leg longer than the other and with pain in his ribs, someone who did not want to make himself known. Her gold chiffon shoulders drifted through the room. She crossed the border again away from English, then returned. "Someone, O Lord."

It was not that Terry didn't recognize his own injury from the first Sunday's rodeo, but that his legs were perfectly normal. He said nothing. She came behind him. She touched his shoulder, leaned him forward, brushed her hand across the back of his rib cage. "It's going to be all right," she said, calmly as the best mother would, before groaning, "We *adore* you, O Lord." She stepped around to his row, moved the empty chair in front of him, and, bending, held one white leather Converse in each hand, drawing his feet toward her on the floor. She paired them, and revealed that the left did not reach as far as the right. The bottom of its sneaker did not match with the other but came only to the seam where leather and tread met. "It's going to be all right," she said again.

She returned to the pulpit and asked the minister in floral to bring Terry up to the front. He didn't need the help, though his thighs felt watery. He laughed to himself. Nothing was going to happen. Sister Jackie asked the other minister to bring a chair, and told Terry to sit down. She told him to stretch out his legs. She told him to lift his arms above his head. She straddled his shins, her black skirt touching them like the hem of a curtain. She prayed half intelligibly, half in that other language. She stepped back, took his ankles, slid his legs apart on the tile. She brought them together. He saw that now they matched exactly. She straddled him again, large body tipping forward, glistening neck near his face and breasts close to his shoulders and palms pressed to the sides of his ribs. His arms in the air were shivering. He felt his chest vibrating, his lips trembling, his chin about to shatter. She hugged him. "It's going to be all right," she said once more, "that's just the Spirit moving through you."

The next day, the third Sunday in October, without pain in his ribs and, conceivably, with legs more evenly aligned, Terry Hawkins won the Guts & Glory. Whatever the physical improvements wrought upon him, they played no role in his triumph. To grasp the chip he simply let the bull knock him down—and was lucky enough to come up in one piece. But he felt himself to be a slightly different person, with different prospects. The money was part of it. "What you need?" he joked with a guard behind the stadium. "Fifty bucks?" The money may also have been the least of it. He felt that between Rev and Sister Jackie he had been drawn down a new path. He was going to "get off into that Bible." He was going to please Ora. He was going to become a good person. And for this, and for his bravery in winning the Guts & Glory and, earlier, the Bust-Out, he would be rewarded. Warden Cain and all the assistant wardens had seen what he could do, what he was willing to do, with those bulls. He would be made trusty. There would be a job with the range crew. He would be assigned his own horse and the freedom to ride along the levee at the edge of the prison grounds. He would rise to the top in this life he was sentenced to.

That Sunday and the next were filled with promise. The sun was bright, and the crowd, overflowing the bleachers, claimed the dirt beside the ring. Earlier they had thronged the hobby-craft tables, bought the cowhide belts, the strange sculptures—shaped like a giant's fingers—made from cypress limbs and etched with scenes of leaping deer, the wallets, the birdhouses. The inmates would make enough money to order wood and leather and dye to last most of the next twelve months. Even the convict who told me his customers haggled over prices as though he were subhuman, as though "something gross" were attached to his body, seemed to be enjoying his brisk sale of zodiac key chains.

And over at the photo concessions, where the fans got themselves locked in that freestanding jail cell—young couples; fathers and sons; toddlers coaxed to press their noses to the bars—the convict photographer looked pleased. In this way, he raised money for the Angola Sober Group. I asked if he was bothered by the element of mockery. "No, it's not like that," he answered with what seemed a twelve-step graduate's rigid oblivion. "This is my chance to have a little contact with the public. I'm not an inmate for today. Today I'm free." Minutes later, two round women smiled uneasily behind the bars. "You remember us from last year?" one of them asked. And the other said,

"Yeah, now you got to hug him, Charlene." Holding her half-clarified Polaroid between two fingers, Charlene wrapped her arms momentarily around his neck.

Inside the arena, on the third Sunday, Johnny Brooks absorbed everything the bull tried. Between its contorted leaps he seemed to loll peacefully in a trough between cresting waves. Because so few inmates had lasted the needed eight seconds, this day the standard was lowered to six. Brooks kept his chest out, his weight centered, his free arm, perpendicular at the elbow, cutting the air in classic rodeo style for balance and points from the judges. When the six-second whistle blew, he was still in full control, and for several seconds longer he worked his arm with immaculate form, to show that he could do this forever, to make clear to everyone his expertise, how much he'd learned in the years he'd been locked away.

There was applause from the spectators. It was not the loud roar he'd described to me back in September, but it lasted a few seconds. He waved his hat and walked back across the arena, surrounded by fading approval.

And on the fourth Sunday he rode still better, on the bull that was the toughest of this year's stock. It gyrated, heaving its tremendous mass into the air. Brooks rose three, four, five times with the animal; when it came down, wrenching, his body snapped but held out against the spin. Then, tipped suddenly to horizontal, he could not right himself. He was on his back on the dirt. Five seconds—not six—had gone by. The rodeo, for him, was over. He would win no all-around buckle. Yet in the crowd's diffuse clapping there was one last measure of acknowledgment, an agreement, perhaps, with what many of the lifers said to me constantly, like a mantra: "I'm still a citizen, and I'm still one of God's children." There was the most fleeting welcome back into the world.

He strained to hear, as well, a single voice among the spectators. Three hours ago, just before the rodeo, while the range crew looked over the bulls in the pen, the wife of an ex-inmate had called Brooks over to a chain-link fence. Through it, she introduced a friend, Belva, a tall, sturdy woman with high cheekbones and a delayed smile, a smile made arresting by the delay and by a slender gap between her front teeth. She wore white stretch pants with a white sweat shirt, and she and Brooks spoke as shyly as homebodies forced to a singles party.

"It's nice to meet you," he said.

"It's nice to meet you. Are you riding in the rodeo?" The question was scarcely audible.

"Pardon?"

"Are you riding in the rodeo?"

"Yes I am."

That was where conversation ran out. The women returned to their places in the stands. Brooks did not have vast experience with emotional relationships. He had no visitors. Based on this exchange, he decided that he and Belva would fall in love. He went on believing it, though he could not hear her voice in the bleachers.

Buckkey Lasseigne, face like an old rancher's, felt hopeful, too. Toward the end of the third Sunday, he was in the running for the all-around. If he won the buckle, maybe his son, Chris, would come see him, maybe their hours together would be easier than the twice-a-year visits of recent times. The last one had been in the park built for trusties to picnic with their families. (Like Johnny Brooks, Buckkey had trusty status and was a member of the range crew.) Buckkey and his only child had played their usual sullen game of one-on-one basketball on the packed-dirt court. As the afternoon ended and the bus came to collect the visitors, Chris, who had Buckkey's blond hair but who was three or four inches taller, responded to some piece of fatherly advice, "Okay, dude."

"Don't call me that," Buckkey had said.

"What do you want me to call you?"

"Dad would be just fine."

"Cool," the boy had agreed. "Dad. I'll call you anything you want me to call you. You want me to call you inmate, you want me to call you convict, you want me to call you Louisiana State Penitentiary?"

Still, the boy had said once over the phone, "I'd sure like to get one of those buckles." So the father had told me. When I spoke with his wife, who had stuck with the marriage throughout his imprisonment, making her all but unique at Angola, she said, "That's just Buckkey." Chris didn't want the buckle at all.

Perhaps Buckkey understood this. Thirty-six years old, his handsome, square-jawed face was so wrinkled, especially across his forehead between his curly hair and hazel eyes, it could have belonged to a man twice his age. Thorough resignation lurked behind the energy that seemed to go with his nickname. He knew the things still said to his son in their small town, the town where Buckkey had grown up, the town of the murder. "Hey," a substitute teacher had yelled out to the boy a few weeks ago, trying to control him in class, "I know where your daddy's at." He knew that outside a Wal-Mart the victim's mother had shrieked her undiminished rage at Buckkey's own mother and then, fury blending with futility, swung at Buckkey's mother's thighs, over and over, with a plastic shopping basket. He knew he could do nothing for any of them. He knew he had destroyed them. He knew what he had done.

And refused to know. He told me it hadn't been him, that it had been the friend he was with, that the two of them, high on PCP and weed, had stopped to get gas, begun arguing with the attendant, a boy they knew vaguely who'd been a few years behind them in school, and that the next thing he remembered the .22 wasn't in the glove compartment and his friend had shot the attendant behind the station. (The murder had been prosecuted as resulting from a robbery. Buckkey had made a videotaped confession, before recanting at trial.)

Just a few minutes before rendering his story to me, Buckkey had said, "I don't consider myself a murderer. Murderers are born. They come out of the womb killing." It was a way of distinguishing evil men from bad acts, of claiming some innocence at his core if not in his deeds. But it seemed an admission that he had done the killing, and the tale blaming his friend made me wince. *You murdered someone's child,* I wanted to scream. *Can't you do any better than this lame bullshit?* I thought: It is a good thing that you will spend the rest of your life here, that you have had your life taken away. I wondered if it shouldn't literally be taken, and I knew, imagining the victim to be my own son, that I would want Buckkey's mother and wife and child to suffer as I did, that I would want Buckkey killed.

Now he climbed from the rail onto the bull. "Ready?" The animal jabbed its head against the boards, and Buckkey, determined to ride one-handed because others had lasted the six seconds, clutched with his free hand to the wall. "Ready?" the gate man urged. Buckkey lifted his hand. "Outside!"

Convulsing, the bull lunged forward twice and hooked left. It rose off its hind legs and whipped the rider's forehead into its own skull. Buckkey crumpled and slid, unconscious. The clowns rushed to lure the bull from the ring. The prison's emergency medical team hurried out to immobilize Buckkey's neck and belt him to a stretcher.

On the fourth Sunday the hope was also this: A rider named Danny Fabre wanted a new pair of ears. He believed that if he mounted a bull, showed he would "do anything for him," Warden Cain might approve cosmetic surgery.

Danny had killed a neighbor of his brother's ten years ago, a woman who tried to help him, this five weeks after he'd been released from Angola following a short stint for simple robbery and probation violation. (His arrest record had been long: armed robbery, assault, burglary.) He killed the woman for questioning his honesty, though he had indeed knocked on her door and asked her for a ride to buy jumper cables, but instead directed her to a house where he "scored some weed." He "exploded," he told me, when she pulled over and said in the car, as he remembered it, "'You been to the penitentiary, you ain't nothing but a con man, you ain't never going to be nothing.'" He punched her in the face and punched her again, four or five times, then began choking her, while she fought weakly and said quietly, almost no voice available, "Danny, you're hurting me." He remembered those words, and his strangling her to death. He dragged her body into the woods and, in the moonlight, mistook the shifting of her limbs over the rough ground for signs of life. He found a stick and drove it through her eye nearly to the back of her skull. He covered her body with pine straw. He set it on fire.

Danny Fabre believed he deserved the death penalty. He felt fortunate for his life sentence. Yet he wanted surgery on his ears. And they did in fact protrude comically, at virtual right angles to his head. He tried to style his longish blond hair to conceal them, but no matter how he combed, the disks of bright pink cartilage sliced right through.

"Hey," another inmate had suggested lately, "you could leave here any time you want."

"What do you mean?"

"Just flap your ears and fly away."

That was what they called him, "Ears." But he'd learned that the teaching hospital at Tulane University in New Orleans might reshape the disks for free, for the education of its students. "Look at me," he pleaded right there in the arena, as we talked amid the convicts waiting to ride. "Look at me. I don't want it for beauty. I got a life sentence. My looks don't really matter. But I'm tired of waking up every day, Ears this, Big Ears that, Dumbo the Elephant—it hurts, man, it hurts."

He was intent on holding my gaze with his own. His eyes were green but flecked disturbingly with yellow. He said that in September he had joined Toastmasters. The captain who sponsored the club had finally given him permission. For months the captain had put him off, told him to go longer without a write-up. Danny was famous among the guards I spoke with. They didn't want him in their camps. Anything could set him off. He'd spent years in the cells, for fights, for burying knives all over the Yard, for painting battery acid over his own feet. Sometimes he'd chosen to stay locked up, broken rules on purpose, because to him the cells felt easier than the dorms. Terry Hawkins's record was rated poor by prison authorities; Danny Fabre's was off the charts. But now he'd done everything the captain asked. He wanted to learn how to give a speech. He'd given a talk once for the inmate chapter of the Jaycees. The subject he'd picked was butterflies and reincarnation. People had told him he had talent.

And he told me of enrolling in school. A year ago he had started with a fourth-grade reading level. Now he was near seventh. His teacher gave him twenty-five new words every week, and on his bed he copied them out thirty times for spelling, looked up their definitions, and wrote sentences for each. He thought he could pass his GED by the end of the year.

But the ears were his first wish, and despite the fact that he was wound extremely tight, despite the disconcerting quality of his yellow-flecked eyes, I couldn't fault him for his perspective. If I'd had ears like his, I would have wanted a new pair, too.

Danny had already begged one of the prison doctors to deem the operation a necessity; now, on the fourth Sunday, he appealed to a higher power. He got himself a slot in the bull riding. With the warden watching from above the chutes, Danny straddled the animal. It tried to scale the chute wall. Danny scrambled off. "Don't be a coward," a clown yelled.

"One thing about me," Danny answered, "I don't fear death. But I ain't stupid."

He tied in with two hands, somehow lasted the six seconds, heard the bull let out a sputtering breath through its nostrils, lost his hold with the next buck, landed face first, pushed himself up to get out of the way. The bull's hoof came down on his back and nailed him to the ground. The following day, three of his ribs snapped badly enough that I could feel where they overlapped, Danny coughed blood onto the gray concrete of the Walk and waited to be remade.

Buckkey, coming to after being knocked unconscious, managed to avoid the medical paperwork that would keep him from riding. On the fourth Sunday, he won more points in the Wild Horse Race, an event in which six unbroken horses were sent into the ring dragging ropes behind them. Three-man teams dodged high-kicking hooves while attempting to grab the ropes, then hold on long enough for one man to leap on and ride. At the end of the day, the end of the month, Buckkey stood second in the all-around. The runner-up buckle was his.

And Johnny Brooks was right. A week after they met, Belva sent him a letter. "I'm writing to let you know I would love to go see and viste you...I know you may get a little lonssome and time-after-time you may need a friend to talk to....Ruby said you were a very nice person and that why I decide to drop you few lines....You was great at the rodeo. I could not belive how you ride a bull lack that." Within a month she started visiting. They talked of her four children, her job as a kitchen-worker in a Cajun restaurant, her desire to become a nurse's aide. Letters were exchanged, three or four every week. "It been a long time now I share my thought with a man and I hope you would let me consider letting our relationship grow and I'll always be there for you." By Christmas they were engaged to be married.

THREE

"DO YOU BELIEVE IN GOD?" CAIN ASKED.

We sat, two days before Christmas, in the small, denlike office in the building everyone called the Ranch House. It was down the road from "B-line," the village where two hundred guard families lived on the grounds, and down the road, too, from the inmate cemetery. With its long bleached-wood porch and mounted deer heads, its stocked pantry and fruit bowl piled high on the kitchen counter, the house borrowed from dude ranch and hunting lodge and fifties suburbia. Cain liked to run the prison from there. (He didn't live on the grounds, as all past wardens had. He preferred the layout of the warden's house at Dixon Correctional, and compelled his successor there to find other quarters. The warden's official residence at Angola remained empty, but the Ranch House served as a daytime home and informal control center.) Outside, horses grazed in a hillside pasture. In the kitchen, a lifer named Forty-Five—the number on his football jersey when he'd starred at LSU—kept the serving trays filled with fried steak and mustard greens and jambalaya and corn bread throughout the afternoons.

Hearing the warden's question, I thought, This is crazy.

I was supposed to be the one asking questions. And if we were going to have a two-way conversation, this subject, for me, was the most intimate starting point.

And sometimes the warden did seem a bit crazy, erratically homespun and overly simplistic, but, finally, he made sense.

"Look," he had reiterated a few minutes earlier, "people have to see that it costs thirty dollars a day to incarcerate a man who committed a crime twenty years ago and is not the same person. We could be spending that same money to change young predators. There's only so much room in our prisons, I don't care how fast you build them. Why not let the changed man go, and put the kid with the rap sheet in Angola for enough time to rehabilitate him, instead of passing him in and out of the system until he goes out and kills someone?"

He leaned back behind his desk, eating Forty-Five's creamed corn from a Styrofoam cup, spooning it out until the cup was scraped clean.

"Now the men I'd let go—and they need to let *me* decide now, let the shepherd separate the sheep from the goats—one or two might fall back. But we'll protect against that. We'll use the parish jails. Use them like a halfway house. Let the convict go to work during the day, get locked back up at night. Till he's definitely on his feet. And the one or two that gets out and does something bad, that's a lot better odds than you'll get setting those young predators loose every six months."

He said that at least five hundred men, probably a thousand, should be released from Angola that day. He said there would be more once his programs took hold, once he instilled morality and a sense of accomplishment.

"These people that commit crimes, they're basically—now there's exceptions to every rule—but look at them, they're poor. White or black, they're poor, and they didn't have the family values. Remember, we gave up the family, and we gave up the draft. We quit taking our young people off the streets into the army, teaching them to say yes sir and no sir, training them for a job. Stopping the draft was one of the worst things this country ever did. Even when there was no war, we gathered them in—everybody had to either go to college or vo-tech school or go to the army, and wherever you went you learned a trade. We gave all that up. And Mama went to work, so we gave up the streets to the kids. Wasn't *Ozzie and Harriet* great? I try to put back some of those values."

I had to suppress my uneasiness with his dime-store analysis. I put aside, too, a suggestion of impropriety: a short-lived attempt, during his first few months as warden, to bring private enterprise to Angola, to allow a canned-food resalvaging company to use inmate labor without paying the state much of anything. And of course some inmates weren't fond of him. I'd heard critical comments here and there. "He's Pharaoh," Littell said. "And he's a businessman."

Grumblings had come, too, from members of the traveling inmate band that had, until recently, performed at fairs and Knights of Columbus fund-raisers around the state. They had been scheduled to play at the rodeo, and I had looked forward to hearing them. Back in September, I had stopped in on one of their rehearsals as the lead guitarist, Myron Hodges, built a thrall of notes beneath the vaulting chorus of an old Motown hit. During a break, he played a rendition of "The Wind Cries Mary." It was my favorite Hendrix song, and the way Myron weaved the quiet opening—one sad, questioning riff answering another—gave me chills. Agile as his fingers were, his throat was not. He was not the band's singer. But he sang for me at that moment, and somehow his limited voice made the lyrics all the more crushing.

The traffic lights turn blue tomorrow....

The band didn't end up playing at the rodeo. The first weekend in October they had been slow to wake for an early-morning rehearsal at the stadium, a rehearsal that was supposed to help the rodeo livestock get used to the music so the animals wouldn't spook during the event. And, depending on who was recounting the episode, one of the musicians had talked back at a senior employee. Immediately Warden Cain had substituted a haphazard outcamp group and abolished Myron's band permanently. He'd announced, "Y'all won't touch an instrument again as long as I'm warden of this penitentiary!" Yet while I sympathized with the musicians and felt almost bereft that I would never again hear Myron play the guitar, and while I wondered always about Cain's excesses, I wondered equally why these prisoners, who'd been given the privilege of touring the state, hadn't just gotten their butts out of bed.

And overriding everything was Cain's intention to lead people who no one else wanted to deal with, men who society wanted to forget. He meant to lead them up from the bottom.

His hope was not based in naiveté. When he spoke of the heart of his program, when he recalled what his mother had once told him, "'The Lord put you in that job—it's a wonderful place to fish,'" he added, "You can never catch all the fish. You might not catch but a few." When he talked of a "religious explosion" at Angola ("And I don't mean just the Protestant religion, I mean all religions, I mean the Koran," he said to me, whose Judaism, he teased, was "like unleavened bread waiting for the right ingredient to rise"), he acknowledged that many attended services only to win his favor. "But at least they're going. At least they're pretending. At least they're acting like God-fearing people. And doing all that acting, they might change from the outside in."

And to all the inmates, whether or not they took part in religion, he had announced his own slogan of behavior modification: "I'll be as nice as you let me, and as mean as you make me."

"If they're going to act crazy and bad," he explained to me, "I'll make it so they don't want to do that anymore. I don't mean physically. I mean, take it to Camp J, do what you have to do. I mean, take

take take—to where they don't get anything to put on but a paper gown, to where they don't eat anything but the food loaf." The loaf consisted of the ingredients in the regular inmate meal, minus all seasoning, put in a blender and whipped into a gelatinous log. It was served without a utensil. "I mean, take their dignity, and then say, 'Here, you can have this back as soon as you behave.'"

Did I believe in God? All kinds of things rushed through my head when he asked that question. As with many of the inmates, I thought of the warden's favor. I needed my own privileges at the prison. He could legally bar me from Angola, his world. Or, wanting only his own version of Angola written, he could decide abruptly that my time with the convicts would be spent with a staff escort, something we had agreed would not be necessary. There was plenty at stake in my answer. But also like some of the inmates, I had my own religious belief, regardless of my need to please. Yet it was never certain or solid; it was the flimsiest thing.

I couldn't tell Cain, I hope to feel God's presence at Angola—I wouldn't sound like much of a journalist, and I might sound plainly manipulative. And because I had been raised without religion, surrounded by people who saw it as the enemy of human progress, expressing anything about God was the last thing I wished to do.

"Warden Cain," I said, in the dark little office, "I come from a different place than you do."

"Okay," he said.

"For all kinds of reasons, my yes can't be the same as yours."

"I appreciate that."

"But I do," I said.

"Well, that's good, that's good."

I knew I had given a self-serving answer. Still, I felt that I had spoken the truth to a man who, in his own way, understood.

■

Cain was a kind of apothcosis. So much before him had been so degraded. From the end of the Civil War until 1900, 10 percent of Louisiana's convicts had died every year.

That was when the state leased its prisoners to private business. The system was used throughout the South, and took a variety of forms. Some state governments stayed responsible, in part, for their convicts, for feeding them, guarding them. In Louisiana, all control was ceded to the lessee, a former Confederate major named Samuel James. Most of the men in his charge were imprisoned for larceny, with sentences ranging from one to five years. Six years was the estimated life expectancy for those with longer terms.

Louisiana preferred not to spend a cent for the keeping—let alone the rehabilitation—of its criminals. It wanted its criminals to turn a profit for the state. Since emancipation, the convicts were increasingly, overwhelmingly, black. The plantation no longer fed and punished. Blacks were poor; many of them stole. In 1860 they made up less than one third of the men imprisoned in Louisiana. By 1869, when Major James signed his lease, it was 70 percent. James hired out his men to lay track for the New Orleans and Pacific Railroad, to build levees which were the responsibility of plantation owners, and to pick cotton and cut sugarcane. For the railroad and the farmers, the rates were cheap and the workers, with whips and guns behind them, were much more productive than the average citizen.

Yet it is important to be careful. Convict leasing was not created for black men. Louisiana signed its first lease in 1844, when none of the state's inmates was black. Still, the arrangement was different before and after the Civil War. Before, the convicts were housed in a new penitentiary building in Baton Rouge, where the various lessees had whipped them into faster production at the prison's textile machines, had readied them for work in society as "manufacturers." The three-story fortress of cells was modeled after the progressive prisons of its era: places where criminals could both learn a trade and find repentance, by toiling in absolute silence all day and, throughout the remaining hours, by contemplating and praying on their sins. This was considered a great stride forward. Not long ago the preferred punishments had been execution (even for many thefts), branding, public lashing, the stocks. And most recently all the state's inmates had been lodged in an old New Orleans jail, described by Alexis de Tocqueville after his touring of America: "We saw there men...in the midst of excrement and filth. In locking up criminals, no thought is given to making them better but simply to taming their wickedness; they are chained like wild beasts; they are not refined but brutalized." So no matter how harsh the Baton Rouge lessees became, the state could tell itself the setting was modern and beneficial.

Only after the war, with the change in the convict population, was the new penitentiary abandoned. Under James, just a few white convicts stayed behind, to sew striped uniforms for the others. The rest of the men lived in camps at the site of their labor, slept shoulder to shoulder and hip to hip on wooden platforms that rose, one above the other, to within a few feet of the ceiling. Workers were replaced (far more cheaply than slaves) as they perished, the causes of death combinations of disease, malnutrition, and relentless over-work—or a gunshot, as James's terse records put it, "while attempting to escape."

Nothing about the system was a secret. The men "are brutally treated and everyone knows it," one Louisiana newspaper wrote in 1886. "Corporal punishment is inflicted on the slightest provocation. ...Anyone who has travelled along the lines of railroads that run through Louisiana's swamps...in which the levees are built, has seen these poor devils almost to their waists, delving in the black and noxious mud....Theirs is a grievous lot a thousand times more grievous than the law ever contemplated they should endure in expiation of their sins." That same year a committee of the Louisiana legislature investigated some of the camps. One convict, having been forced to work without shoes through the previous winter, had no feet. Frostbite and then gangrene had set in; one foot had rotted off, the other had been amputated with a pen knife. The committee's report did nothing to inspire restrictions on Major James.

With his profits, he bought the plantation of Angola, named for the African region most of its slaves had come from. He set himself up in the Big House, put some of his convicts to work as household servants and others in the fields with the sharecroppers. He had made himself among the richest and most powerful men in the state. He had, in a sense, reversed manumission. He was Louisiana's last great slaveholder. When he died suddenly, of unknown disease, in 1894, he was sitting on the Big House porch, talking with his family, surrounded by his land and by the men he effectively owned. Without warning he lurched toward the rail, seemed to be trying to vomit, spewed blood instead from his mouth and nostrils, and was gone.

Again, it is important to be careful. Angola's beginnings cannot be told as a story of race, not simply, anyway. Major James was condoned by a Reconstructionist legislature: Black representatives voiced no objection to his brutality, only to the encroachment of his cheap labor on the jobs of their constituents. And even at his death, when the percentage of black convicts had climbed near 80, there were still plenty of whites enduring—or failing to endure—his regime. Just as plenty of whites continued to suffer Angola's cruelty after the end of convict-leasing in 1900. The point is more that race has always been one crucial underlying factor at the penitentiary, in the way it is run, in the way it is viewed by the public. The preponderance of blacks, the reflexive link of "convict" with "black" in almost everyone's mind, helps to allow certain attitudes, certain things to happen. Like, perhaps, a rodeo that borders on the gladiatorial.

Of course, the factor of race in the world of prisons is not limited to Angola, to Louisiana, to the South. At Angola, however, race sometimes rises to the surface with unique flair. During the late 1960s at the rodeo, after the playing of "The Star-Spangled Banner," the emcee would ask everyone to remain standing. The inmate band began, "Well I wish I was in the land of cotton..." An old black inmate climbed onto a wooden platform painted with the Confederate flag. Dressed in a Confederate soldier's gray uniform and cap, he tap-danced for the crowd.

When Louisiana claimed direct control of its convicts in January, 1901, the motive had little to do with scattered cries for prison reform. The change came through political infighting and a desire for direct profit. In 1914, the man who ran the state's penal system considered the possibility of rehabilitating his convicts. He concluded that in Louisiana "the vices and defects of the negro race are well known," that it would be wasteful to apply "what are called the advanced systems of treatment in use in some wealthier states, where only white men are dealt with."

Angola was expanded from 8,000 to 18,000 acres through state purchases. Farming gradually took precedence over levee and railroad work for Louisiana's inmates. When floods made a mockery of financial goals, there were calls for more efficiency. The security staff at Angola was cut from 150 to 11 in 1917; the inmate population was 1,600. Convict guards, given rifles and shotguns and later submachine guns, replaced paid employees. Through the 1960s these trusties were the only armed men in the fields. (Black convicts were placed over black work lines, whites over white.) Even as recently as the '60s, the warden offered them a six-month reduction in sentence (this before the passage of life without parole) for any escaping inmate they shot.

How often the convict guards defined "escaping" to suit their own purposes is impossible to sort out. Much more certain is that they themselves rarely tried to flee the prison or even disobey the freemen. They knew their punishment would be loss of weapon, that they would be "swung" from their special dorm back into the main population. Among the men they had lorded over, they would be left to fend for themselves.

Through the first half of the century, the state remained desperate to operate Angola, if not for profit, then at least without appropriation. Warden after warden failed this standard; whatever else happened at the penitentiary drew little interest. At their camps every morning, men were called out for floggings—twenty, forty, sixty lashes. "Incorrigibles" were kept in a new unit called the Red Hats (named because the inmates wore hats dipped in red paint at the crown, to identify them in the fields). Each of the Red Hat cells was closed off by a steel door and ventilated, in the 95-degree summers, only by a twelve-inch-square window covered by a steel flap. A convict guard had control of the flap. The toilet was the pail you washed in, and you stayed with it through the night.

Then, in 1951, thirty-seven white inmates severed their achilles tendons with razor blades. They hoped somehow to rescue themselves from the beatings they received in the work lines and the conditions they lived under in the camps. When news of the self-mutilation leaked out, the local and national press swarmed. "If the present efficient leadership at Angola is left alone," Governor Earl Long spoke in response to the crisis, "Angola will be on a paying basis before I leave office...." Quickly, though, he realized that the public's indifference to inmate life did not go quite this far. State investigations began; recommendations were announced; plans were drawn up. And the plans were funded. By 1955 *Life* magazine came down to document a miracle. "Bad Prison Goes Straight," the headline celebrated, and beside pictures of brand-new buildings the article read: "If any prisoners ever have the right to be happy, then the men at right do....New Angola has an up-to-date library, schoolrooms, bright modern dormitories…" One caption noted, with a kind of corporate optimism, that the inmates, who had finally shed their broadstriped uniforms, would soon be issued shirts with pinstripes.

What they wore, by the late '60s and early '70s, was dinner trays and mail-order catalogs taped to their chests and backs—for protection from one another while they slept. A few years of state generosity had been followed by renewed neglect; this, and then the phasing out of convict guards, brought pure chaos. By the early '70s, about 400 employees, spread over three shifts, supervised 4,000 prisoners. A liberal warden, Murray Henderson, had been hired from outside the state. Nobly intentioned, he tried to enlighten security and bring self-help programs to the inmates. But while some in his new team of classification officers lit candles, turned out the lights in their offices at Main Prison, and gathered convicts in circles on the floor to express their feelings, men stabbed each other freely in the dorms. Between 1972 and 1975 there were at least 40 inmate murders. Recorded stabbings totaled 360.

One man, John Whitley, who began his career in classification in 1970 and later became warden, remembered the convicts, with blankets for stretchers, rushing the wounded toward the hospital. "Back then when you stabbed someone you stabbed him pretty good, and blood would be trailing as they came down the Walk. It was just part of the working conditions. At first I thought this was ridiculous, unbelievable, how could this happen all the time? But it got to the point where I saw a man sitting on a bench in the main hallway trying to hold his intestines in, sitting there waiting for someone to take him over to the hospital, and I looked up and saw a guard on his way down the Walk to take care of it, and I just had no interest. I just walked away and went to work."

Four inmates sued the state in federal court. Inside Angola, they claimed, arbitrary discipline, poor medical care, racial segregation, and pervasive, anarchic violence deprived them of their civil rights. The men had spent months, between 1970 and '71, gathering evidence and conferring secretly with one another, speaking sometimes in pig Latin through the heating ducts when they were kept in cells. At last they described their world to a young lawyer they found: convict guards beating inmates with mop handles in the Red Hats (and men living ten to a 4 by 7-foot cell there); pummelings by groups of paid employees; unchecked rape and murder among the inmates; segregation that kept blacks picking crops while only whites were promoted out of the fields; an often doctorless hospital staffed by a convict named O'Dell Causey. As the lead plaintiff would later recall, Causey had worked as a mortician's helper before coming to Angola. "And that's how he learned to sew human bodies. If you were cut, O'Dell would stitch you up. He'd try to save your life. Everybody depended on O'Dell, even the free people. O'Dell couldn't read his name in boxcar letters, but if you took all the pills in the pharmacy and dumped them on the floor, he could pick each one up and tell you its street name, medical name, and what it was used for."

A federal magistrate, Frank Polozola, heard the case in the visiting shed at Main Prison. When questions of witness credibility came up, the plaintiffs' lawyer suggested that he see for himself, that he walk over to the hospital, the cells. Polozola rose from his makeshift bench and went to inspect. He harbored no soft spot for criminals. "He wanted prisoners to be prisoners," the lead plaintiff recounted, "but man, he had to do right."

In 1975, his findings led to federally mandated reforms and increased spending. The state did not readily take heed. The legislature voted funds to expand the LSU football stadium and claimed there was none available for ordered improvements at Angola. But after defeat on appeal, and under the threat of released inmates when the court set impossibly low population limits at the prison, the state surrendered. Angola's security staff doubled (and soon doubled again), new buildings relieved overcrowding, disciplinary procedures were regulated, doctors were hired, and through earlier agreements worked out during the course of the lawsuit, the last of the convict guards were gone, the dorms and inmate jobs were desegregated, and seventy-five black employees joined what had always been an all-white work force.

Suddenly, under federal oversight, Angola became what *Life* had once rushed to call it: a model prison. At least, it was about the closest any large, state penitentiary could come. Within two years, violent deaths dropped to zero. And this at a time when the state became a pioneer in natural life sentences allowing no chance for parole. As my year there began, inmate violence had stayed low, killings remained an exception, and homosexual rape—at least the overt kind, where the victim is simply overpowered—had been largely eliminated. As for abuse by guards, reliable comparative statistics are impossible to come by, but incidents at Angola were, according to Keith Nordyke, a federally appointed civil rights attorney for the inmates, fairly few. And since efforts at redirecting convicts' lives are a thing of the past all over the country, inmate safety and tolerable conditions are the standards by which penitentiaries are judged. With continued court supervision, Angola excelled.

Warden Cain had inherited an atmosphere of peace, a place where a warden could, if he wished, focus on something beyond security. Without his sanity being questioned, Cain could turn against prevailing cynicism, declare his mission the uplifting of men. He owed this latitude not only to the court mandates, but to a pair of former wardens who had brought the calm—and something more than calm—into being.

Ross Maggio, wearing a cowboy hat and cowboy boots and

known as Boss Ross, took over Angola in 1976, soon after the court rulings. Short and puggish, he took his mandated budget and defied tradition, hiring and quickly promoting as many men with two- or four-year college degrees as he could lure to the prison. It wasn't many, but he set a tone. Guards used to condoning rape, to arranging dates for the marriages of new inmates, to authorizing shanks for their favorite convicts, were retrained and, if necessary, fired. As for the prisoners who needed retraining, Maggio built Camp J. It was filled before the contractors finished screwing in the door handles.

A work buck filled it. The inmates, accustomed to an idleness that had taken hold over the past few chaotic years, protested the centerpiece of Maggio's program: labor. He believed in the tranquilizing value of sweat. And they, one afternoon following lunch, refused to return to their jobs. Maggio responded with his new emergency team, trained and armed with his new money. "Shields, helmets, and I had just bought some AR-15s," he reminisced with me, from behind his tinted glasses, in the office where he was now vice president of a private corrections company. "Shoot, I was ready for war. The inmates, they'd never seen anything like it. Until then, the tac team was whoever with baseball bats. My guys came marching in cadence. Boom boom boom boom. The inmates thought the army had been called in."

Maggio herded all one thousand protesters into a small fenced area. They demanded that the media be called, that the governor come, that a prison-rights advocate be allowed to negotiate. Maggio told them to elect sixteen leaders. He told the sixteen there would be no audience. "Whatever happens here tonight it's going to happen between us," he remembered saying, and no other version I heard contradicted his showdown rendition. "You all want to be inmate leaders? We have any trouble, anyone in that crowd does anything, and you sixteen are doing hospital time. That's a promise. Hospital time."

One of the elect, a contract killer there for attempting to murder the mayor of Baton Rouge, asked to resign.

"Un-unh," Maggio said. "Ain't no resignations."

Magistrate Polozola had already been called. He had told the warden to do whatever necessary. Maggio chose the early opening of J. "They cut up when they got there," he said to me, "so security gassed them till they were dishrags."

Listening to the stories of domination emerging from this small man, I felt vaguely nervous and weak, as though I belonged to a less clear-thinking species. I felt this even while he spoke about Angola's flower beds. The botany had been his idea. Before he started as warden, smashed windows had stayed unfixed. Screens were torn. Every surface was filthy. The grass had been two feet high around the administration building. Maggio decided that the first thing he would do was clean up the grounds. He wanted—and got—everything pristine. It was that way still. I had seen the disciplinary cases, in their white jumpsuits, mopping the Main Walk twice daily. They even dusted the cinder-block walls. But Maggio had wanted something more, and found it on a family trip to Disney World. He came home with dozens of pictures, documents of the landscaping. "I want Angola to look like this," he told the wife of one of his officers, a woman he knew "liked to fool with flowers." He put her in charge of a beautification crew. He promised her all the inmates and all the security she asked for. "And she did a great job," he told me. But then, as if the unmet goal still nagged at him, he added, "It never did meet Disney World. Really, Disney World is outstanding. I don't know who they have in charge of those grounds."

And I felt the difference, my own lack of clarity and strength, as he toyed with a letter opener while recounting the most famous incident of his career.

The night before the rodeo's last Sunday in 1982, his parents were staying with him at the warden's house, on the hill at the edge of the prison. At one end of the house, his wife bathed their four-year-old son. In the living room, Maggio and his father listened to the LSU football game on the radio. His mother went out to the carport to get a suitcase. There were screams. Maggio bolted to the sliding glass door, saw his mother held by two inmates. They yelled at him to back up. They shoved her into the house, into a corner of the living room. One of them ordered Maggio to lie down, and straddled him with a knife to his neck.

With me, in his office, he raised the letter opener and pressed its point against his carotid artery. Through the rest of the story, which took about five level-voiced minutes to tell, he held the point there.

His wife had seen the men from the bathroom window. She took a .357 from the gun locker and, leaving their son in the bathroom, came through the kitchen's swinging door, aiming at the convict on top of her husband. The man threatened to cut if she didn't leave. Maggio's mother was shrieking, the second convict clutching a screwdriver in front of her. His wife backed out through the swinging door. One of the inmates demanded the warden's car keys. Maggio pointed to his truck keys on a shelf. They walked him and his mother back outside. One convict opened the driver's side of the pickup. "What's that," the man peered down, "a hydromatic?" Maggio had no idea what he was talking about. He realized only later that the inmate was confused by the four-wheel drive's floor lever—he'd been imprisoned seventeen years. "Give the keys," the other one seethed, "and let the warden drive the truck."

They pushed his mother under the dash with the knife at her back. The man next to Maggio grabbed his hair, put the screwdriver to his throat. "Now you gonna drive us out the front gate. You gonna get us out the front gate. The warden tells them let us through, they'll let you through."

"And I want to tell you, Warden," the man above his mother said slowly, "if anything goes wrong I'm gonna kill her."

Maggio drove down the hill. They got curious about the prison radio, the microphone on a cord from the dash. They wanted to know how it worked.

"Well, what you do is you grab this mike, and you have to push this button." Maggio pushed, said a few cautious words into it. The man beside him slapped it from his hand.

"Mother*fuck!*"

"Y'all calm down," Maggio tried. "That wasn't nothing."

"Anything goes wrong, *anything…*"

"That wasn't nothing."

"You stupid stupid fuck, I'm going to cut her, I'm going to *cut,* you hear me?"

"We're going to get through the gate," Maggio said.

They neared the main road. He told them to lie down, told them he was going to speed up.

"Motherfucker!"

"We're going through," Maggio shouted.

"Anything. See this? *Anything…*"

Maggio turned toward the gate. "Now crouch over," he told them.

As he jammed down the gas, they huddled low. Yanking the wheel hard, Maggio whipped the truck into a wall opposite the gate-house. He squeezed fast out the crumpled door while the convicts sat dazed. Two guards rushed from the gatehouse, pistols drawn. He ran toward them. One of the inmates started to flee. "Shoot, shoot that son of a bitch!" Maggio screamed, but the guard didn't fire and Maggio grabbed the pistol, shot and missed, and then he heard the truck door slam and looked back to the other convict inside with his mother. He ran up to the window and shot him dead. The second guard finally shot the fleeing man, stopping him. Maggio's mother was tucked under the dash, unhurt.

That, except for the wounded convict begging the warden not to kill him when Maggio came by the hospital a few days later, was the end of the story. But something had always bothered me, whenever

I'd heard the incident told. And it confused me now. Hadn't Maggio worried what would happen to his mother when he wedged himself out the truck door? I understood why he'd rammed the truck, that once they were outside the prison both he and his mother would likely be killed. But why, with the convicts stunned by the crash, hadn't he tried to wrestle their weapons away? Why had he left his mother alone with them? It seemed he'd forgotten all about her.

I phrased my question in a delicate way. He didn't seem to glean my point. In his mind, he had taken the only reasonable course. "What went through my head was, that guy told me if anything went wrong he was going to kill her, and I didn't give him a chance to find out if he meant it or not. He had a knife in there with her."

I saw that the same logic did not prevail for him and for me. His thinking was straightforward, and he had run toward the guards, toward their guns, to carry it out. What had gone through his mind was: Kill the problem.

We talked, after that, about rehabilitation, and about Murray Henderson, the liberal warden who had preceded him. I had heard that one evening, a few weeks after taking over, Maggio put on his cowboy hat and ventured out for an impromptu inspection of Main Prison. Halfway through his tour, he opened the door to classification, a department whose role had always been ill-defined. It was supposed to assist in determining the status of inmates—big-stripe or trusty or cellblock. It was supposed to help convicts navigate the prison bureaucracy. It was supposed, generally, to maintain a slightly closer relationship to the convicts than security could. When Maggio opened the door, found the lights off, candles burning, and a group of inmates gathered on the floor around the classification man, he posed what even to me would have been a logical question: "What in the fuck is going on in here?"

He asked me now, "What rehabilitation? Henderson was going to be a big rehabilitator and all that, but all I saw was the prison falling down around him. You can't play patty-cakes. I was looking

for results. In fairness to him, he didn't have the money. But even if
he'd had it, he wouldn't have done it the way I did. He wouldn't
have got the results. I left that place one of the safest maximum-
security prisons in the nation."

Ross Maggio had eliminated the unremitting sense of danger. He
had killed the primary problem.

John Whitley was Maggio's protégé. Fresh out of college, hair down
his back, he had started in classification six years before Maggio's
arrival. He planned, back then, to change all the inmates. "Yes, all
they needed was a little understanding." The guards despised everyone in his department, threatened them, sometimes made them wait
an hour before walking over to open the internal gates. But they had
a special disdain for Whitley, who favored a pair of striped bell-
bottoms in red and gold, and a bandanna-like scarf, hip in Baton
Rouge, fastened by a ring at his throat. Those scarves had a particular significance at Angola. They were a badge, worn only by the gal-
boys. "Oh, we got a good one here," the guards muttered before he
caught on.

The scarves went first, followed by the long hair and the bell-
bottoms. And as the inmates took advantage of him, and as he wit-
nessed their violence and the therapeutic flailing of his colleagues, his
"liberal ways were left," he said, "somewhere down the Walk."

Maggio promoted him, transferred him into security. He continued to rise after Maggio's time; in 1990 he became warden. "I would
never have hired the me I was when I came to Angola," he said,
wearing a white button-down shirt, brown slacks, cowboy boots.
Half-hidden by his mustache, the corners of his mouth gave way to
an almost imperceptible tremor as he related his stories, possibly
from some physical ailment but seemingly from repressed laughter—
over the lunacy of who he had been.

"Finally it dawned on me. These guys are not here to learn a trade. They're here because they're pretty bad people."

I asked about the sincerity of the religion many of the inmates adhered to.

"You've been up there awhile," he returned the question, "have you seen Jesus yet?" His lips quivered briefly with sly mirth—at my lunacy as well.

During his later years there, he confided, if he saw some horrible crime on the TV news he sometimes wrote down the name of the man arrested, thinking, "Now when he gets here, I'm going to be waiting for him." He had to fight to put that part of him aside. "They have to be just another inmate in your presence." But sitting in the cramped, street-level office in Baton Rouge where he now worked as Polozola's specially appointed prison expert, his thinking was a very long way from Warden Cain's ("You have to forgive to be forgiven"), from Cain's offering to every prisoner a new beginning, a kind of free grace.

"When I first got to Angola," Whitley said, "I didn't believe in the death penalty. There was no way we should claim a human life. I didn't even believe in carrying guns. And right now I could hold off a National Guard unit from my living room. That's the change you go through. I've gotten to the point where I'm not that sociable anymore. When you work in a prison for twenty-five years and you see nothing but the bad, when you're reading inmate records, checking them out for specific jobs, and you see the crimes they committed, you finally just get disgusted, and you start thinking this guy here"—he pointed toward a man crossing the parking lot outside his office window—"might be packing a gun, might do something. You have to have been there, and you have to have gone through it, to understand what I'm talking about. It just kind of turns you off from wanting to be with any group of people at all.

"No, I have no problem with the death penalty. I could stack them all up at one time, and if there was enough voltage, or enough poison to inject, I would give the signal."

He said all this, spoke much like Maggio, but with Whitley I did not feel the same sense of my own inferiority, of my own tangled thinking. His lips quivered not only about the past but the present: his arsenal of weapons; his embrace of execution. His current self seemed as comical to him, as extreme, as his old one. The huge change itself seemed ridiculous. His frequent, barely detectable laughter was a way of confessing that nothing seemed right.

Whitley revered Maggio, but he had left Angola's inmates with a very different sense of the man who governed them. There were many who actually remembered Whitley with affection. That he had run Angola after Maggio's era gave him a huge advantage—he didn't have to fight so hard for mere control. And then there was the residue of the past, the naiveté—or hope—he had "left somewhere down the Walk." The residue hadn't fully evaporated. Some of the programs Cain described proudly and talked ardently of fostering had gotten their start under Whitley. He didn't mention it, but I knew that the CPR team had come together under his administration. Inmate tutors had begun working with illiterate convicts. And to death row, Whitley had brought one day of contact visits each year.

He was remembered, most of all, for what happened in 1991 when the state switched from the electric chair to lethal injection. A gurney had to be built, a table where the man would lie while the chemicals flowed in. Whitley toured state prisons in Nevada, Colorado and Texas to find the best design. He resolved on one resembling a slightly bent cross, to give easy access to the veins in the arms.

He returned to Angola, discussed blueprints with the officer in charge of the prison's industrial complex, and was told the metal shop could handle the project. The next thing he heard, one inmate, then two, had refused to work on the gurney. Whitley sent an assistant warden over to the complex. By then the entire metal shop had balked, and before Whitley could think what to do next, he learned that a D.B. court had been convened right in the middle of a prison passageway (rather than in the remote, closet-like rooms where the mini-trials were usually held). Every inmate walking past could watch as the entire metal shop was convicted of disobedience and sentenced to the fields. Worse, they could find out why. And news spread fast: that the brother of a recently executed man had been one of those assigned to construct the gurney, and that the metal-shop officer had tried to trick the men, telling them the gurney was a new kind of bed for the mental-health ward. That afternoon, four hundred inmates protested, would not go back to work.

Whitley responded as Maggio had fifteen years earlier. He knew that to lose hold here meant losing command of the prison. The tac teams marched in. Special marksmen aimed down from the roofs. All four hundred were locked up in cells. But then Whitley did something Maggio would never have done. He let every protester go. He announced to the inmates that he'd "screwed up." He took the blueprints and contracted them out.

The admission and reversal were unheard of. They created an unprecedented trust. For the next four years, Angola's peace was based on communication as much as militaristic order. When Whitley stepped down, Cain's appointment came with this advantage. Just as Whitley had benefited from Maggio's resolve, just as Whitley's reputation for candor was made possible by the lasting effects of Maggio's control, so Cain inherited both legacies. He was given order, and he was given trust. His improbable mission had a great head start.

F O U R

STRINGS OF CHRISTMAS LIGHTS FANNED OUTWARD from the top of the guard tower near the front gate, and giant, luminous angels éncircled the base. More angels trumpeted through B-Line. In their camps, the inmates were on vacation from their jobs, hoping for—or refusing to hope for—visits that would not come. Those who were surprised sat for a few hours with their mothers or sisters or children, gazing at a four-foot tree and the words "Merry Christmas" written in a sweeping curve, in gold tape, on cinder block.

Buckkey was the exception. Eighty percent of Angola's inmates never saw their families at all; Buckkey's stayed in close touch and drove the two hours regularly to the prison. He had just designed the invitation for his youngest sister's wedding—fancy lettering and swirly adornments. He had worked with the fountain pen his mother had sent. The day after Christmas, when he was taken to the trusty park, he saw his wife, two of his brothers, one sister-in-law, three sisters, and his mother waiting for him at a picnic table on the hill. The gift of the runner-up buckle had changed nothing. His son was not there. The buckle, his wife later told me, sat in a box where she kept it for whenever Chris wanted it. So far he didn't.

"You didn't bring your kids to prison?" Buckkey asked me, when he returned to the range-crew headquarters, to immerse himself in welding trailer hitches, after his family's visit. He liked to jab at me with deadpan questions.

"Not this time," I said. "Maybe for my daughter's fifth birthday party."

"Where are they?"

"Home."

"Well, what the hell are you doing down here then?"

"Came to see you."

"Yeah, you've got your priorities straight." He rolled his eyes.

"Thanks, Buckkey."

"Take it from an all-American dad like myself."

That holiday week, I went to find the convicts I'd met at the rodeo, the men who would show me what it meant to fashion one's life inside a maximum security prison, the men who would show me what people pushed to the absolute limit, pushed by their own deeds beyond the edge of human society, to a place that felt like the edge of the earth, were capable of. What life, what striving, what humanity, was possible here? In what ways, direct or indirect, would Warden Cain's leadership touch them as the year unfolded? And could a man like Littell Harris—hurler of feces in Camp J—find a way to rejoin society?

But first I wandered through death row. There one inmate had cut out a small construction-paper Christmas tree and asked the sergeant to pin it to the bulletin board on the tier. Little by little the inmate had dressed the tree with more cutouts. A guard tower took the place of a star at the top. The light in the tower glowed. Shackles and handcuffs and jailer's keys hung from the branches.

Otherwise, the holiday didn't make anything much different. In the death-row cells, the men lay inert in their boxer shorts twenty-three hours each day. Once or twice during the week they shuffled off to a religious service, their legs in chains and their hands not only cuffed but restricted, by means of a belt and metal loop, to within inches of their navels. When they greeted one another in the meeting room it was with the most abbreviated, waist-high wave or fist pump. When they turned the pages of their Bibles they might have been afflicted with M.S. The chaplain, as always, brought his acoustic guitar. They requested "I Can't Feel at Home in This World Anymore," and he sang in a loud, plaintive, unmelodic wail. When the inmates tapped their feet slightly, the leg chains, surprisingly delicate, shivered between their ankles or slapped almost inaudibly against the floor.

Out among the general population, an old skinny man with a long gray beard jogged for hours. He circled the Main Yard over and over, in one-mile laps, following the dirt path worn at the base of the fence line. In the middle of the yard, eight or ten men worked out at the weight pile, a crude setup of rusty benches and lat machines with broken pulleys. The winter influx of sea gulls had descended on the grass. A pair of stray cats humped on a ledge outside one of the dorms. "That bitch is getting her issue," someone said. Inside the dorms half the beds were filled with men dozing, white sheets pulled up over their eyes, up over their heads.

Various inmate clubs—the Toastmasters, the Toy Shop—put on holiday banquets for their members, served special meals they had paid for: a chicken cutlet; pound cake and ice cream; plenty of donuts. Of those lucky enough to belong to the clubs, a few had family to sit with, a handful had wives or girlfriends to make out with. By next Christmas, their families encouraged them, they would be out. By next Christmas they never were, but again put their wispy hopes in some glitch they'd found in their trial transcripts, or in the process of clemency. The lifers' would mail off their applications to the pardon board. (Many could barely write well enough to fill them out.) Months later the fortunate would be issued a hearing date. Following their sessions in front of the board, the still more fortunate would be recommended to the governor. Then they would wait for what everyone knew as "the gold seal," a letter bearing the executive's embossed insignia in the corner. It commuted the prisoner's life sentence to a fixed number of years. It did not mean that the inmate would be released anytime soon, only that, as the convicts said, he had "numbers instead of alphabets." Through his first eleven months in office, the current governor had approved none of the board's sparing recommendations. During the weeks leading up to December 25, when Louisiana governors had traditionally commuted at least a few life sentences, he had still reduced none.

The men held no expectation of release. Many refused so much as the wish. The newest member of the range crew said, "I look to die here. Period. One day I hope to be as good a cowboy as Johnny Brooks." They just didn't want to be buried in the powder-blue pressboard coffins the state provided for those bodies not taken out for family funerals. The older men had all heard about those coffins, how the burial crew had to lay the dirt down in spits, because any stray rock would crack right through the lid that was no sturdier than Styrofoam.

But Littell knew he was out. His life in the punishment cells five months behind him, this Christmas Day he lay on his cot in the dorm, cushion of dreadlocks beneath his head, and counted the days until release. The dreadlocks had been a seven-year project, had nothing to do with any Rastafarian beliefs, were a declaration to himself that he was untouchable at the core. Nothing that happened, nothing about Angola, nothing that was done to him or that he did, could matter. His rarely cut beard completed the statement.

When he had first come to Angola in 1984, after serving two years of his sentence in a parish jail, he had been stunned. He had never seen so many black people in one place. Yes, his neighborhood had been all black, and the detention centers of his youth had been mostly black, and so had the jail. But this felt different, overwhelming. Blacks marching off in the field lines, hoes slung over their shoulders; blacks shining the guards' shoes. Even back then Littell was not completely uneducated. He'd done moderately well in his detention-center classrooms. He knew, as he was shown to his first Angola bed, that Louisiana's population was about one-third black. He knew, seeing that this huge maximum-security prison was filled with black people, that something was wrong.

Much later, at J, he would start reading some history. But right away he had decided there were only three kinds of inmates at Angola: field niggers and house niggers and those who rebelled. Field niggers were everyone from the obedient cotton picker to the trusty with the range crew. House niggers were everyone from the dorm orderly to the editor of the *Angolite*. The rebels were harder to identify. He sensed—rightly—no uprisings in the air. So he decided that the rebels were simply those who would not play by the rules. It didn't matter whose bones they broke in the process, the guards' or each other's. Mostly they broke each other's. Littell became one of them and stayed one of them, his mission to avoid being taken advantage of by freemen or convicts. He felt sure that his nickname, "Outlaw," was a sign of his success.

The dreadlocks were part of his defiance, his resolve never to be the freemen's slave. But he hoped the uncut hair protected him, as well, against the violent person guards and inmates had turned him into. He hoped it was like a buffer, forming a private zone. He tried to persuade himself that within that zone he was someone else.

Yet he couldn't be sure who that someone else was. He knew that for the past several years he had read far more than the average convict; he believed he could pass his GED; he told himself that once these last weeks were over he would never, never, be back in prison. Beyond this brief list, his private self was vague. And he knew that

Angola hadn't quite created his public, violent one. He knew that white people hadn't quite created it. Once, just two or three years ago, one of the three black inmates who had attempted to spark racial protest by randomly choosing and killing a guard in 1972 had lectured him from the next cell, "You a pretty intelligent guy. Did a white man hold your hand and bring you in that store and put a pistol in your fingers?" Littell worried his public self was his only one.

And how would he change when he got out? He would have no money to speak of. He had spent so much time locked-down in the cells, his savings account had almost nothing in two-cent set-asides. When he was let go, the state would give him ten dollars and the price of a bus ticket back to the city of his crime, his home, Lake Charles. He hadn't seen his mother for ten years. He hadn't seen anyone in his family for six. Who was going to be waiting for him? What was going to turn him into someone different?

His Christmas gift was a rush of reminders about who he was. The memories ended, after the feces and the batterings with padlocks and the stabbings and the recollection of unzipping his bloody sweatshirt and of a guard passing out at the sight of him half-disemboweled and of being driven to an emergency room in Baton Rouge and of losing forty pounds and almost dying in the hospital, ankles ever shackled to the bed rails, and still, when he returned, carrying on as he had—the memories ended with a cellblock orderly who had stolen his radio to pay off a drug debt. The orderly denied it. "He played me cheap," Littell explained to me. "He knew I was going to know that it was him, and he was thinking maybe I'm going to let him get away with that."

Littell didn't deal with retribution right away. A year later, they both wound up living at the same outcamp, where Littell enlisted the help of a towering, pumped-up convict named Popsickle. He had another accomplice distract the dorm guard in conversation—it wasn't difficult; the guard faced twelve solitary, woozy hours in the steamy air. In the game room, Popsickle threatened the orderly with a knife. Littell intervened. The orderly was so terrified he was willing to believe in this act of kindness. When Popsickle backed off, apparently respecting Littell's reputation, Littell told the orderly, "Just make it look like you're my bitch. That way he won't do you nothing. Just go in the shower and make it look like I'm fucking you in the ass. Just take this tube, just greaze up, I'm not going to stick it in."

Then, as Littell recounted it, "I got him in the back of the fucking shower and slid my dick in his ass and claimed him for ho."

Littell had no doubts that he was heterosexual. Lately his most regular fantasy centered around an old, torn-off cover from *Vanity Fair*. It showed the nude profile of the actress Demi Moore, eight months pregnant. "I never wanted to have no fucking sex with no man, bro. I just did that to totally humiliate somebody. When somebody was to make me angry, I fucked him in his ass."

But about who he was, he was worried.

I risked expressing to Littell what I sometimes felt, that Angola was an unexpectedly positive place.

"Man," he said, "Angola is a fucking super-negative piece of negative fucking shit."

I didn't persist. I planned to follow him out. Even if I hadn't, he wasn't someone I cared to antagonize. As to his analysis of Angola, it was all a matter of perspective and degree. I had anticipated the worst and was finding much that was better. But it wouldn't have been difficult to prove Littell right. Though his existence as a "rebel" was the exception, I knew there were others like him and those who did what he did with lesser frequency. I knew as well that while most of the guards tried to offer some measure of vigilance, of deterrence, there were plenty who tried only to get through their twelve-hour shifts without dozing off, and some who made themselves willfully oblivious, and a few who took payment for their oblivion, and a few who, in their daily interactions with convicts, went beyond the typical brusque handling, the kick at the bedpost to wake an oversleeping inmate.

Since I had first arrived at Angola four months ago, two cellblock guards, in separate incidents at separate camps, had been arrested for forcing inmates to perform blowjobs repeatedly through the bars. Both had eventually been bit— the convicts knew that damage to the guard's penis was generally the only way they would be believed. In other, similar cases, inmates had held the semen in their mouths, spit it into the cellophane of a cigarette wrapper, folded the wrapper tightly, and mailed it to a lawyer with their plea for help.

Forces seemed to conspire against the better impulses of the employees. Their pay was low, with a scale that began around $15,000 a year, and awarded captains, who'd put in years of service, about $30,000. At night they were locked alone inside dorms with sixty-four convicts. The guards were unarmed and, in most cases, didn't even have a walkie-talkie, just a signal box that would bring help guaranteed to arrive within three minutes. As a means of containing disturbances, the doors were bolted from the outside. The "key guards" were instructed *not* to free a colleague until backup was present.

Combined with this vulnerability was a kind of authority few people could have anywhere else. The lowliest guard could tell a great number of men what to do. He could be extremely blunt in giving his orders. And if he was put on one of the shakedown teams he could, in searching for weapons and drugs, clear out entire dorms and tear through the belongings of those inmates, ransack their "houses," their locker boxes, leaving everything from rolls of toilet paper to photo albums scattered across the floor along with the upturned benches (to check for contraband stashed in screw holes) and the contents of overturned garbage cans. In fact, he *would* do this, was *expected* to leave their homes torn through, and probably couldn't help being aware that he had this control over *killers,* couldn't help feeling, as one assistant warden put it, "that superpower, like your chest grew six inches under that badge." (Any softening of the atmosphere that might come from female employees was limited. Most women were stationed in the towers or at the control panels.) It was the very rare guard who stuck his erection through cell bars and demanded service. It was the very rare guard who gathered a colleague or two and beat an inmate for some past wrong. But a mixture of indifference and hostility seemed a requirement of the job.

Yet within this place, to whose negative-fucking-shittiness he had contributed a good deal, Danny Fabre—ears jutting at right angles and ribs healed poorly, still overlapping—appeared to have turned a corner. At the Toastmasters' Christmas banquet, in the Main Prison visiting shed, where the club president delivered a hearty welcome to the scattered family members and sang a hokey version of "Chestnuts Roasting on an Open Fire," and where dinner began with onion soup, a slab of unmelting cheese floating at the surface, Danny took his Forgotten Voices Toastmasters club card out of his jeans pocket. "See here what it says?" He read from the back. "'The mission of a Toastmasters Club is to provide a mutually supportive and positive learning environment in which every member has the opportunity to develop communication and leadership skills, which in turn fosters self-confidence and personal growth.'"

He stood close as we spoke at the back of the room. Everything about his features was exaggerated. Besides the yellow-tinged eyes and the ears ineffectively curtained by a back-sweep of blond hair, his cheeks were inordinately hollow above a chiseled jawline. And his hands were heavy, broad across the top of the palms and long and thick in the fingers. He showed me his "Communication and Leadership Program" manual, issued by Toastmasters International. He turned to the evaluation pages for his first few speeches. Next to the questions "Was the speech topic appropriate for this particular assignment?" and "Did the speaker employ vocal variety to enhance the speech?" Danny showed me that he had received, from the inmate evaluator, checks under "satisfactory" and "excellent."

Ten years ago, I reminded myself, he had been so volatile that during his trial his feet were not only shackled to each other but chained to the courtroom floor. And only this past summer the Toastmasters sponsor, Captain Newsom, had refused to let him into the club. "I know I've been King Asshole," Danny had pledged to Newsom, "but I will prove to you that I'm Toastmasters material." In September the captain had relented.

Danny pointed out, in the manual, the guidelines for earning "Competent Toastmaster" status within the organization. He pulled over one of the members, so I could see the "CTM" pin—a red laminated tag with a royal blue T etched into a gold circle—he would be able to wear on his white T-shirt after his tenth speech. He talked about the first one he'd given, the big traffic-light timer in his face and the other members in the school chairs around him. He recited the beginning: "Growing up is a hard thing to do, especially when you have one eye, one leg, retardation, or even ears like myself. When one has things that's wrong with you, that's out of the ordinary, kids in school, and all around you, seem to pick on you to get a laugh. You have a low self-esteem. You feel like everybody hates you. When one has a physical disorder, you should never tear them down. You should always upgrade them...."

For the first time, I took note of Danny's voice. It was sonorous, intensely inflected within a confined range, emphatic without ever being loud. It carried just the hint of a southern accent. He bent the word "why." I heard this over and over when, later in the week, we found an empty attorney conference room and shut ourselves in to talk. But before we came, without any prompting from me, to that question regarding his choking his victim and spearing her through the eye—"Why? I don't know why I did it. I can't tell you why I did it. She was a woman, I could have raped her. I didn't rape her. I didn't rob her. Why did I do this?"—before all that, he said, "I'm going to tell you something I've told to only one other person."

I thought, You're going to tell me something that isn't true.

He began quietly, slowly: "When I was about eight years old, one morning I wasn't fixing to go to school 'cause I felt sick. And I told my dad, and," he paused, "my daddy ended up," he paused again, "molesting me. And it went on for about four years. But it wasn't an on and on thing. It was every now and then. And I didn't know what was happening in my life. But I knew this wasn't right. And he always scared me about, If you tell your mama, if you tell your brothers, it's gonna bust the family up. You know, this is why I want to work with children if I ever get out. Because a child can hold something in his mind for so long. And then they explode. See, this is what the world is drawing to. I mean, probably eighty percent of the world has been through some type of abuse. But they don't talk about it. But I remember when I was twelve. It was a cold night. And my daddy woke me up. I was in a room by myself. And I told him, I stood up in the middle of the bed, 'This ain't right. If you touch me again I'll kill you.' Where I got that, I don't know. But he left me alone. And my daddy's a well-respected man. He's a beautiful man if you meet him. I forgive my father for what he done. 'Cause in order to be forgiven for the things I've done, I had to forgive that past. But it started out that I had to prove, to everybody, that I was a man. I wasn't going to be no punk. I wasn't going to be no queer. I was going to prove that. And I started all kinds of fights. Fights, fights, fights, fights. Kicked out of school. I always was a violent person. I hated people. I loved my mother to death…."

He veered on. The story seemed a clear attempt to win my sympathy, my forgiveness. Or his own. Maybe he had convinced himself of the story's truth. Maybe he needed the delusion to tolerate his own living. But then again, some inmates had surely suffered through such childhoods, some greater percentage of men in prison than elsewhere....

"My mom knew something was wrong. And I never told her. She always used to ask me, 'What do you have hanging over your daddy's head?' Because Daddy—from when I said I'd tell—every time I'd get in trouble, he wouldn't whip me or nothing. She kept asking me. So I had to say something. And I told her Daddy was mixed up with the mafia. And he blowed up a house full of people. And killed them all. And that's what it was. She didn't believe me. But I said no, that's what it was."

My skepticism dissolved, partly. The detail of what he'd told his mother—the Mafia, the house blown up—seemed far too ludicrous, too perfectly childlike, to be his later invention.

"Why did I do this?" Danny asked now. He'd been saying he could have killed any number of people, any of a dozen men he'd fought brutally, battered or slashed outside of bars, anyone who had triggered him in any way, "because that's the kind of person I was, but I never thought about killing no one....

"Why did I murder this woman I didn't even know? All she'd done was let me use her phone. Two times. All she'd done was give me that ride. I think my mind was overloaded. And when she said that? That about I wouldn't never be nothing?

"I exploded."

It was easy to imagine how quickly Danny had killed her. Besides "Ears," his other prison nickname was "Popeye," for the lumps and ridges of muscle he'd once had all over his lean body, and for how suddenly he would put his strength to use. (Lately he had told other inmates about the chance of surgery for his ears. "Don't go getting that operation now," they sometimes called out to him, and the first time he'd heard this Danny asked, "Why?" "'Cause then you wouldn't be Popeye." They would miss the entertainment of the fights he was goaded into.)

He had let the distension of his body shrink over the past year. Still, his shoulders were broad and his forearms were solid and he had those hands. But he said he had gained self-restraint. "I done taken control of myself," he told me. "That's what I like about me." And while he had few kind words for the guards in general, he talked about the staff who were helping him.

There was the Toastmasters sponsor. A tall man whose uniform pants reached only to his ankles, Captain Newsom carried his skinny body without a hint of physical assertion. And he did not like to speak. He had seventy pen pals—"some full-time, some part-time," he said—and spent his off hours at his computer, communicating with his unmet friends all over the world. At the Toastmasters meetings, he sat in a corner, sipped his coffee, and never so much as made a comment. When the members forced him to the lectern for "Table Topics," their competition in impromptu speechmaking, he droned out a few sentences and reclaimed his seat. He was like the high school tennis coach who'd never touched a racket. Newsom took pleasure in watching those meetings. He took pride in Danny's improvement, and in his own gamble that Danny could keep his destructive emotions under control and function within the club. He told me, when we spoke alone, "Danny's come a good way since September." And Danny said gratefully, "He took that chance."

Danny praised, as well, his first teacher in the literacy program: "That woman drove me." When he tested out of the lowest level, she insisted he stay another few weeks, to be sure he was ready. Now, with a new teacher in the next phase, he was learning to use a computerized study program. Last month, the instructor had taught him to use a mouse. "I like hearing that music that plays when I get the right answer," Danny said with a laugh.

And he told me he had talked with Warden Cain since his bull ride at the rodeo, walked up to him after a Lifers Association meeting in the visiting shed. Danny had spoken about his ears, how tired he was of "waking up every day with all this picking on me," about the teaching hospital he had heard of and the surgery being free.

Cain, Danny said, had listened. He hadn't walked away. He had focused.

"I'm going to look into it," the warden had promised. "I'm going to see what I can do."

Terry Hawkins had lost the jumpy bravado I'd noticed when he first explained his Guts & Glory strategy to me in September. Since late October, when he had felt unqualified to approach Sister Jackie's pulpit for salvation, then been healed in the ribs and legs at her insistence, he no longer slouched with jiggling knees wide apart as we talked. Now his long body remained upright, still. At first, I thought he'd grown more composed. But as I got to know him better at Christmastime, I realized how far he was from calm.

Terry couldn't study his case without being haunted. And studying their cases was something the inmates liked to do. Any mistake in the testimony against them—that the crime had happened, say, in a "strip mall" instead of a "shopping plaza"—gave them a sliver of hope, and they would stare at that bit of their transcripts, trying to convince themselves that it could mean reversal and freedom just as soon as they paid one of the counsel substitutes a few packs to file for them. Or, if they had pled guilty, as Terry had, they stared at their police reports, hunting for misstatements there. Often there were many, and so the pleasure of removing these documents from the safe bottom of their locker boxes, and of rediscovering the errors, could be experienced many times each year for decades.

But whenever Terry started to read his paragraphs, the image of his boss, Mr. Denver Tarter, on that hall floor came at him. The way the gash had been so deep into his throat. He'd almost chopped the man's head off. The way the blood from the wounds to his forehead had streamed across his bald spot. The way, before Terry had thrown the ax behind the hog-scalding tank, he'd seen Mr. Denver Tarter's hair stuck to the blade.

The sound of his boss's desperate breathing had been half like gagging, half like the air suction in a dentist's chair. Terry had stared down long enough for the blood to pool on the floor. Then he had seen that his own boots and clothes were covered in it, and felt where it had splashed onto his face.

A few weeks before Christmas, Sister Jackie had returned to Angola and asked again for all those who would give themselves to the Lord. Terry rose, balance tenuous, sat back down, decided to stay sitting, felt himself pulled strangely forward to be saved. With six or seven other inmates he stood before her. Waiting, he held himself together, trying not to disintegrate as the praise team attacked him with singing so slow each note seemed to last minutes.

> O the blood of Jesus
> It washes white as snow....
> O the love of Jesus
> He freely gives to me

At last Sister Jackie began to address the unsaved, to teach them that faith and submission were all that Jesus required. She spoke and made them recite the Bible's words, led them away from Romans 6 and back again, away from "the wages of sin" and back to "the free gift of God." She asked the entire congregation to repeat along with the men up front, so that Terry heard his own mumbled need and willingness multiplied by fifty voices, made huge, overwhelming, something he couldn't possibly contain, and he began to lose the battle against disintegration, the shivering starting to happen like when he'd been healed, moving outward from his chest to his shoulders, the congregation not only magnifying his longing but making it melt into theirs, making *him* melt, making him wish they would stop, that Sister Jackie would stop, that they would let him fit the pieces of himself back into place, fit them hard and tight. "While we were still weak...the righteousness based on faith says...on your lips and in your heart...that Jesus is Lord and that God raised Him from the dead...His love for us...His love for us..."

Her hand was on his forehead. Faith City's assistant ministers had taken the hands of other convicts, but Sister Jackie had moved toward him. The heel of her palm braced against one eyebrow and her fingers seemed to enwrap his skull. The rest of his body lost still more control, chest threatening to tear open and shoulders to spasm. "I call out the spirit of demons in Jesus' name," she spoke over Terry. "O Karishira. I call out Satan, O Lord, I command those forces loose their hold, I call them back to their place of origin, O Lord, I give this man strength in Jesus' name, O Lord, strengthen him, Lord, strengthen him, O we give You praise, O Lord, O we glorify You..."

It did not work. Not according to Terry. He told me that she had said quietly that he was not ready. "She said I got too much devil in me. She said that's why I was doing too much trembling." She had said, by his report, that he could not yet be saved.

Later, I told Sister Jackie of Terry's account. She cautioned that she could not be sure what had happenend, that during her services her words were given by the Spirit and were not easily recalled. But she was, for all her charismatic faith, a perfectly reasonable woman, and she added that it was extremely unlikely, even close to impossible, that she would ever declare anyone unfit for salvation. "His trembling was the power of the Lord," she said. "That's what happens in my church. That trembling was God's love. I would never have told him it was the work of the devil. I prayed for the devil to come out. But when I proclaimed all those men delivered by the authority and in the Spirit of Jesus, I meant every one of them. All men are worthy of Jesus' love."

Every Tuesday night since the end of October Terry had been attending Bible study in one of the two or three small meeting rooms at his camp. Now, after his failure to be saved, he told me he needed to "get more with my prayers and with my Bible," and he concentrated still more deeply during these Tuesday night sessions.

And all over Angola, all through the year, in a tradition old as anyone could remember, inmates read and explained verses to one another in these scripture groups, watched by no guard, their attendance marked by no record—a suggestion that Angola's worship was about more than conning those with control over their lives. For some, it was a way to keep an afterlife in mind. One man spoke of heaven's reflective gold pavement. "Here I look in the mirror and see what I see, but there, whenever I look down, I'll see my face coming back in that gold." For others, it was an effort to distinguish themselves from prison churchgoers they saw as insincere. ("They confess it but they don't possess it.") One inmate, who confided his rage when a clock he'd made in the hobby shop had been stolen, taught himself restraint. He read his passage, then lectured, "We have to pray when demons come to tagulate us. Lord, keep that clock! I don't want it!" For almost all, it was a way to reinforce their belief. "Faith is paradoxical," I heard one convict announce. He asked whether anyone knew the word "paradox." When no one answered, he read a definition, then proceeded. "In faith being paradoxical, it goes beyond reason. Faith believes without understanding why. Faith glorifies in tribulation. Faith chooses to suffer. Faith is a surrender."

I was never sure how much Terry understood of what was said by the other men around the table, their quoting and analyzing. Afterward, he could never talk in much detail about it. He rarely spoke during the meetings. Others shared their thoughts furiously ("He will tell you what you need, He will plant you with the true desires, that's what it means right here: 'He shall give thee the desires of thine heart'"); mutely Terry turned in his King James Bible to the verse called out. Sometimes he had to shift the letter and certificate he kept between the Bible's pages. They were from his daughter, Jamonica, who wrote of wanting "some gold for my teeth." The certificate said, "Student of the Week," and had her name written by hand above the line. Terry slipped these papers within other biblical chapters, and stared at the passage being read. Sheer comprehension must have been a struggle. Once, I'd seen the drafts of a letter he'd sent me. In the margins, he had practiced the spelling of words like "dinner" and "Saturday." The word "finished" had emerged as "frinst," "alcohol" as "ocall." He could not have had an easy time with the language of King James. But he had an orange marker, and neatly highlighted every passage cited. On his cot before bedtime he would read the lines over to absorb them.

A few weeks after Christmas Sister Jackie returned. When she beckoned the unsaved to come forward, Terry kept to his seat.

The day before, he had been alone in the shower after his shift in the kitchen. (The bathroom in Terry's dorm was half-hidden by a partial wall from the rest of the quarters.) Another inmate, a man he'd been friendly with for years and "didn't know was no freak or nothing," began showering a few nozzles down, staring at Terry's penis. Soon the man burst out, "I got to have me some of that." Terry gave little resistance as the man applied his hand and then, down on one knee, his mouth.

It was not Terry's first sex at Angola. He'd had, as he calculated it, "one or two relationships." He recalled a man he'd known at Main Prison. "Yeah, I fell in love with him," he said, and tried to explain: "He looked just like a little woman. And he acted just like one." He had made Terry's bed and fixed his snacks.

Whatever Terry meant about the man's appearance (to my eye,

the inmates looked and dressed invariably like men, though the gal-boys had their flourishes—an extra seam stitched down the center of their jeans, or hair plaited a certain way), and whatever he meant by love, there had been a strict division of sexual roles, as there was in nearly every Angola partnership. The punk did the sucking and the punk got fucked. He had either come to prison a homosexual or been maneuvered ("thrown into a cross," the way Littell had maneuvered the orderly) into serving as one, to be passed or sold from convict to convict for the rest of his sentence. Or, as one inmate urged me to recognize, "After ten years of no attention or affection, you might just give up and decide to be gay." You might decide to let go of your "manhood."

The one who did the fucking never returned the favor. Nor did he ever use his lips or his hand. Whatever love meant here, the punk masturbated later, by himself, or paid for one of the underclass of prison prostitutes who would service him. As Terry put it about the inmate he'd been in love with, "He would never even ask me. He knew better. He respected me as a man."

Terry said he hadn't felt much of anything for the inmate giving him a blowjob in the shower. There was no stirring of attraction. "There wasn't nothing to be attracted to." But, to borrow the phrase other convicts had used in discussing their sexuality, it had been a long time since he had been "inside some warm flesh." The inside of that mouth felt too good, the sheer contact too precious and power-ful—the plain heat of another person against his skin. He let it go on and on. Until an inmate walking in to use the toilet—though unable to see what was happening on the other side of the four-foot partition—pushed the level of Terry's shame too high. He set his hand against the punk's forehead, and shoved him away.

He did not feel Sister Jackie's palm on his own forehead the next evening. He did not step anywhere near her. To everything else, he had added another reason he was unworthy.

■

"Sometimes I can't believe it," Johnny Brooks said. Engaged to be married in an Angola wedding come next September, at Christmas he listened to Marvin Gaye on his Walkman and dreamed of Belva.

Had Warden Cain been willing to name inmates he thought should be let go, Brooks would surely have been near the top of the list. Other highly ranked staff were willing, and they told me that Brooks was fully rehabilitated, that if he was released, he would never be back. But his particular rehabilitation—his mastery of horses and cattle—and the support of Angola authorities had come at a price.

The magnitude of that price was impossible for me to judge: because I was white and he was black; because the price had been paid in dignity; because I could never tell how deeply the payment cut within him as he went on smiling and saying "Yassuh" and never, even after he opened up about other things, speaking a critical word about anyone of importance on the prison staff.

That staff—especially the range crew boss, Mr. Mike Vannoy, who had taught Brooks to work livestock—were fond of saying, "There's only one Johnny Brooks."

"Yassuh, Mr. Mike," he would answer.

"They threw away the mold," Mr. Mike, with his squashed-down, stocky, resilient body, would say.

"Yassuh."

"Do what you do when that bull comes out of the chute," Mr. Mike would request, as employees and inmates stood around the barn getting ready to start their day.

And Brooks would bug his eyes and stiffen his neck and quiver his head and quake his knees in fear, and Mr. Mike and everyone else would laugh.

"Threw away the mold!"

Mr. Mike had requested him for the range crew after watching him in the rodeo years ago. Brooks had taught himself to ride long before that. There had been a pasture, with a few horses, across the dirt road from the small clapboard house where he'd grown up. A field of sugarcane grew behind the house, and every fall Brooks's parents made some extra money by cutting the cane for their land-lord. They had lived that kind of existence, putting together bits of income. The horses in that pasture were the joy of Brooks's child-hood. Their owner lived somewhere else in town, and at nine years old Brooks coaxed one of the animals to the fence. He leapt on with-out saddle or halter. He was thrown fast. With a clump of grass in his hand, he lured the horse back to the rails—he needed the height of the slats in order to jump on. He was pitched again. But soon, with scavenged hay string for a halter and reins, he stayed on; soon he had won over all the horses. Every day, checking to make sure their owner wasn't around, he stole across the road, prepared his chosen mount with the hay string, and galloped from fence to fence, imag-ining himself like the cowboys he'd seen on TV.

He had become that cowboy at Angola, on the range crew. Show-ing him around the prison's graze land, Mr. Mike had galloped after a dodging calf, slung his rope, and lassoed the neck as neatly as if both horse and baby cow were standing still. "Think you'd like to do that?" Brooks heard, and was schooled, first, on the ground, with a bucket for a target. When he could fling his rope around that every time, he graduated to calves held within a pen, and quickly to the open land. It took two years, he said, for him to "get good" out there. By the time I met him, and watched him work, he was easily the best roper on the crew, far better than any other inmate, far better than any employee, far better than Mr. Mike.

And his boss took a certain pride in having found him, in having trained him. That was part of the sentiment in Mr. Mike's refrain, spoken as the crew herded cattle or groomed horses or stacked hay, "Only one Johnny Brooks." The other part was that among the group of trusties he controlled, only Brooks, the quickest and most muscular athlete, was so completely his boy.

When I rode out with the crew, I watched Brooks, in prison waders, charging across a puddled field on Sonny, the quarter horse permanently assigned to him, reins in one hand, rope in the other, and tag held in his teeth. The sky was low and dark with clouds, its ceiling close to the tall trees out toward the river. Otherwise things seemed, for a moment, limitless, as though we weren't in a prison at all: The pasture was so huge no fence lines were visible and, steering around scrub growth, we came to hidden rivulets and deep gulleys, and staring into the distance we saw the hills, so densely wooded; it was as if we were riding across some unclaimed western territory of the nineteenth century, rather than a penitentiary farm. The hooves of Brooks's horse skidded three or four yards on the waterlogged ground as he stopped, then chased a calf again, and for an instant, the hooves hydroplaning, Brooks had no connection to the earth.

Seconds later he had maneuvered the young cow exactly where he needed it, in front and to his right and away from its mother. Still galloping, and with his target still sprinting, he flicked his wrist, aiming the loop at a spot five or six yards from him, aiming perfectly. Seemingly in one motion with halting the calf, he leapt from his saddle. He did this so quickly, in fact, that I never saw it. The next thing I registered he stood over the young animal. "It's a bull calf, Mr. Mike," he called up.

"All right, Johnny."

With a tagging gun Brooks clipped a numbered tag through the calf's right ear. Then he flipped the animal onto its back. He straddled it, splayed its legs with his own knees. From the pocket of his waders he took his boss's jackknife, given him for the day. He pinched the calf's scrotum. He sliced, yanked the testicles from the sac, and tossed them onto the mud, a pair of elongated blue-gray bulbs with silvery tubes trailing behind them.

The calf was the fourth or fifth in a row Brooks had roped on the first try. During the next few minutes, though their interchange was somewhat playful, it was hard not to think in symbolic terms of what Brooks had just done for his boss: strung the animal up, and cut its balls off.

Saying that Brooks's head was getting too "swoll," Mr. Mike flicked his own rope near Brooks's face. Brooks laughed. He kept laughing as the rope whacked a few times against his shoulder, in a way that couldn't have hurt much, but that made him flinch. "Only made one like Johnny Brooks," Mr. Mike said, and went on cracking the rope. Brooks stopped his horse to let his boss continue out of striking distance. Mr. Mike stopped too, and went on snapping. Brooks voiced no objection.

Later that afternoon, as Mr. Mike and I rode back alone, he said to me, "It must surprise you how well we get along with the inmates, fooling with each other." We were just passing one of the large barns. On the outside wall, under the peak of the roof, hung a painting done on plyboard. Buckkey had made it: a cowboy roping a calf. Everything about it was predictable. But back when Buckkey had started it, Mr. Mike had wandered by and seen that the cowboy was going to be black. He had told Buckkey to change this. "Shoot," he had said, with Johnny Brooks standing beside them, "I don't want no nigger on the side of my barn."

Johnny Brooks believed, perhaps rightly, that his boss appreciated his skill. He believed that his boss's brother, Mr. Darrell, a man with a softer edge who was one of Angola's assistant wardens, cared for him as a person. During Brooks's first years at the penitentiary, Mr. Mike's and Mr. Darrell's uncle had been Brooks's supervisor elsewhere on the farm. He believed their entire family felt a certain indebtedness. He believed that Warden Cain respected him and valued him and felt affection for him.

Whatever the link between his beliefs and reality, it was true that Brooks's faithful service paid off in small dispensations and liberties, in a life closer to normal than the average inmate's or even the average trusty's. He could breach the dress code to wear a royal blue T-shirt with a large, jersey-type number 1 stenciled between his shoulder blades. Sometimes he wore a cap with the bill turned backward. These tiny allowances were grand by prison standards, especially for someone who'd been measuring his life by those standards for almost a quarter century. But there were bigger dividends, some that added to his intimacy with Belva, that gave this reformed convict the chance to build some fraction of a full existence. There was the possibility of sex in a state where conjugal visits were illegal....

Brooks's relationship with Belva had grown, at first, mostly through letters. She knew three or four women with boyfriends or husbands at Angola, so while she was terribly shy with Brooks in person, she was not uncomfortable with the idea of loving a prisoner. She pushed things along by mail. "Hi, Johnny," she wrote. "How are you doing today I hope find.... Me and my girlfriends stayed up late talking about how they found happinniss there and they are feeling good about themsefe and hearing the girls talk it make me feel even better.... Bonnie said she told Billy that I said something about your hair and that not true however you choose to ware you hair dose not worry me at all becase hair dose not make a person. I wont to get to know Johnny and only you. Like you said you need someone you can trust and I wont to be that woman to share every thing life have to offer us life is so precious...."

After work, Brooks would put Marvin Gaye or Isaac Hayes or James Brown into his Walkman, lie back on his cot, and read and reread Belva's most recent letter. Often he took the entire stack from his locker box and read through those as well. Every other evening he wrote back, going to a friend, Derricks, an inmate tutor and librarian at the outcamp's closet-size room of torn paperbacks, for help with phrases and spelling. Sometimes he went so often Derricks would lock him out of the library. (Brooks's nickname among the convicts—used sparingly—was "Ignorant." He insisted he didn't mind.) Lately Derricks had convinced him to take a few sessions of Saturday tutoring. If he wasn't needed with the range crew, Brooks spent an hour on Saturday mornings with his spelling, then returned to his Walkman and his wishes.

The visits with Belva became easier. He was almost as reserved as she was, and conversation could be a struggle, but he was at least used to prison's absolute lack of privacy, and could feel some self-assurance in drawing her out, urging her, "You can't hold back 'cause of all these people around. If we're going to be together, we're going to be visiting like this for a long time." They talked about the two men who had fathered her children. The second had been violent, had hit her. Brooks ducked his head as they sat kitty-corner, holding hands under the edge of a table.

"I'll leave you before I hit you," he promised, imagining some future life outside Angola.

She looked at him, her high-cheekboned face expressionless. She tilted her head to one side. She pursed her lips slightly, almost sadly, then smiled. "I'll kick your ass," she said.

They laughed. Brooks gave a mock pout. They kissed with the guards looking on. Belva told him, "Johnny Brooks, you have a beautiful personality."

The oversize Christmas card she chose for him had not a bit of white space in its design—baubles and candles and garlands and stars and an effusion of gold light filled every millimeter. The card he sent in return was a hand-me-down, because he had so little money in his account. He bought it from another inmate. Brooks borrowed some Wite-Out, dabbed it over the date and name, and mailed it with his declaration of love.

The visitors were always bussed to the sheds first, then the inmates brought. When he walked into the shed the next weekend, he didn't see her in the cavern among the thirty or forty people. It took him a full minute. She was at a back table, just waiting.

"Wow! That you, baby?"

"Yeah. That's me."

"Wow!" He had a way of saying that, half laughing with pleasure. "You look beautiful today."

She wore a long, glossy blue dress with high heels. She paid $2.50 to the guard handling concession money, and she and Brooks had a Polaroid taken in front of the mural with the stream and the low, luminous shafts of light. They sat down, held both of each other's hands, his under hers, cradling her palms. They talked of her daughters, the oldest of whom, at fourteen, had just been sent to a detention center, and of her sons, the youngest of whom, Marcus, at four, couldn't wait to meet Johnny. Brooks said he couldn't wait to meet all of them. He promised that as soon as he had money in his account, the next time his sister sent thirty or forty dollars, which she did on occasion, he would have someone in the hobby shop make belts for the boys and pocketbooks for the girls.

And next year's rodeo wasn't going to be like this last one. He had let himself get overconfident. He had quit running three or four miles after work. That wasn't going to happen again. By spring he would ask to be transferred from the range crew, because the long hours didn't always allow time to stay in shape. He would work at the car wash by the front gate, and jog and hit the weights. And next October he would win an all-around and a bull-riding buckle for Belva's two boys.

"When you bringing them up here to visit?" he asked, for the third or fourth time that morning, partly because they still ran low on conversation, but also because he wanted badly to be part of her family, fantasized himself called "Father," and because he needed to be more deeply inside her life, that much less easy to abandon, to just quit seeing, quit visiting, one day, any day.

"As soon as there's room in the car, Johnny."

She rode up—it was a two-and-a-half-hour drive, each way—with the group of women from near her town who had men inside the prison. She reminded him, yet again, that she did not have her own car. Then, ignoring the guards and the inmates and the families around her, she touched his newly shaved head, held it between both hands, stroked it.

Brooks said, "I sure would love for you to be the mother of my child someday."

She searched his face for many seconds, head tilted, lips midway between uncertainty and one of her wide, reluctant smiles. She needed to know something, that he wasn't talking about the special visits she'd heard about, that he was trying to ask something else.

"I would love for me to be the mother of your child someday," she said, finally knowing.

And that was the way he proposed marriage, and that was the way she accepted.

As for the sex, I do not know what Brooks and Belva did over the coming months, or did not do. I know only what almost everyone at the prison was aware of. Down the road from the Ranch House, Butler Park, with its dozen or so picnic tables and bits of playground equipment, had been built eleven years ago to give trusties something to aim for if they avoided all write-ups: surroundings less bleak than cinder block for them and their families. There, some convicts led their women to the crest of the gentle hill, just outside the guard's vision as long as he didn't look too hard. He rarely did. He knew that no one wanted him to, not the administration and of course not the inmates. Mostly clothed, couples could seize a fast physical intimacy on that knoll, with no more privacy than the oblivion of their own love or lust could afford, with other couples doing the same hurried thing around them.

The prison's tradition of sex at the park may well have been the only way to allow conjugal visits in a state so rabidly harsh in the sentencing of its convicts. And surely the inmates weren't complaining, were happy to take what they could get. They and their

women may even have felt some—maybe even a great deal of—
extra electricity in their lovemaking, because of its speed and setting.
Every touch may have been fraught. And afterward, during the
weeks or months when the couples didn't see each other, or couldn't
schedule a day at the park, the memory of every touch may have carried a powerful reverberation. No routine, bored, forgettable sex
here. But not much dignity, either. As the prison had designed it, the
convicts fucked under the trees, furiously, amid other humping
couples.

Because he was such a favorite among the authorities, Johnny
Brooks could expect not only that his applications for park visits
would be readily approved, but that if, as infrequently happened, the
guard did look too closely, he would not be severely punished for
any indiscretion. His faithful service had brought him the chance at
a certain quality of closeness with Belva.

It also brought them a constructible dream. Like a reliable chorus running through the sporadic conversation of their visits, Brooks
described their future. Mr. Gerry Lane, the Baton Rouge Chevrolet
dealer who sponsored the rodeo, who sent the cowgirl in the blue-
spangled jumpsuit to ride around the arena during the national
anthem, and who kept his favorite horse at the range-crew stables,
had promised Brooks a job whenever he was set free. Brooks wasn't
the only one who saw his future in Lane's hands. Many convicts
believed that the car dealer, who drove up from Baton Rouge to trot
his jet black quarter-horse stallion along Angola's levees and to take
part in cattle drives as though on a dude ranch, wielded so much
influence with the governor that he could guarantee a man's pardon.
Lane had, to be exact, arranged the pardon of one lifer under a previous administration. Yet he was going to win everyone's freedom.
And Brooks could believe he was first on the car dealer's list. Not
only had Lane admired how well he handled the livestock, not only
was Lane a good friend of the warden's (which meant that he'd

heard Cain speak highly of Brooks's character), but Mr. Gerry Lane had entrusted his stallion, Little Man, to Brooks's care.

Little Man had tremendous jaw muscles, articulated veins, a deep cleft dividing the muscles of his chest. He was strong and quick enough that, working the cattle, he could lift a calf into the air with his teeth, swing it around, and set it on its way in the right direction. But most enchanting to Lane and Brooks and everyone else who dealt with the horse, Little Man was unruly. He would not let himself be ridden unless you knew exactly how to manipulate him, as Lane and Brooks did. The stallion's father was said to have stomped a man to death. And Little Man himself, when breeding, was almost uncontrollable, even with the chain rigging that could be cinched into his nose to force him back. Most stallions, when put in with a mare who wasn't quite ready, would give up when she kicked out with her hind legs. Not Little Man. His approach, as one of the range crew put it, was "I don't care. I'm going to stick it in you anyway."

When Lane called the range-crew bosses to say he was coming up for a ride, Brooks shampooed the horse, then applied ShowSheen to his coat to make it gleam. The coat wasn't really a pure black. It was an extremely dark brown with a white streak over one nostril. Lane liked the stallion kept in its stall as much as possible to preserve the appearance of black, and to minimize the white hairs that grew pronounced with the sun. Brooks sanded Little Man's hooves to remove the grain, and painted on layer after layer of polish to blacken them. When Lane arrived Brooks presented him with the sleek, gorgeous animal, then outfitted Little Man with Lane's red saddle that was studded with antique silver coins.

As soon as he got out, Brooks told his bride-to-be, he would go to work for Mr. Gerry. He wasn't yet sure what the job would be—taking care of Lane's other horses, working in his dealership, it didn't matter. And he would start at minimum wage if he had to, climb his way up. But he would be working, that was the definite thing, and at the end of every day he would arrive home to play with the kids in their backyard, to make sure they did well in school, to make sure Belva was always happy. A life of family bliss was just a year or so away, just on the other side of his next pardon-board application.

By January Belva had bought their wedding rings on a layaway plan. She wore hers to the visiting shed, making it double as an engagement ring. Because of prison regulations about the wearing of gold, Brooks would get his on their wedding day. In a kind of ceremony of engagement, she slipped her chiseled band halfway down his pinky finger, where he turned it at the knuckle, digging it into the skin, to leave a mark. They discussed, not for the first time, the preparations they had to make, the procedures they had to go through. Brooks had already asked Rick LeDoux, the Cowboys for Christ minister who came to preach at Camp F, to officiate at the wedding. They had to get a list of possible dates from LeDoux, then set a definite one with the warden's office. They were aiming for early September, because in that time they could get to know each other better, track down a copy of Brooks's birth certificate, which they needed for the marriage license, have the required interview with one of Angola's staff chaplains, and request approval from the warden. Even with Brooks's favored status, these procedures could take time. Not much happened fast in Angola's world of lifers, but Brooks and Belva were sure that their wedding would, eventually, happen.

If it did, it would not merely be what some of the ten or so weddings performed each year at Angola clearly were: attempts, on the inmate's part, to secure a link to the outside world, to needed legal papers, to a lawyer who might be convinced to appeal his case, to a source of money. Partly for this reason, several of the prison chaplains were reluctant to approve or perform the ceremonies. But this marriage would bring together a woman who, however shy, had said, "I'll kick your ass," and a man who had said to me, "Ever since I been here I wondered if anything like this could ever happen. She done changed my life. I love her, Mr. Dan. I love her."

Between visits he counted the days, and once, waiting for the prearranged time when he would call her collect, I had sat with him on his cot as he counted the minutes and checked his watch every twenty-five seconds. How many of these intervals would there be until September?

He began to picture the ceremony in detail. He wondered who would be there inside the chapel. He hoped his two sisters would come; they were the only family who kept any contact. He wasn't sure they would make the drive from their coastline town three hours away. They no longer visited. But he knew that his boss's brother, Mr. Darrell, the assistant warden, would be there for him; he knew how that man felt about all the work Brooks had done for his family. In fact, Brooks planned to ask him to be his driver, to take him in the assistant warden's long, white Department of Corrections pickup truck, the closest thing around to a limousine, from Camp F to the chapel at Main Prison.

And Brooks knew that on his biggest day, when he held Belva's hands and spoke his vows, Warden Cain would clear his calendar to be there.

I had to find one last convict I'd met before the rodeo, a rider who'd embedded himself in my mind. I wanted to follow him through the year.

"What made you come here tonight?" I'd asked Donald Cook back in September, standing at the rear of a Pentecostal service in the Main Prison visiting shed, as a hundred inmates sang along with a convict choir.

"The a.c.," he had answered, leaning toward me across a pinball machine, a spiderweb tattoo on his wrist, other designs devouring both arms.

Then, at the rodeo in October, determined though all the other men were, Cook had seemed even more so. One Sunday, in the Wild

Horse Race, he hauled himself partway up onto the animal's back and rode the bucking horse with his body pitched sideways, virtually parallel to the ground. He was simply unwilling to let himself fall. As he crossed the finish line he *did* fall from that fully vulnerable position—for the rest of the day he couldn't move his left arm at all. Yet he walked out into the ring for the Guts & Glory, stalking the chip with his useless arm held straight to his side. "I want to take that chip off *him*," he had told me, pausing before that pronoun, seeming perhaps to capitalize it, as if he felt himself in a battle with his maker.

Cook's dorm guard told me I could find him in the Toy Shop. I went along the Walk to track him down. After building and giving away 2,500 toys just before Christmas, the members were catching their breath. Over the past year, the club had grown from a temporary, November-December group that constructed a few hundred toys in a hallway outside the prison gym to a year-round organization with its own workshop. Its collection of tools had expanded from the makeshift—a hammer made by welding a piece of compressor motor to a stray metal cylinder; a meat saw found in the kitchen's Dumpster and rigged for cutting wood—to the traditional. Now there were table saws and a full tool closet. Local businesses had donated some of the equipment; Toy Shop fund-raisers (a cheeseburger, potato salad, and a PG video shown to any inmate with three dollars to pay) had bought much of the rest.

The club was still hardly sophisticated or well supplied. Material consisted of scrap lumber, of scavenged mop handles that would be turned into stick ponies. But those ponies were beautiful! Their spotted wooden heads were like something you might hunt for in expensive boutiques. And the cars and trucks and dragsters and military tanks—all their wooden wheels were impeccably balanced and had been made, one at a time, by inmate and saw. All their gleaming surfaces, their racing stripes and camouflage spots, had been painted by hand.

The workshop was almost deserted when I looked in. Two inmates geared up for next December, aiming past 2,500. A saw shrieked. A hammer pounded. Donald Cook lay curled on an old vinyl couch, amid the sawdust and noise.

I was surprised Cook had been accepted into the organization. It was a selective club. You had to show good discipline to be approved by the members and the security sponsor. And just four months ago, he had finished a year in the punishment cells for dealing marijuana.

Six years earlier, in the small Louisiana city of Alexandria, Cook had lured a man from a bar with the promise of sex. A friend of Cook's drove them to the Red River levee. Cook was married, had one child and another coming, and for several years had been letting men suck him off, partly for money, partly for pleasure. Burglary supplied the rest of his income. He had been charged with at least thirty separate thefts. Once, a group of tavern owners had arranged to have him beat up, they were so tired of his daytime break-ins. He spent his nights in those same rough bars. And once, at a place called Cleve's Lounge, when a man stroked the belly of Cook's pregnant wife, Cook had taken the gun from his belt, shot between the man's feet, and then shot out the ceiling above the bar mirror.

On the levee above the Red River, Cook wound up beating his trick to death with a tree branch after trying to rob him. He dragged the body down the embankment into the water. He hurled large rocks to make it sink. The corpse was found three days later. Meanwhile, Cook changed out of his blood-soaked clothes, hid at friends' houses around Alexandria, discovered from the TV news that he was the prime suspect, and fled to Texas. He returned with the hope—grown quickly stronger than the wish to avoid arrest—of killing his wife and two friends who, he figured rightly, had told everything to the police. He was in what he called his "don't-care mood." He planned to torture them first, give them plenty of time to think about what they'd done to him, while he put them through pain. He found his wife at another friend's house. She answered the door when he rang. He said, "Come to Texas with me." She, sensing he wanted to get her alone to kill her, slipped off to call 911. The cops stormed the house before he could do any harm.

From his time at Angola, as well as many stays in parish jails, his short, wiry body was covered with tattoos. The spiderweb was among the smallest. An animal half lion and half monster, with a mane of fire, occupied most of his back. A Viking dominated his chest, a helmeted woman his shoulder. From hip to hip across the bottom of his back, in fancy calligraphy, a tattoo read: LOUISIANA CRACKER.

For each of these he had paid a convict artist to burn a plastic canister, usually of Speed Stick, with a paper bag held over the plastic to catch the rising soot. Scraped from the paper, the soot was mixed with toothpaste and water to make the ink. A steel guitar string was threaded through an empty pen shaft. The artist rigged a tiny motor, taken from a cassette player, to jab the steel string thousands and thousands of times into Cook's skin.

For work, Cook had not progressed off the field lines since coming to Angola, partly because of fights with black inmates. "I won't let these niggers get racial with me," he said, reminding me of an element of life here that I rarely saw or heard about. The blacks were so dominant in numbers that the whites never challenged them in any concentrated way. Yet the whites didn't seem to feel overly stranded—there were enough of them, and enough mostly white clubs, to keep them comfortable. Quiet avoidance marked the relations. But the quiet didn't mean the anger wasn't around. Trying to capture the beauty of some property his brother owned in Missouri, fields he showed to me in pictures and spoke of like the Promised Land, Cook emphasized, "There's no niggers up there."

Besides the tattoos and the fighting, he had spent his time in prison smoking and selling marijuana. The drug, like the harder narcotics, came in through guards (who might leave it behind one of Angola's unused buildings, to be picked up by an inmate and buried in the fields, unearthed by another convict, and brought to the prisoner who'd made the deal with the guard in the first place), or it came in through visitors (who buried it in their rectums). When Cook heard of a new delivery, he put out word that he was willing to handle the sales if the inmate was too nervous to deal for himself. Cook divided the drug into sugar bags—the little packets meant for coffee, emptied of their contents. This was the prison's standard measure. One sugar bag, scarcely filled, cost ten dollars, about four times what the same amount of marijuana would have brought on the street. It furnished what the inmates called a "mosquito" joint.

The day he'd been caught, Cook had taken some sugar bags out to the fields to distribute. On a break between picking rows, a few men had huddled together to get high. They positioned themselves so the breeze would keep the smell from their guards, who chatted with one another and ignored what they didn't see. At lunch, relaxed and hungry, Cook decided to risk the mess hall. He knew he might be frisked, but it was Wednesday, chicken day, and he didn't want to miss his favorite meal. The lieutenant outside the doors stared straight into the face of every inmate. Cook glanced away.

He knew he was finished. He prided himself on handling all pressure. He should never have let his eyes slip.

The lieutenant told him to step out of line. He ran his hands over Cook's back first, then his underarms, down his sides, his thighs....

"What you got in your pocket?"

"Chap Stick," Cook said.

More eye contact. This time Cook's held.

"Let's see."

Cook drew it out, showed it, a tube of Chap Stick.

Again eyes, again steady.

The lieutenant ran his hand over the same place. "What's this?"

"Nothing."

"Empty it."

Cook leaned to the side, dug into his jeans pocket. He squeezed the sugar bags in his hand, swung up with his other forearm. The lean giving him extra momentum, he knocked the lieutenant into a wall. Cook ran up the mess line, through the open gate, across the Walk, and through another gate and onto the Yard, where he tossed the sugar bags under a ledge as he sprinted toward the basketball court, toward the softball diamond, toward the hundreds of yards of open grass, toward nothing but fence, he realized, with three or four guards behind him, as he leapt over a drainage ditch, slipped on some mud, fell and just lay there, waiting to be cuffed.

They couldn't find the sugar bags. When it came to sentencing in D.B. court, this meant the difference between J and a working cell-block, where he got an hour of communal rec time in the early evenings. The working blocks also had circulating air. Standing against the vent at the back of his cell, and knowing the guard had to walk his tier only once an hour, Cook went on getting high. He did it for the gamesmanship. Much of his life had been ruled by the pleasure of adrenaline. His childhood had been poor and disordered enough (his family's trailer home, which I visited, stood in a weedy lot across from the railroad tracks, the worst house in a run-down, all-black section of Alexandria, and his schooling had ended in the ninth grade), but his crimes had been driven by more than poverty. He had liked robbing people he knew, sometimes while they were asleep in their houses. And he had liked robbing his tricks, men who could identify him and who he would see again afterward.

This tempting of fate, along with plenty of anger, ran through much that he did: spraying bullets around Cleve's Lounge; brutally robbing an elderly neighbor a few weeks before the murder; sleeping with his brother's wife because he suspected his brother had slept with his; smashing the skull of the man on the levee, a man he'd had sex with at least twice before; vowing to torture and kill his wife and everyone else who had given evidence against him; phoning from the parish jail after his arrest, promising them that he would escape—from the jail before he was sent to Angola, or from Angola if he had to—just to get at them. His calls, as he knew full well, were recorded: "I will be out there.... There's many a ways.... It might take me thirty or forty years, but I'm coming.... Arson...."

And now he was curled sweetly, dark blue eyes opening slowly, short black hair rumpled, on the Toy Shop couch. He said he'd been part of the club for several weeks, that an inmate he knew from Alexandria had invited him in. He claimed he had decided to change, that at twenty-nine he felt worn down. "I know twenty-nine don't seem old, but it's old to me." He spoke of his mother, who was sixty-three and sick with arthritis. He needed to give her some hope, some thought that in return for good behavior he would someday be released. "I'm going to die here," he said. "I know that. But I don't tell her. I'm the baby of the family. She's living for me."

One of his brothers was in prison. Another had been. He showed me a picture of his mother in her cluttered trailer home: white, flow-ered housedress; cigarette; sunken mouth; the blue eyes. He said she'd run fairly wild in her day, spent as much time in bars as he later did. Now she tried to "garden," though a picture of her yard showed more debris than greenery. "I'm living for her," he added, and men-tioned the certificate he'd received for participation in the Toy Shop—he'd sent it to her; she kept it on her refrigerator door.

From his reluctant, inward speech, he seemed thoroughly honest. He said he'd gotten the certificate for nothing, that he'd hardly worked on any of the toys the club had given away. He had painted a few cars, that was all. Most he had done in simple patterns, accord-ing to other inmates' instructions. But one racing car, as yet unfin-ished, he had begun to decorate with an underwater-looking design. He brought the car down from a private spot, on top of a high cabi-net, for me to see. One side was painted a dark purple, almost black, and adorned with slender tentacles like seaweed that were only a few shades lighter than the background. They were nearly invisible, but the twisting, waving strands were beautiful. It was as though he was painting his version of the bottom of the ocean. It was as though in the slow painting he was purging a former self: one that sped wildly, as if in a racing car, through an ocean's darkness.

The car was, at any rate, an accomplishment, a hint of talent, but I saw even more hope in his mere presence in the workshop, in his sleeping on that ratty couch. He left his dorm every morning before sunrise, and napped or lay awake here. He remained in the workshop through most of the day. Much of that time was spent lying on the couch. A new job on the kitchen paint crew had him working odd hours, often in the evenings; between the job and the waking up at three A.M., he was in the dorm only a few hours each night. Which was how he wanted it. He needed to escape the men who knew him. His closest partner had started whispering "model prisoner," but Cook could hardly be called a showcase for rehabilitation. So far, hibernation was about as far as it went. The workshop was a refuge. Like a dog on a familiar piece of rug, or a child who likes to nap in the living room, he rested amid the comforting tumult of life, was reassured by the accumulation of sawdust.

If Donald Cook makes some sort of personal progress this year, I thought, Warden Cain will have worked a minor miracle. The credit would belong, as well, to the inmate who'd brought Cook into the Toy Shop, and to the assistant warden who supervised the organization and helped it grow. But finally, I reasoned, if Cain hadn't put his energy and encouragement behind it, Cook—and surely others like him, in other stages of transformation—would have had no sanctuary. From his position as ruler over 5,000 inmates and 1,800 employees, Cain's benevolence was filtering down to the bottom.

The warden would have been less pleased by another development in Cook's life. Cook told me he'd fallen in love with an inmate he'd met while doing his year in the punishment cellblocks. Alberto was one of the handful of Hispanics at the prison. Cook said Alberto's accent turned him on.

Every other afternoon, around five o'clock, Cook hurried to a fence at one end of the Main Yard. On the other side of the barbed wire and chain link was the Walk, then another fence, then the area where the cellblock inmates were let out for exercise. Cook's lover was still serving time in the cells, so they arranged to meet at their opposite fences, about fifteen feet apart. There were always ten or twenty men meeting in the same way—to catch up on news, or to run business of one kind or another, or just to sit and pluck at the lawn and let the time pass. Cook ignored the men around him. And though everyone had to call across such distance, all the conversations did seem intimate, even private, as though the convicts had honed some inflection of voice that mingled in a special way with the Angola air, muffling and channeling their words so that they barely carried outside a direct line.

One warm afternoon in the last days of December, Cook asked his lover, whose buttery, unmuscled chest showed beneath a work shirt open to the belly, "You heard from your mom yet?"

"No, Donald."

"She's doing all right. You'd feel it if she wasn't."

"She's bad sick."

"You'd feel it, though. If she got any worse you'd feel it. Like my mama with that pancreas. Soon as she got it, I started getting them cramps. Started cramping up. We're like twins. You're the same way with yours. You'll know. Trust me."

"Mine's farther away."

"It don't matter."

"She's bad."

"Don't start being all depressed now."

"I know."

"You better be strong."

"I know."

"You know, you lose your head they got places they're going to put you. Places worse than them blocks."

"I received your brother's card."

"He wrote you?"

"You know."

"Yeah. I told him to."

"It was a nice Christmas card."

"Yeah."

"He say how special I am to you, sweetheart."

"Yeah. That's true.

"It was a very caring card."

"I told him about your mom and all."

As Alberto's hour wound down, Cook said, "Turn around and show me your ass."

Alberto pressed his jeans against the chain-link, rubbed for a second against the metal. Cook did not reciprocate. Nor was he asked to. Whenever his lover made it back into the main population, their sex would follow the code: "There's always a man and always a punk." "He'll take care of his own self," Cook explained. "He better never disrespect me."

Within those parameters, Cook had found love at Angola.

F I V E

HE ORDERED ME TO HIS OFFICE. I HUNG UP THE
phone in the range-crew headquarters. It was late January. In muddy
boots, pants, shirt after a ride with Johnny Brooks, I drove right away
to the administration building. I tried to brush the caked dirt from
my clothes as I steered. I did not wish to keep the warden waiting.

"Mr. Bugner," he began, never quite having learned to pronounce
my name, "I want to know what you're up to." His white hair was
luxuriant. His voice was affable. His stomach, as he pushed away
from his desk, made him look still more relaxed. "'Cause you might
be hearing too much."

We exchanged smiles.

"That depends what I'm not supposed to hear." It was easy to
keep my tone light. I hadn't heard much that reflected badly on him.
And I wasn't hoping to.

He chuckled, then let his smile fade. "I've given you the run of
this prison. I haven't put an officer with you. You're out there driving
from outcamp to outcamp. But why do you need so much privacy,
anyhow? How much are you going to put homosexuality in that
book? Or drugs? I'm starting to wonder. And what are you going to
do if these inmates say bad stuff about me? You're coming down here

from New York. I don't know who you are. How much are you going to believe what they say?"

"Warden Cain—"

He cut me off, politely. He radioed for two assistant wardens. He said he wanted their input, wanted them to hear my answer. This did not seem a good sign. Maybe I could reassure him during a long-winded, personal chat about religion, regeneration. But with a pair of Angola veterans to keep the talk on practical terms, I thought the meeting might end with me led permanently off the grounds.

As we waited amid the dustless, gleaming surfaces, Cain turned his attention to signing documents. And I thought of the coverage he was used to in the national media. ABC, PBS, the Discovery Channel—in the past year they had each run programs featuring him as a warden unlike any other: balanced, sensitive, deeply thoughtful, a hero to anyone who still believed in the basic humanity of violent criminals. And it was no secret that he loved the publicity, adored the way he came out on camera. He'd urged the teams from ABC and the Discovery Channel to return for more stories. My book, he'd been certain, would bring him even more serious attention. He would be recognized as the leader of a "moral revolution" in criminal justice.

What had triggered his nerves? We had discussed, up front, my dealing with all sides of prison life, homosexuality and drugs included. Those issues alone couldn't have set him off. But the difference between me and a TV crew—maybe that had just dawned on him. No inmate was going to speak critically about him into a camera. With me he had no guarantees.

Or maybe, I thought, he'd been remembering one of the few print journalists, a reporter for the *Boston Globe,* who had displeased him. The man had written about the food can relabeling plant the warden had tried to establish at Angola. He had mentioned, too, private business brought to D.C.I. while Cain was warden there. The writer's suggestion of corruption, of kickbacks, had been unstated and without proof. But the suggestion had been unmistakable. For months I had tried to keep that article out of my mind. I recalled it now, as the assistant wardens, forearms thick below the short sleeves of their sportshirts, took chairs close on my right. "We've got his name at the front gate," I'd heard Cain say with easy satisfaction about that reporter. "He won't ever be back here again." I didn't want my name recorded there.

"All you have to do," the Warden set aside his documents and resumed with me now, "is put me in my comfort zone." He leaned far back, seeming to speak past his belly, which had grown during the months I'd known him.

"I'd like to."

"Well, that's good, that's good. 'Cause all I need is an editorial agreement. So I can read through your book before you turn it in to your editor, and make sure it's all accurate, and make any changes I need to make, 'cause I want it to be a good book."

"I understand your worries," I said, trying to stay calm as I imagined what his sanitized treatment might look like. Warden Cain no longer entering in his chariot. Terry Hawkins no longer getting that blowjob in the shower, no longer needing to be "inside some warm flesh." And none of my fear, growing minute by minute as I sat in Cain's overly air-conditioned office and sensed the extent of his desire to keep something hidden, that the *Globe* reporter had been right and, worse, that the corruption wasn't a mere human flaw but might be the defining quality of the man. What if all the humanitarian talk was a smoke screen?

"I understand how important it is to represent Angola and your administration correctly," I went on, keeping my voice steady. "I know that books and movies usually turn prisons into sensationalized places, with all kinds of rapes and killings, and wardens are always sadistic villains. But I haven't seen any rapes, and what I'm hearing about you is eighty percent good. Eighty percent's not bad when you're dealing with inmates talking about their keeper. So I really do understand, but I think it would be a mistake for both of us if we had any kind of editorial agreement."

"But it would put me in my comfort zone."

He sipped from his Dr Pepper, and I entered into a long explanation: Everything positive I wrote would be put into question.

"You don't have to tell anyone about the agreement," he offered. "I won't. All it'll be is a piece of paper."

"But everyone will ask. How did he get such access inside a maximum security prison? How did he convince the warden to let him roam around for a year? And I'm not that good a liar."

"All right. Well, you're an honest man. In that case I'm going to have to put an officer with you. But you don't have to worry. It won't be a man in blue. It'll be someone from classification. Because I don't want to intimidate the inmates. I really don't. I want them to talk to you. I do. I want this to be a good book. But they're inmates, let's remember that. They're liable to say any old thing. So let's put someone with you, to make sure they say what's right."

"I am skeptical of what they say every second."

"All you have to do is give me editorial review."

"That would be another kind of book. 'Warden Cain as told to.' No one would take it seriously."

"Then," he looked to the stone-faced veterans, "shouldn't I put someone with him? To make sure they don't say anything too bad about us? Isn't that the right thing to do?"

They nodded.

"It would be much better," I turned back to Cain, trying to keep the plea out of my voice, "if I could write on the acknowledgments page, 'And many thanks to Warden Burl Cain, for allowing me unlimited access to the prison and unmonitored time with the inmates.' Then everything that really matters to you, the humanity of the convicts and the value of your programs, all your accomplishments, will be trusted by the reader."

"You can write that anyway," the warden said, finishing his Dr Pepper. "That way we'll all be comfortable."

The air-conditioning was turned way too high. I wanted a sweater, I wanted a cup of coffee. I was freezing. I couldn't give him editorial control, but a staff minder was nearly as impossible. It didn't matter if it was someone from classification. How well could I get to know Terry Hawkins, how well could I get to know Danny Fabre, with a prison employee sitting beside us as we talked, and following me as I followed the inmates through their days? Everything I wanted for my year would be lost.

"This might sound crazy," I started, "but if you want to be sure I'm not on some muckraking mission, why don't you give me a lie-detector test? Why don't you hook me up right now, and ask whatever you want to ask about my intentions?" I held my jaw tight, my teeth clamped shut, to keep from shivering.

"A lie-detector test?"

"I'm serious. Your investigations unit must have one. Put the machine right on your desk. Hook me up. Ask whatever you need so this project can go forward the way it should. Let's clear the air."

He smiled. "How much are you getting for this book?"

"How much?"

"How much is your publisher paying you?"

I had been surprised back at Christmas by his question about God; now I was caught completely off guard. We had gone from the intimacy of faith to the intimacy of money. I laughed nervously. "All right," I heard myself say. "I guess I owe you an answer."

Why? Why did I owe him anything? I felt I did, I suppose, because he had let me into his kingdom, because, in a country whose laws and courts gave him nearly unmitigated say as to who in the media his prisoners spoke with, he had given his prisoners to me.

But my playing along in what became a guessing game—"More

than twenty-five?" he asked. "More than forty?"—came, as well, from a need to retain some feeling of strength. My advance was neither large nor small, but it was about the same size as his yearly salary.

"Well, that's good, that's good," he said. "That's more than I thought."

He ruminated silently on the figure.

"Look," he continued, "here's what we'll do. We'll let you finish your visit like you want. You can have your privacy. And then next month, I'm going up to Amherst, Massachusetts. To the university up there. They want me to come speak. It's a symposium. So what we'll do, we'll meet up there. That's your country. That's Yankee country. So I'll meet you on your grounds, and we'll work out all this editorial business. We'll get it straightened out. It won't be any problem. Everybody's going to be happy. You're going to write a good book. The right book. I know that."

We would work it all out in Amherst, and then I could drive with him to the lecture hall. There he would speak on a subject that tore at his heart, the death penalty.

I spent the final day of that trip to Angola—my last day at the prison before the warden opened himself up to me—with Danny Fabre. Hair newly cut, making no attempt to conceal his unconcealable ears, he sat before a computer in his GED classroom.

On the screen, a wolf leapt off a cliff, pounced toward a house belonging to little pigs. One pig popped up onto the roof with a bow and arrow. Danny searched the multiple-choice answers in his computerized study course. If he picked the right one, the arrow would glide across the screen to annihilate the wolf. There were ten questions in each section—math, science, history, and spelling and grammar. There were ten wolves waiting on the cliff, three pigs in the house. If Danny missed three questions, the house was destroyed.

Math, at the moment, was a good subject for the wolves. Com-

mon denominators had just arisen in the curriculum. One third plus
three fourths, four fifths minus two tenths—more than one home was
consumed. Danny switched programs to one that awarded fork-
toting devils for every correct answer. If he did well, he could assem-
ble an entire satanic legion. He amassed a squad of three.

"Can you ask your teacher for help?" I suggested.

"I might," he said. And didn't.

Twenty computers were placed around the perimeter of the
room. The twenty students worked independently, on whatever sub-
jects they chose, each facing a screen and, behind that, a bit of blank
wall. The teacher, one of the handful the prison employed through
the state education department, sat at the front of the room and did
not move. Not once, in the hour I sat with Danny that morning, did
the teacher lean over a student's shoulder to guide him through a
problem; not once did he address the class from his desk, which was
mostly walled off from the inmates by a book-lined hutch. Yet Danny
spoke highly of him. Danny spoke, in fact, with gratitude and affection. Two months ago, the man had taught him to use the mouse.

I had to wonder just how much effort Warden Cain put into carrying out his mission. How much did he try to inspire his staff? So
far, I'd never actually bumped into him on the grounds, never actually seen him stop in at the Toy Shop to offer his encouragement,
never seen him stroll the Walk to remind his staff of his goals by his
mere presence. Probably it was sheer chance that our paths hadn't
crossed. But one thing was certain: He hadn't influenced this instructor. If he had, Danny might have learned to assume, at the late age
of thirty-three, that teachers were there to assist him when he
couldn't figure out an answer.

Yet Danny seemed able to thrive, or at least inch upward, on the
minimal attention given him. And on the good fortune of a spot in
that classroom. Since October he had climbed two tenths of a grade
level in reading, from a 6.9 to a 7.1, and despite today's demolition
of the little pigs' house, from a 6.2 to a 7.2 in math.

Giving up on fractions, he moved on to science. He read a passage that would lead to questions, to another try at earning an army of devils. "Look at this," he said. "Are you reading this? Did you know this? I think I'm going to use this tonight." He copied down the three paragraphs in deliberate handwriting.

School ended at ten. After count and lunch, he went to his job turning dirt on the yard. The job entailed a good deal of hoe-dragging, slapping at soil already turned, yet it involved occasional teamwork, or at least working side by side. Each man was given a "cut," a section of ground about seven feet across, to till. The men worked in a line, but not all that close. Danny did not do well at such collaborative effort. He often felt the world was crowding around him, misusing him. The other convicts got in his way, the freemen planned the projects inefficiently. Usually, by around two in the afternoon, Danny wished the man next to him would say something, start something, so he could let loose. He wished the freeman would bark at him one more time—Danny would teach him a lesson in respect, the kind of lesson he'd quit teaching lately. He wouldn't care what happened to him afterward; let them lock his ass up; he would do it; fuck Toastmasters and GED and all that; people didn't call him Popeye for nothing.

But today he chopped at the dirt without even noticing the crew he usually perceived converging around him. He thought of tonight's speech, was thrilled by his topic. Until this morning he hadn't quite known what he would speak on, a particular problem because this assignment, from his Toastmasters "Communication and Leadership Program" manual, was supposed to be written out and read aloud. There would be no hiding his lack of preparation. He'd almost been ready to find one of the Forgotten Voices executives, to own up. The admission would not be treated with sympathy. A sonorous voice was Danny's natural strength; preparation wasn't. The members had urged him, after recent speeches, to spend more time organizing his thoughts and rehearsing key points in advance. If he admitted that he had nothing written at all, they might put him on probation. They would, at the very least, lecture him on his responsibilities, on the limited space in the club, on the Forgotten Voices' goal: to prove to everyone the positive things convicts could achieve. *Well, fuck them,* Danny had been thinking over the past few days. Fucking rat check-out model prisoners. How many weak assholes were in that punk organization? All of them, it looked like.

Now he thought that if this speech went well they might elect him to the team for their next outside competition. He might represent Angola at the next Battle of the Institutions against chapters from other Louisiana prisons. And if he could make trusty before the Forgotten Voices traveled to the Holiday Inn for the next District 68 Toastmasters convention like it had last year, he might step up to the microphone and hold that free-world audience spellbound.

Back at his cot, he wrote out the paragraphs yet more carefully in his spiral notebook. I let myself speculate—because of his Toast-masters ambitions and his short haircut that granted his ears their extraordinary prominence—that his desire for cosmetic surgery might be fading. I knew he hadn't heard anything more about approval for the operation, and I asked if he still thought about it.

"Yeah. I think about it all the time. Have I ever told you about the way I got picked on when I was a kid?"

He'd tried to give me the details. I'd deflected his attempts. I'd told myself it was because the phrases of torment would be so predictable. But I think I didn't want to hear him out because I knew his pain would be absolutely basic, fundamental. I couldn't bear to find myself standing with a murderer who was also a defenseless child. Now, again, I showed no interest in the specifics of his childhood.

"Yeah, I think about it," he said. "Wouldn't you?"

I answered that his ears weren't that noticeable. But perhaps the more straightforward response would have been more comforting: Yes, I would.

I asked if he planned to ride in next October's rodeo, if he would try again to win the warden's okay on the surgery if he didn't get it this year.

"I really don't know if I will. Some of us were talking about the rodeo the other day. It just makes us look like a bunch of monkeys."

He tore out the two pages of copied words, folded them into his pocket. He headed down the Walk and climbed the stairs to the A Building meeting room.

Through narrow slats, the windows in the room offered one of the few second-floor views at Angola. They looked down on the passageways of Main Prison, the coils of razor wire in the blue-gray dusk. The walkways were clearing. Most of Angola's inmates were already locked down in their dorms.

About thirty old school chairs with attached desks were arranged in a semicircle. On a table against one wall stood an electric coffee maker along with a stack of Styrofoam cups. Beside the cups were a battered collegiate dictionary and a pink cardboard hat in the shape of a tall cone, the hat decorated with Magic Marker drawings of a cartoonish man saying, "Uh," "You know," "Um," "Ah," and "Well." The inmate who uttered more of these "clutch" words than anyone else would wear the cone at the end of the meeting. The evening's designated "ah-counter" was in charge of keeping track.

The Forgotten Voices' blue-and-gold banner was tacked to the lectern at the head of the room; the American flag hung from above a window. In a back corner a timer like a traffic light—green, yellow, and red—rested on a pole five feet high. All of the setup, from the formation of the chairs to the exact placement of the dictionary, had been approved by a member specially appointed and trained by the club to make certain the room was in order.

The club's inmate officers put great emphasis on organization. Like the Bible students who said, "They confess it but they don't possess it," this was the Toastmasters' way of distinguishing themselves from the rest of Angola's prisoners, of declaiming, *They, those others out there, are the bad ones.* Long minutes were taken at the executive sessions; motions were made and seconded; and at the general meetings the leaders beckoned each other formally, by officially worded rank, to the lectern, "And now I welcome Distinguished Toastmaster Mr...."

The leaders, and every member on down to Danny, told me repeatedly of the club's success. It had begun only five years ago, the inspiration of a state court judge—and Toastmasters International devotee—who sometimes visited Angola. There had been just enough interested convicts who could pay the Toastmasters dues: forty dollars initiation and four dollars per month. (Danny paid his with money his father sent periodically.) In the last year the Forgotten Voices had not only won the Battle of the Institutions. It had been given "Select Distinguished" status by Toastmasters International, and *The Forgotten Voice Articulator,* the group's monthly newsletter, had been named a Toastmasters International Top Ten Publication. The Forgotten Voices members had earned forty CTM ratings and six ATMs—Competent Toastmasters and Able Toastmasters—and the chapter was ranked first in District 68.

Just before tonight's meeting officially convened, Danny motioned to the club's sergeant at arms, a bony young inmate with a mustache that did little to toughen his mouth of bright, flawless teeth. They stepped out into the hall. Danny needed help with certain words: "circulatory" and "respiratory" and "dioxide."

"Circulatory," the sergeant at arms pronounced quietly, so the other members in the hall wouldn't hear.

"All right," Danny said.

"Don't you want to practice it?"

"I'll be all right."

"Say it."

"Circa— Damn! I hate that word."

"Try it again."

"Circalutary."

"Once more. Cir-cu-la-tory."

"Circulatory."

"That's it." The sergeant at arms, half a head shorter than Danny, reached up to pat his shoulder.

They hurried through "respiratory" and "dioxide," then went in just as everyone stood and faced the flag, placed their hands over their hearts, and pledged allegiance. The next words, too, everyone recited by heart: "The mission of a Toastmasters Club is to provide a mutually supportive and positive..."

The meeting began with "Table Topics." The sergeant at arms called a series of inmates to the lectern, picked a Toastmasters International subject slip from a cap, and read it aloud to the inmate, who had to deliver a two-minute speech. One man in his sixties, gray hair greased back, drew the question "What does friendship mean to you?" His quavery, heartfelt answer went like this: "Friendship is something you can't buy.... You earn friendship by being a friend.... A friend in need is a friend in need." The members applauded loudly. Captain Newsom, uniform pants exposing his shins and thin hair dragged across his scalp, clapped along.

The next man up, by contrast, gave a dazzling mock oration on the importance of thumbs: "My fellow Toastmasters, I am talking about that finger left out of every fist, that pacifist, that voice of independence and reason that stands opposed to the four-man posse...."

The formal part of the evening began. "Mr. Forgotten Voices President," the sergeant at arms said, "Mr. Master Evaluator, Captain Newsom, fellow Toastmasters. Since September Danny Fabre has proven to a lot of people that he is not who he used to be. The title of his speech tonight is 'An Introduction to Science.' But with every speech, he is introducing himself to us. He is introducing himself to himself. Danny, you've begun to show everyone who you really are. Come on up and show us some more."

Unlike the others, Danny had no laminated CTM or ATM pin

on his chest. In his dingy white V-necked T-shirt he accepted the lectern, took the two sheets of paper—with their tattered spiral notebook edges—from his jeans pocket, unfolded them, spread them, and looked long and steadily around the room. "Mr. President, Mr. Master Evaluator, Mr. Sergeant at Arms, Captain Newsom, fellow Toastmasters," he opened, "this evening I would like to give my introduction to science."

He glanced down at the sheets and smoothed them on the lectern. He checked one and the other, confused about which came first. He put up his hands, palms outward, close together, a shield. Stepping out from behind the lectern, he clenched one fist. His biceps seemed swollen with all the words waiting to spill out. His ears were a brightening pink. "I'm a little nervous, but I'm going to talk from the heart." Then he remembered that this was supposed to be a written speech. He stepped back to the lectern, searched his two pages again. "Well, I just learned this here today," he said, "and it really made an impression on me."

At last he found his starting point, and read what he'd copied from the computer. "'Introduction to Science.' Simply defined, science is the study of ourselves and everything around us." His voice occupied the room without effort. It carried a strange conviction. "Science is concerned with questions such as: How does a tree in Brazil affect people living in Chicago? How do human activities affect the world in which we live? Science is also a way of thinking." When he announced, "In the following minutes I'm going to explain to you some of the broad questions that scientists ask," the line had an ungrounded resonance, as though Danny perceived some profound emotion encoded within the textbook words.

Yet he couldn't string the sentences together. He paused between each one, wondering if anything he read made sense, and now, peering down at his handwriting, he paused still longer, finally blurting another title. "'The Most Marvelous Machine.' I don't think I copied this off right." He put up his palms again, extending his arms, shielding himself, pushing his audience away. "But this is really what I wanted to tell you about.

"Mr. President, Mr. Master Evaluator, Mr. Sergeant at Arms, Captain Newsom, fellow Toastmasters, let me interest you in a wonderful machine." He pointed his long, thick forefinger at his listeners. With that hand, he had punched and choked a fifty-one-year-old woman to death. With that hand, he had rammed a ten-inch stick into her right eye through her brain, leaving the stick protruding from the socket. "It can run on many different kinds of fuel." He gathered momentum. "It can operate in blazing heat or cold. It seldom breaks down, but when it does it often fixes itself. In fact, it is constantly making and replacing parts that wear out. It has powers that the largest computer cannot match, yet it is completely—" He came to a halt. "Port. Able. Wait a minute." He lifted his head. "Because this is important. This is what I need to tell you about." He pointed. "It is completely port-able. Well, I guess that's what it says. It pumps liquids. It filters air. It removes poison. It fights off attempts to break it down. If you haven't guessed by now, 'it' is you. The human body is the most marvelous machine ever made."

He listed the organs, the systems. "Respiratory" gave him no trouble, but "circulatory" remained a tongue-twister and carbon was paired with "dinoxide." He lost his place and found it with several uh's. "Can you guess what the largest organ in the body is? This is what blew me away. My fellow Toastmasters—" he slapped his chest loudly with his open hand, left his hand on his heart, ventured again from behind the lectern, remembered himself, returned to reading. "Well, the answer may surprise you, even though it is right under your nose. In fact, it is also behind your ears, on the palms of your hands, and between your toes. The largest organ in the body is the skin. It can weigh seven pounds and cover twenty square feet. Amazingly, this largest of organs is completely replaced about once a month. If you are looking for a new you, you don't have to wait. You grow about a thousand new skins during your life."

He studied his audience, the president with his arms folded and Captain Newsom without expression. (Newsom had encouraged him, by Danny's thankful count, twice in the five months since Danny had joined, saying, "Don't let me down" and "Just take one step forward at a time.") The sergeant at arms, who'd welcomed him so enthusiastically, didn't look so enthusiastic. They didn't seem to get it. They seemed to be waiting for something more. "Isn't that amazing?" Danny added. "That blew me away. I never knew that before. A thousand new skins. Hey, I like the way they put that." He glanced again across their faces.

"Well, thank you, Mr. President, Mr. Master Evaluator, Mr. Sergeant at Arms, Captain Newsom, Fellow Toastmasters," he said, and soon, after the rest of the formal speeches, he was awarded the cone hat by the ah-counter.

It was presented in a joking ceremony ("And now, that dreaded moment..."), and accepted with a jolt of laughter from Danny himself. He placed it lightly on his head. He was supposed to wear it for the last half hour of the meeting, while club business was discussed. He tried not to think of what he looked like. He tried to remind himself that other people had worn this same hat. He tried not to let every voice reverberate and distort and echo and bounce back off the walls in a way that bent and blurred a comment about club finances into a comment about his hat and his ears. He tried to avoid, as he put it to me later, "bugging up."

And what kept him from lashing out or simply leaving the room was the memory, from a few years ago, of waking in the middle of the night and seeing his dorm in a way he never had. The men slept, as always, with their white sheets pulled over their heads. But for the first time it had struck Danny that the dorm, with its rows of shrouded bodies, looked like a giant morgue. His change had begun slowly then, led him to GED school and Toastmasters. He forced himself to recall those corpses now. He had been one of them. He had felt he was among the dead. He set his palm on the point of the cone, pressed down to stop the tall hat from wobbling, and stayed.

S I X

I DROVE FROM MANHATTAN TO AMHERST, MASSA-
chusetts, thinking hard of Louisiana's most heroic politician, Huey
P. Long. His career as governor and senator in the 1920s and '30s
had been marked by corruption—but also by benevolence. He had
brought schools and services and enfranchisement to the poor. I
thought of Long because during early February, as I tried to reach
the warden by phone to win his promise that I could complete my
year without interference, and as he ducked my calls and finally said
he didn't want to discuss anything over the phone, I had read the
story of the can-relabeling plant. That is, I'd read it with more care
than I had previously allowed myself. In an old *Boston Globe,* and in
a series of old articles in the *Baton Rouge Advocate,* it had been waiting for me.

Around the time he took over Angola, about eighteen months
before I first traveled there, Cain had met a California businessman
who hoped to take outdated or damaged cans of evaporated milk
and tomato paste, bought indirectly from Nestlé, and sell them under
a different label. Such resalvaging was not, in itself, illegal. That the
old, rusty cans failed to meet Nestlé's own standards for taste and
safety did not necessarily mean they fell short of federal require-

mcnts. The businessman, Charles Sullivan, planned to sell them in less than prime markets—state agencies and third-world countries. All he needed was some cheap labor to spruce up the cans.

And quickly, at Angola, a team of fifty inmates was scrubbing off rust and pasting on labels: "Veronica" for the tomato paste and "Pot o' Gold" for the milk. For the prison facility, the requisite guards, and for each eight-hour shift of fifty workers—for four hundred man-hours—Sullivan paid the state a total of $220.

It could have been a lucrative arrangement, at least for Sullivan, except that an inmate paralegal soon wrote to the U.S. Department of Health and Human Services. He inquired about the legality of both the resalvaging itself and the practice of paying inmates four cents an hour for work done on behalf of a private company.

The letter wound up with Louisiana's own health officials. Unthinking, they revealed their inmate source to Angola's administration. Right away Cain transferred the convict from his trusty job as counsel substitute to a spot in the field lines, and from his quiet, trusty dorm to a rougher section of Main Prison known as "The Wild Side." It was too late, though, to save the relabeling plant. Cans were seized as unsafe and the enterprise was shut down. Sullivan pled guilty to minor charges, paid a fine of five thousand dollars, and assured the public that the cans already resold had gone mostly to Russia and Latin America.

And Warden Cain maintained, during court hearings, that he had encouraged the business only in order to create jobs for inmates too weak for regular farm labor—because "idleness is the devil's workshop." The hearings were held by Frank Polozola, who had risen from magistrate to federal judge since the 1971 civil rights suit, and who retained oversight of Angola. Cain testified that he had been unaware of any illegalities in the operation; that he had transferred the whistle-blowing prisoner only because the language of his letter had been insultingly strong, not because he wished to punish anyone for raising concerns; and that the whole incident had left him feeling betrayed by private industry and by those now doubting his ethics. "Believe me, Your Honor," he said, "you would have to fight me to bring an outside factory again. I am snake-bit."

He had brought up the episode, early on, with me. "That really caused me a lot of grief." He held my gaze. "People wanted to say it was my deal. They found out it wasn't. It's obvious. I wasn't involved in anything wrong. It was federally investigated and I'm still here. But it grieved me greatly, that hint of impropriety—that the Bible warns you to stay away from, and for good reason—because it cost me credibility with the inmates, and they're my only job. The inmates."

I'd never quite accepted his words as truth, but I had focused mostly on the transfer of that convict. The retaliation, I'd decided, was just one of Cain's excesses, his sizable ego slipping out of control. It did not outweigh the good he was doing at the prison. As for the possibility of his receiving kickbacks, there had been no hard evidence.

But after our January meeting, as I sensed issues about himself Cain desperately didn't want explored, I no longer knew how to weigh anything, and felt that I had been fingering the scales too hard in Warden Cain's favor. I concentrated on a fact I had thus far scarcely acknowledged, that the can operation wasn't the first private business Cain had introduced under his leadership.

As warden of D.C.I., he had established a chicken deboning factory. For a company owned by a man named David Miller, an associate of then governor Edwin Edwards, and co-owned by Charles Sullivan's son, the meat of chicken thighs was stripped from the bone by a group of about eighty-five inmates. By Cain's arrangement, the company paid the state the same $220 per shift as the relabeling plant later did, though this time, with the greater number of convict workers, the rate was even lower. During a legislative investigation into D.C.I.'s contract with the company, an investigation which led to nothing and which left the factory running, the legislative auditor reported that the company had saved $3.3 million in labor and other expenses during the thirteen-month period examined. It had wound up paying the state only $113,300, and once security and electrical expenses were figured in, the state had actually lost money.

It was David Miller who introduced Charles Sullivan to Warden Cain as Cain was promoted to Angola. At both prisons, the entrepreneurs could expect the help not only of the warden but, if any trouble arose, of Governor Edwards, by way of a top gubernatorial aide, Sid Moreland. During the legislature's investigation of the chicken contract, Moreland was reported to have called the committee chairman to discourage him from demanding too much information. Edwards himself had been indicted twice, though never convicted, on charges of racketeering. And Cain's career had flourished under Edwards, flourished beyond the traditional power of a warden. Cain had boasted to me that in laying the groundwork for his "moral revolution" in penology, he had arranged with Edwards to place a loyal Cain supporter as Secretary of Corrections. Cain had no one except the governor to answer to.

Wary and yet still optimistic, I reached Amherst. Even if the warden had taken kickbacks for inmate labor (and there was no proof), would that make meaningless his message about the convicts or his goals for the penitentiary? Weren't all men corrupt in one way or another? Didn't we inhabit a fallen world? Couldn't he remain a kind of hero?

And in any case, as long as I kept my access, my privacy with the inmates, and kept free of editorial intrusion, I could go on learning and writing about the lives of Terry Hawkins, Danny Fabre, Donald Cook, Buckkey Lasseigne, Johnny Brooks....

At a bed-and-breakfast, I took a room across the hall from Cain's.

The quaint wing chair he sat in, I noted with sympathy, was too small for him. His belly was squeezed, forced outward, looked like a package on his lap. Such were the cruelties of bed-and-breakfast furniture.

The short speech he entered into—never mentioning editing or overseeing my work—was also sympathetic. His parents, he said almost introspectively, had been small-town people. They had been simple people, not poor but definitely not well-off. They hadn't retired with much. He hoped he could retire more comfortably than they had. "And I have to think about that. 'Cause I'm in my fifties. I'm not such a young guy anymore like you."

He wanted, he explained, to build his wife a barn for her dressage horses. It would cost about fifty thousand dollars. Could I see my way clear to contributing?

Faintly, as he'd come to his wife's desire for a new barn, I'd sensed the request in the air. When he asked for money, I wasn't shocked. I only stared, thinking, *So it's true,* and listened in a fleeting calm, adrenaline in momentary remission, as he made it plain that my continued presence at Angola depended on my paying him. If I couldn't come through, he would give himself and his prison to another writer.

"And I've got a good thing there," he reminded me, for I must have been a second delayed in my response. "I've got another rodeo coming up next year. And I've got those inmate clubs, the Toastmasters and the CPR, and that's good, that's good. And I've got Angola's history, all that drama and all that blood, and that change.

"And I've got another execution coming up in April, and that's good, too."

Adrenaline surged. I thought fast. But this time the room didn't feel cold, this time I wasn't freezing, only scrambling in my mind for some way to navigate. If I gave him money, I would break a journalistic taboo against paying for stories. If I didn't, my year was finished. What if I paid and then wrote about it openly, as *part* of the story? Maybe, maybe if it came down to that. But in the meantime, my words and voice somehow effortlessly composed now that we were dealing on the most basic level, far, far from any talk of redemption, I deflected his demand. First I suggested gingerly that there might be "ethical concerns" raised by any arrangement between us.

He said he wasn't worried.

I didn't want to press, didn't want to change my phrasing from "ethical" to "legal," didn't want him to realize what he'd just become in my mind: a brazen extortionist. We'd gotten along so well at the beginning of the year because I'd seen him the way he'd wished to be seen. My implying that he was a criminal wasn't going to keep me inside his kingdom. I said that I couldn't possibly pay him up front, but that we might work something out in terms of future royalties. "So you'll want to get a lawyer—"

"I don't want any lawyers."

"Well, in fairness to you—"

"I don't like lawyers." He spoke as though attorneys were an affront to Southern honor.

"No one does," I said. "But to protect your own interests you're going to need one, to make sure whatever we might sign is valid and to review the sales figures, to make sure you're getting your fair share."

He thought this over. The fear of losing out on proceeds seemed to overwhelm his desire for secrecy. "Well, that's true. I really will need one. Now, what we'll do, we'll just call our deal a consultancy, and that way it won't be any problem. I can get it past the state ethics board."

"All right." I tried to invest my voice with a slight hint of warning, just enough that he might reconsider, but not enough that he might think I harbored any ill-feelings.

"I sure hope we can make some money off this thing," he said, as though we were now, fully, joined.

■

In a lecture hall at the University of Massachusetts that evening, he spoke with gravity, even agony, about the executions his job forced him to carry out. He told his audience of students and professors about the second of the two men he'd put to death: how that convict had changed, was no longer the person he'd been seventeen years earlier, when he was convicted and sentenced for murdering two men in robberies that netted seventy-seven dollars.

"And when the time finally came, and it looked like there wasn't going to be any more appeals, Antonio was scared," Cain remembered, in a tone that seemed private and confidential to everyone in the hall, to the girls with their neo-'60s hair parted down the middle and to the professors standing with their table of leaflets calling for an end to capital punishment and the beginning of prison reform. He even seemed to confide in the empty chairs, vacant because the night was frigid and full of snow, and because even here at a liberal college, in a liberal college town, no one cared all that much anymore.

"He was scared because he didn't know if when he died Jesus would be there right away, and he asked me would he have to wait. And I told him, I said, 'I've read in a book where a band of angels will take you right away.' So we made a deal: that when the IV was ready and the lethal injection was about to go in, I would tell him, 'The Lord is waiting for you,' and that way Antonio would know Jesus was there.

"And that's exactly what I did. I can't tell you anything else for sure. I can't tell you what I do, when I carry out the law, is right. And I can't tell you it's wrong. I just held Antonio's hand. Now some people say to me, What about the victims? How could I hold this man's hand when that same hand took two lives? Where was I for them? Well, I wish I'd been there when they were dying. I would have got down on my knees on the pavement and held their hands, too. But I only had Antonio. He was the one. He was the one who needed someone to hold him."

"But what if Jesus was sitting next to you right here?" a girl asked from the audience. "What would Jesus say about *your* killing?"

There was a pause. Cain was unruffled, but when he answered he sounded yet more pained. "That's just it," he said. "I don't know. We make earthly laws. They're not God's laws. We are imperfect. Our society is imperfect. Our knowledge is limited. But we do as best we can, and I am a public servant. I have to serve both God and man, that's the problem with being a warden. But when it comes to executions, if someone has to do it, I'm glad it's me in a way, because at least I do it with compassion. That might sound horrible to you all, but that's how I think."

As the program ended, the audience wouldn't let him leave. He stood near the doors, carrying no overcoat, wearing just a tweed sport jacket, the warmest winter clothing he had for this trip to the North, and he was surrounded. They wanted to know everything he knew, wanted his wisdom, not only on capital punishment but on all his prisoners. He told them how the inmates had grown up without fathers, without anyone positive paying attention to them, rewarding them for the good things instead of the bad, and how he paid attention, walked the penitentiary, listened to the men. "It's just common sense," he said. One of the professors, handing out his newsletter condemning the Massachusetts state prisons, whispered to me, "We could use a few people like him." And finally Cain invited two of the students back to the bed-and-breakfast so he could give them Angola gate keys. An ACLU lawyer who'd spoken as part of the symposium, and who was taken like everyone else by Cain's open heart, tagged along with us.

"Come down and visit," the warden urged the students, presenting each with a heavy five-inch-long brass key. "It's a real interesting place. We'll show you around. We'll treat you right." He turned to me. "Won't we?"

"He will," I confirmed, smiling.

It was almost midnight by the time the kids left. The ACLU lawyer wanted to take Cain out for coffee. I made a move to return to my own room.

"We're going to try to work all this stuff out," I promised Cain as the lawyer started down the stairs ahead of him. I waited until the man was *almost* to the vestibule. I wanted the warden aware of his presence. "But can I schedule my trip for Easter in the meantime? I'd really like to be at Angola for that week."

"Let's get this deal worked out first," he said.

I had nowhere to maneuver. I all but begged, saying that airline tickets would be too expensive if I had to put off reserving till the last minute. And that my story of regeneration at Angola would be left with a terrible gap if I couldn't include Easter at the prison.

I kept at it.

Cain relented.

Home, I pursued the background research I should have done months before. While in charge of D.C.I., Cain had become involved with a recycling company just as local parish officials were facing new state recycling requirements. Lobbying the parish to hire the company, he argued publicly for its plan to use convict labor. He meanwhile signed a contract with the company, guaranteeing him a commission on its business. And soon he had invested his own money in the enterprise. Later, the recycling prospects having fallen through, Cain was questioned by the *Advocate* about his ties to the operation. "My relationship had nothing to do with my state employment," he replied. "I avoid any conflict of interest at all costs. I know better."

His moments under judicial, legislative, or local journalistic scrutiny never seemed to deter him. He had no reason to be deterred. The problems came to nothing; the bad publicity just melted away. Though the governor who succeeded Edwards had few ties to his predecessor and was a conservative Republican while Edwards was a populist Democrat, he kept Cain on at Angola. It seemed that as long as there was no rash of escapes, and no return to the embarrassing violence of the early '70s, the new governor felt it best to leave things alone. The public wasn't clamoring for a change. Men who committed crimes were sent away; it was easiest not to think, in any way, about where they went or who was in charge. They went to another world. The god there was largely on his own.

After the relabeling plant closed, Warden Cain had encouraged the use of a soy-based meat substitute to be served at Angola and throughout Louisiana prisons. The Department of Corrections, effectively under his authority, bought 20 tons of the mix and planned to buy 480 more—close to $4 million worth—all from a company called VitaPro. Then the deal hit two snags.

Another company bid to supply the same product at a much lower price. And a scandal broke in neighboring Texas: The head of its prison system had, over the past five years, purchased $33 million of VitaPro's soy without taking bids, then had retired and accepted a job with the company paying $1,000 a day. Suddenly, unable to buy from VitaPro, Louisiana's Department of Corrections lost interest in any meat substitute at all. "VitaPro wasn't my deal," Warden Cain told the *Advocate*—exactly what he had told me about the relabeling. As I read the stories, it was hard for me not to wonder what kind of sinecure he had worked out with VitaPro for his retirement.

How could I have deceived myself for so long, diminished so thoroughly what now seemed Cain's primary interest in running prisons? My only, marginal comfort was that other journalists, too, were eager for delusion. One local reporter I spoke with assured me that Cain's brief scandals had arisen from naivete rather than greed. He endorsed Cain's explanation that the need for inmate jobs had led to the relabeling and deboning. Cain just hadn't foreseen how the arrangements would appear. There had been nothing sinister behind the contracts. "If that's not true," the reporter kept telling me, "then I don't know Burl Cain."

And the producers of those glowing Warden Cain portraits shown on ABC, PBS, and the Discovery Channel (with a new one in the works for A&E), whose underlings must have run press searches before film crews were sent down, seemed to have made hopeful calculations, like my own, that the warden's ideas on punishment and rehabilitation were far more important than any small transgressions. It was easy to think that they were, especially when you might want to film another program requiring access to a maximum-security prison, and when you knew that so few welcomed journalists past their gates, and when you knew that you had no legal right to be inside, no First Amendment standing at all, and when you knew that a flattered Warden Cain would allow you to return.

But perhaps there was still another reason. The journalist himself, at least in my case, felt flattered by the warden. It felt good to be trusted—and liked—by a person in such absolute control of his world.

S E V E N

THE LOWER MISSISSIPPI HAD BEEN SURGING. WITH Easter six days away, the river at Angola's bend climbed past record height and was starting to flood the prison. I traveled again into the warden's domain.

I carried the notion that one of the inmates I knew might, on Holy Thursday, kneel down in church to wash another convict's feet. The rite of forgiveness was limitless in need. It was an effort to love perfectly, if only for a minute, as the self dissolved in servitude. It was an obliteration of the origin of all sin and wrongdoing. And for the one whose feet were being washed, it was a touch of this unmitigated love which, for the vast majority of humanity that feels undeserving, was hard to welcome, even painful to absorb. I went down that week to see men healed, for an instant. I found the penitentiary about to be washed away.

"We need to talk tonight," Cain said quietly in passing, on Monday, before he went off to battle the river. It was above the level of 1922, when it had swept over the levee in a bank of white water that looked, in pictures, like a mini-Niagara. Back then, the inmates had been packed on barges while their camps were submerged. By the time the river crested, parts of Angola were under sixteen feet of water, and all you could see of the buildings were the peaks of their roofs. The main levee was four feet higher now, built up over the years by inmates and the Corps of Engineers. But by Monday a secondary, peripheral levee had already been flooded; the Mississippi had claimed something closer to its natural shape; and a paddle boat full of roulette-playing tourists had lost its way amid the wider channel and cruised onto prison grounds, gamblers waving at the guard towers. One fifth of Angola was already underwater. The river wouldn't crest until Friday.

But the big problem wasn't height, it was pressure. While the Mississippi sat just a foot or two below the main levee at Camp C, while alligators lolled near Camp F and hundreds of white pelicans converged on the fish that had been sucked over when the outer levee became a waterfall, it seemed that an unusual northern snowmelt had added as much to the river as it could, and that the local rains had stopped, that the Mississippi couldn't rise much more. So it tried to break through. The main levee couldn't hold the force of all the extra water. The banks were saturated and starting to let the river tunnel in. Brown water boiled up from the ground on the prison side. Tiny lakes formed around the percolations. There were fifty, sixty, seventy of them, the count growing every hour. Teams of inmates stacked sandbags around the pools, trying to create enough counter-pressure to stop the inflow. Then the river drove at another spot. If the levee caved, the prison would be under twelve to twenty feet within twelve hours.

If there was time, the convicts would be trucked to tent cities, one on Angola's only high ground, beside the administration building, the other in the forest six miles outside the gates. The inmates were almost finished building them. Vets Incarcerated, one of the convict clubs, directed the staking of tents, while hundreds of prisoners raised new cyclone fences around themselves and then, with long poles, hoisted coils of barbed wire to the fence tops. It was a delicate business, the placing of that barbed wire. If one man wavered with his pole, the length of coil would come down like a net of razors. But the inmates were careful. And they built the makeshift prisons to specifications. Above them, guards poked their rifles from temporary towers made neatly with planks and two-by-fours, all cut and nailed together by the lifers.

No one tried to escape. Convicts were driving tractors and trucks out the gates of Angola, down the state highway and onto the dirt road that led to the forest site, and they were driving them back out of the woods, but no one turned left at the highway instead of right, no one tried to make it to some bus depot or to a house where he could steal a car; they went to pick up their next load of lumber or barbed wire. Nor did anyone bolt past the sleep-deprived guards into the trees. When I asked if he ever thought about fleeing, one man laughed hysterically, rolling backward on the plywood floor he was building under a tent. He had to catch his breath before he could answer. He had to wipe away the raucous tears. "Man, I thought about running every day I been incarcerated. And when we out here, and that fence ain't finished…But where am I gonna get to? Just 'cause we outside the gates don't mean we outside Angola." He elaborated the theory, so often mentioned, that the prison property extended far beyond its supposed lines, in this case all the way to the nearest town, St. Francisville.

Most of the inmates hoped only that they wouldn't have to move from their dorms to these tents, that they wouldn't be forced to live for months here, that they wouldn't lose the photo albums in their locker boxes, and, if the levee did give way, that they would be let out of their dorms before they drowned. Every morning, when they were taken to their work sites, they saw the exodus from the guards' village, the two-hour traffic jam at the front gate. The guards with mobile homes were driving them out. The rest had their TVs and kitchen tables and box springs stacked in their pickups.

On Monday evening Cain called a meeting of convict leaders—
the club presidents and inmate counselors and editors of the *Angolite*.
Angola's wardens had always sent word outward through this group,
and Cain loved the tradition. "I want the inmate leaders in A Building," he said into his prison radio, and all over Angola assistant wardens passed this down to captains and lieutenants and finally to the
low-level guards who barked into meeting rooms and kicked at bed-
posts and told the men Warden Cain wanted to see them right away.
Once the inmates had funneled into the Main Prison visiting shed,
once they'd settled themselves in the plastic chairs and waited a
while, slouched indifferently but dutifully silent, Cain walked in,
with his assistant wardens trailing behind him.

"The other night," he started, his voice big and relaxed and needing no microphone for this crowd of seventy-five, "I was out with our
man from the Corps of Engineers. We were standing on top of the
levee and looking out over those sand boils. That's where the Mississippi is seeping through, and we've got ninety of 'em now. And we
were hoping no alligators were going to climb up and bite us, and we
were putting sticks in the ground to check how damp that levee was
getting, and he said to me, 'Warden Cain, I feel the Mississippi River
right under my feet, and there's only two people I know can walk on
water. That's Jesus Christ and you.'"

He smiled and waited for the laughter. It came.

"So we're prepared to move out if we have to, but meanwhile
we're working to save this prison. Everyone is working together.
Inmates and freemen, side to side, man to man, even friend to friend.
We had a little scare last night, where one boil looked like it wanted
to make us run, and we had inmates working underwater, all night,
to stop that leak. And that leak is stopped. We've got Warden Bon-
nette out there driving a front loader, and we've got Wilbert taking
those *Angolite* pictures, documenting all this for history. Wilbert's
scared of heights and he begged me not to make him go up in that

helicopter to photograph, his knees were shaking and his teeth were chattering and he was just begging me—isn't that right, Wilbert?" And Wilbert Rideau, who had been in Angola thirty-four years, and whose articles in the *Angolite* had won some of the nation's most prestigious honors in journalism—the George Polk Award and a National Magazine Award nomination—nodded and grinned. Or rather, grimaced, his face stiffening. "But Wilbert went up there. And we're going to blow up an aerial shot of the tent cities, put 'em up in all the visiting sheds, so y'all can show your families what you built. We're going to do that."

As soon as he stopped, the convicts wanted to know how quickly they would be let out of the dorms. "How do we know we're not getting trapped inside there?"

"Isn't there a guard in there with you?" Cain answered.

"He doesn't have the key."

"Well, we're not going to lock him in there to drown. Think about it. If you're hearing we're going to leave you in there, that's just rumormonger, rumormonger, rumormonger."

"What about the ones can't swim?"

"Can't you swim?" Cain joked with his questioner.

"*I* can."

"We're not going to be swimming. We're not going to let it get that far. Everyone's going to be safe. That's what I'm thinking about first. I've got a commitment to you all."

The men asked what they could bring if there was an evacuation.

"Take your blankets. Take all the clothes you can put on your body. Wear two pairs of jeans if you can. And bring your Bibles. That's everything."

He asked for more questions. He was in no hurry to leave. He enjoyed standing before them, responding to the same worries again and again. He recounted the reinforcement of their prison, praised the shoulder-to-shoulder effort, promised he would protect them. He confided, "Two nights ago I went out on a boat, and I yelled to that water, 'Kiss my ass, River' three times. And last night we had that scare, that boil. So I won't yell at the river anymore."

He announced that when the crisis was over there would be a day of unlimited Coca-Cola served at all the camps, and that every inmate would be given a Moon Pie. With that he left for the prison radio station.

The inmate deejay, in his cubby of albums, stood from the turntable when Cain walked in, and faded out Otis Redding when Cain was ready. The warden delivered the same message he had to the inmate leaders. "Well, sir," the deejay broadcast, summing things up, "you've been with us all along. And we just want to thank you for stopping the rumormongers, and for all you're doing to stay on top of the situation. I think you're our greatest asset, Warden Cain."

Otis Redding faded back in.

"You deejays been asking to expand, play your music all night instead of like you do now?" Cain asked.

"We would like that, sir."

"Well, that's good. We'll make that happen."

At the end of that evening, Warden Cain led me into the Ranch House bedroom. Motioning me to a chair, he sat on the unmade bed where he'd been catching what sleep he could during the crisis. We discussed money once more. At first he backed away from his earlier demand. "It might not be ethical." Then he claimed he'd found a publisher for his own book about his leadership of Angola. I asked which publisher. He wouldn't say. I asked again. He admitted he'd spoken with no publishers at all, approached none. He asked what percentage of my royalties I would be willing to pay if we did arrive at some arrangement. He asked and asked and asked.

"Warden Cain," I kept saying, "it's been a long, long day." I extricated myself without answering, and managed to avoid any time alone with him for the rest of my visit.

Gunshots echoed across the fields at night, the only ones I'd heard at Angola since September. The guards hunted beavers and any other animals that might gnaw at the precarious levee. They rode the embankment in pickup trucks, searching with floodlights and taking aim. They had a grand time, razzing one another when they missed into the water.

Under a full moon Cain delivered sandbags in an army personnel carrier. He'd bought two such carriers for the penitentiary when he took over; he liked to drive them along the dirt roads in the Tunica Hills. Now, happier than the riflemen on the levee, beaming behind the wheel of the immense, tread-borne, open-bed tank, he bounded across the prison, a general at war. He stopped at the levee's edge. Tank idling loud, he yelled down at a crew of inmate sandbaggers, yelled down to the base of the hill, "Where you want your drop?"

Whose voice was that? Was that Warden Cain up there in the cab window? Yes, lit by the moon, that was him! That was his white hair! That was his wide face looming out! And he was talking to *them,* not to their guard; he was asking *them!*

He was asking Buckkey.

Errant strands of blond hair lit by the tank, and his rubber boots covered in muck, Buckkey climbed the levee's hill. He stood at the rear corner of the tank, raised his gloved hand. He signaled tentatively. "Pull back a little, Warden Cain."

"What's that?"

"I said, pull back a little," he risked shouting at the warden.

The face floated out again from the window. "You just tell me where you need me to go."

"Come on back a little more," Buckkey motioned with his hand, then held it flat. "Wo. Okay. A little more. Wo."

The inmates started to unload, passing the white sacks down the levee to the boil. At the bottom they were thigh-deep in water, setting the bags at angles atop one another, building the walls. From the dark pool a neatly squared white fortress rose to the surface. Cain gazed down, and soon put his tank into gear and went for more supplies. An hour later they heard and then watched him return out of the darkness, the carrier approaching across the sodden, glistening fields. Buckkey directed him again, waving easily. "Right there, right there is good."

It was every boy's dream, being indispensable to his father, guiding him into the parking space. Except that this was eight times better and eight times worse; here they were saving the kingdom, here they were saving the prison. The cab door opened. Cain stepped down. He walked around to the back, where Buckkey was the point man, swinging bags from the tank. "You guys really do good work," he said, before his radio called him: "Angola One. Angola One." And afterward, at midnight, riding in a pickup back to their dorm, Buckkey looked at the inmate who'd stood right below him on the bank, the man he'd handed the bags to, the man Cain had been talking to along with Buckkey.

"Yeah, I know," the other said, catching Buckkey's glance.

But Buckkey wanted it spoken. "It was like we were needed. It was like we weren't prisoners."

The evacuation began two hours later.

The Corps of Engineers had spotted something more than seepage—a part of the levee seemed to be softening toward collapse. The lights were turned up in the dorms, the guards announcing, "All you need in your hands is a blanket and a Bible." Loaded onto cotton trailers and cattle trucks, the inmates began the seven-hour journey to the tent cities. There was lots and lots of waiting. Armed convoys had to be formed, because no weapon—and for that matter no guard—could be put amidst the throng on the truck beds. And the inmates had to be counted as they were loaded, and counted when the trucks were ready to leave, and counted as they were unloaded and marched, all of them, to the tents outside the administration building, and counted before half of them were sent down the highway to the tents in the forest. "Spruce One …Ash Four…Hickory Two…," the guards called out the names of the dorms, followed by the name of each convict. The front gate was plugged tight, a mobile home steered poorly and wedged across one lane and all the pickups full of kids' bicycles and old chests of drawers lined up in front of the other. The morning sun was bright. The fields were serene with yellow blooms and white clover. Jammed within the fenced siding of the cotton trailers or the slats of the cattle trucks, the inmates felt a numb lethargy beyond the palpable depletion of will that seemed to affect every one of them, always, even the most tightly wound or determined. They wondered if the evacuation was really necessary, and at the same time wondered if the few things they owned, everything they'd been forced to leave behind, would be ruined. They hardly spoke during the seven hours. The place they inhabited seemed larger than it ever had, the land already being limitless and the Warden supreme and now the Mississippi coming alive to tell them, once and for all, that they had no control.

Cain marshaled them to the tents and, almost immediately, back along the same seven-hour route to their dorms. The danger had been declared a false alarm. But the evacuation had been, he would soon announce, the largest mass movement of prisoners in U.S. history. The river hadn't whispered any message of submission into his ears. His will was historic in scale.

The following afternoon he convened another audience of inmate leaders. He radioed an officer to bring me to the meeting, and I was pulled abruptly away from an inmate interview and rushed through Main Prison. After his speech of reassurance to the convicts, Cain led me outside to the Main Prison parking lot.

"I want you to sign that editorial agreement," he said beside a row of white D.O.C. vans. "I want you to sign that piece of paper or sign out."

I had, in fact, seen no actual piece of paper, no actual agreement, and he had none now—it seemed he'd realized suddenly, that day, that I might write about his retirement and barn-building plan, about our Amherst meeting, and the agreement had become a matter of full panic. "It's going to be real simple. You'll have it in the morning. So you just be ready to go ahead and do the best thing."

I told him I couldn't.

"Warden Peabody," he called.

His pallid and dour first deputy stepped over.

"Is this fence galvanized?" Cain asked rhetorically, turning from me to run his thumb over the nearest chain link.

"Yes, it is," Peabody answered.

"Does this fence looked galvanized to you?" he asked me, brushing at the metal.

I concurred that it did.

"Well, sure as this fence is galvanized you're going to be on the other side of it if you don't sign that piece of paper." He spoke metaphorically, as we were nowhere near the front gate.

It amazed me that he was willing to threaten so hard in public, that he didn't worry I would turn to his deputy, or to his press secretary, who stood close, or to the few other employees passing by in the parking lot, and describe his demand for money. But, apparently, he didn't worry, not within his universe.

I made no accusations. My only hope was to win back his favor.

I told him I would think things through overnight. He told me to think hard.

"I love you like a brother," he said, "but this is just business."

The next morning, Thursday, one of Cain's men walked me silently to my car, then watched to make sure I drove out the front gate. And as I headed away from Angola, knowing that I could never sign what the warden needed, I tried not to see too much significance in my own loss. When he had first requested money, I had been at least as panicked about my project as I should have been outraged by his use of the prison and its inmates in attempted extortion. (And I hadn't thought about the human spirit or the possibility of God. I had thought about my book.) Driving past the bloated swamps, I was no defeated champion of inmate concerns.

Yet I felt that the convicts I knew were now underwater behind me. Littell Harris was out. Littell I would spend time with. But the others would remain forever where they had already been for a decade or much longer, submerged. Voiceless, unknown, they existed far below the surface, on a deep river bed.

EIGHT

LITTELL UNWRAPPED HIS DREADLOCKS. THIRTY-eight years old, free from Angola after serving fifteen years, he lived, that Easter, at a halfway house in Baton Rouge. There, in a narrow vestibule, he brought out his cut hair to show me how he had saved it. He was clean-shaven now, the slight cleft in his chin exposed, his jawline hard, the corners of his lips almost undetectably yet constantly retracted in a suggestion of universal disgust. His short Afro revealed small patches of gray.

While I thought wildly of how I could soothe or trick or fight the warden, Littell was all I had. I'd wanted to know something about human possibility. It was this.

The dreadlocks, two feet long, he protected within a sheet of newspaper surrounded by a tissue-thin piece of plastic that seemed to have been torn from a dry cleaner's bag. It had about that resiliency, and was dingy and streaked, as though he had taken it off the street. The wrapping was closed by a single bit of masking tape, which Littell removed slowly with his long fingers so as not to damage too much of the plastic. Stooping, he set the bundle at our feet. He crouched and parted the wrapping. He turned to glance up at me. Then he gazed back down.

"There it is," he said. "There's my hair."

Other residents squeezed past us. They had not come from Angola. They were, most of them, not ex-convicts; they had arrived at O'Brien House, in this run-down neighborhood adjacent to downtown Baton Rouge, to shed their drug and alcohol addictions. Littell had found his way here from a state-run treatment center he'd asked to be sent to back in January, when he was two months short of completing his sentence.

He hadn't considered himself an addict in prison. He had only smoked marijuana when he could afford it and drunk Angola's white lightning (mashed rice or fruit fermented in his locker box, with a bottle of bleach beside it to kill the smell) once in a while. But he worried about his enemies taking revenge during his final weeks, when he would hesitate to defend himself. The treatment center was a way out. There, he told his counselor about his life before prison, years dominated by drugs, mostly angel dust and an injected synthetic called "T's 'n' Blues" that had been popular in Lake Charles before he was put away. His counselor, afraid he would fall back as soon as he was free, helped to place him at O'Brien. Littell was eager to go. He didn't know if he was still an addict, but he knew that his mother wouldn't want him living with her. He never called her as his release date approached. He knew that once he completed his sentence he would have no home.

As he spread the dreadlocks, laying the ropes of hair side by side, he didn't seem aware of the men and women edging by. Perhaps his lack of embarrassment came from all those years in a place where nothing was private. Perhaps it came from knowing that these people, too, had so little, had begun without much and lost nearly everything, and that they would see nothing strange or shameful in his adoring some long-nurtured hair preserved within a sooty plastic cocoon. But also it was because the loss from cutting that hair went so deep.

"This is the first time I've actually taken it out."

There were seven or eight ropes, each with a sort of bulb where the hair had bunched near his head, then a long, thick tail that looked like strips of old rug-backing or a worn and matted alpaca blanket. The bulbs were tinged with gray.

He arranged them evenly in straight lines, on the newspaper. He ran his hand along the ropes to smooth them.

"There's me in that hair."

He shifted, from crouching to kneeling. He lifted one of the ropes, brought it to his face, smelled it, kissed it. He set it back down.

"Man, that hurt me, it hurt me," he almost whispered, thinking back to the cutting, as he began rolling the package again to store it. "My counselor at the treatment center convinced me. She saw I was determined to get myself established. She was a white lady, and she told me, people judge you by first impressions. She told me, 'You can't change the way people are going to judge that hair, but you can change your appearance.' She told me I looked bizarre. And I hated to hear that. I hated *her* when she said that. But this woman was genuinely interested in helping me. I clung to her, man. So I did it. And I don't regret it. I can't wait to see me in a business suit. But after this dude clipped it off, when I went to my group session the next morning, I was like a dog when you shave him. You know how he'll sit with his tail tucked between his legs? Right now, I'm living my life in the nude."

Littell had left Angola sometime after midnight on January 21. The guard kicked at his bed and told him to pack his stuff. That was the way they always did it, late and without notice. Whenever an inmate was transferred to another facility—and the state treatment center counted as another lockup—the prison gave him no chance to call, or have anyone else call, his family or friends. That way the bus couldn't be ambushed and the prisoner freed.

There were no other transfers that night. The old school bus, requisitioned by the prison and painted blue and outfitted with steel mesh over the windows, was empty. Littell asked to sit close to the front so he could see out the windshield. The guard had no objections. Littell was cuffed and shackled.

"I guess you've earned your choice of seating."

"You can believe," Littell said, "I'm never going to see this road again."

No one spoke for the rest of the trip. On that night of gauzy rain, Littell watched the forest going by, the headlights of the few cars coming toward the prison, and, after twenty miles, when the bus turned onto another two-lane highway, a man getting out of his car at a gas station. Littell turned his head to keep that man in sight through the steel mesh. That vision—a man stepping toward the pumps in the glare of the station's lighting—injected Littell with the knowledge that Angola was behind him, as though the awareness were now surging through his body rather than merely lying in his mind. Here was life.

"I felt like I was coming out of a cave after being lost underground for a long time. I felt like weights had just been lifted off me. I felt like I could have jumped up and just flown right out the roof of that bus.

"Because let me try to explain the way you feel in Angola. Can you remember the most upset, the most depressed you've ever been in your life? When a loved one died? Has your mother died? Or someone that close? Can you put yourself back into what that felt like? Well, that's the way you feel at Angola. That's the way you feel every day."

Over the years he had dreamt in his sleep, sometimes, of freedom. The dreams took repeated form: He sat under a tree, by a river, with friends he'd known, and suddenly he was alone beside a woman. The sensations were easy, fine, heated. But always, just before the actual sex, another consciousness crept in, telling him this couldn't be real. He woke to his cell, or to the rows and rows of cots in the dorm.

That other consciousness crept in now, about the man at the gas station, about a traffic light, about the billboards and the stores on the roadside—*This might be real but not for you; you will never touch it, never be out in it*—and kept insinuating itself even after he had finished his final two months and was officially discharged from the state treatment center and the Department of Corrections, and was living on the second floor of O'Brien House.

At O'Brien, a fragile gray building that stood across a vacant lot from a Greyhound depot, he slept in a cramped four-man dorm room bearing little resemblance, in his mind, to the dorms at Angola. The floor had carpet, his bunk a thick mattress. His locker box—the same size and shape as those at the prison—where he kept his clothes and his hair, was made of painted wood. He actually slept only a few hours each night. He didn't dream at all. Until two or three every morning he lay awake on his left side, so he could stare out the window at Florida Boulevard. The headlights went by between the trees that framed his view. Car after car after car after car, it took hours for him to grow tired of those passing lights; they might have been meteors.

Awake before dawn, he dressed in jcans and a new turtleneck. He'd bought the shirt with money from the bit of yard work he'd found through O'Brien's director. He sat on the front stoop to stare at the dusty peonies in the flower beds or the Mardi Gras mask wired to a pipe or, with the fixation of an entomologist, at bugs in the grass. Sometimes he walked to the corner and back. In O'Brien's voluntary program, from which he could legally walk away at any moment, he was permitted to venture past the corner only with a resident "buddy," unless he was looking for work and had the director's permission. The rule was stifling, but hardly a challenge after Angola, and he was half-grateful for the restriction. Listening to the other residents recount their crack binges at O'Brien's group meetings, and glimpsing the drug trade in one of the buildings across the street, he recognized himself from fifteen years ago, knew that his unraveling drug life had been part of what had led him to stick a gun in that cashier's face (though the immediate reason had been rage when she seemed to ignore his request for cigarettes), and he couldn't be certain that old self was relegated to the past.

"My name is Littell and I am a drug addict," he said when everyone else had awoken and O'Brien's day had begun and its first meeting gathered in a sunken room two steps down off the first floor hallway, a room with two cheap prints of birdlife on the walls and some old board games on a shelf and a Formica coffee table in the middle and not enough tattered couch space for all the residents, so that the coffee table was a crowded bench. Littell's voice was hoarse with tension and low on volume. He sat near the door to the backyard.

"I was out on the stoop thinking, like I do all the time, and I know I don't say a whole lot in these meetings, but I want to tell you all thank you for your support. I've been incarcerated for so long, and I've done a lot of things up there I don't even like to think about, but I know I can establish myself. If I just stay away from drugs. And I know I can. 'Cause when I was coming up I got into that angel dust, that was the thing back then, and my daddy got so frightened of me, so frightened of his own son, he run me off with a pistol. I just hope you all can understand. I been in Angola. There's no love up there. There's no support like this here, like Miss Katherine tries to give us. So sometimes I just don't know how to speak. I don't even know how to smile. People ask me, 'Why do you always look like that? Why is your mouth always looking like that?' And I try to undo it. I try to pull at my lips to make them look some other way."

Even now, giving a demonstration, prying at his lips with his fingers and, in the process, pushing at his cheeks in what should have been a comic moment, he did not smile. The other residents did not laugh. He seemed to make them uneasy. He did not belong among them. Their vulnerabilites floated around them like an atmoshpere they exhaled, while he seemed inviolable. Through the entire meeting, hunched on the two steps leading down into the room, a woman in white stretch pants kept flicking her cigarette lighter and running the flame along the hairs of her forearm, up and down, up and down, as though to distract herself with imminent singeing from the drugs she would rather be taking or the alcohol she would rather be drinking or the thoughts about herself she wished would burn away. A man whose round head seemed to sit directly on his round torso had spoken for ten desperate minutes about his television needs for the coming weekend; no one so much as sighed with impatience. There were sizable men in that room who might have shrunk away and drowned themselves at a critical word. But Littell's expression looked unchangeable. The cigarette-lighter woman could have held the flame against his mouth, and his lips would have kept their harsh composure.

"But I'm learning," he said. "I'm trying to learn how to bend my lips the right way, do that smiling thing. Just give me a little time. I'm just a little throwed off. But I'm learning."

"All right, Littell!" the director, Miss Katherine, bony, exuberant, one of the few whites in the room, burst out. She was a recovered alcoholic herself.

Her piercing optimism had no effect on his face. Nor did the residents' applause.

"Thank you, Littell," she spoke more calmly. "Those issues that you talked of, that feeling that you just can't allow any positive emotion, might be masking all kinds of things, all kinds of hurt. And feelings of abandonment, because of where you've been…"

Still his features showed no reaction.

"And this community *can* help you." She leaned forward in her chair. "We're here for support. If we're trying to understand ourselves on our own, we're going to go nowhere fast. My best thinking when I was on my own was getting me into trouble. Into that downward spiral. We need each other. You just give *us* a little time."

Her voice, even in her calmer moments, had the insistent energy of someone still fighting off her own collapse, though earlier in the meeting she had mentioned her fifteenth anniversary without a drink. However precarious her own life, she sounded undaunted by the lives of her clients, by the isolation of Littell. Her graying hair a helmet of feathers around gaunt, animated features, she threw herself at them.

"You all ready to link arms?" she asked, and answered herself, "Yes, you are, because I am the Boss Applesauce!" She let out a trill of nervous laughter.

Everybody stood in a tight circle, elbows intertwined, and prayed in unison:

…Thy kingdom come
Thy will be done…

And then, still joined, chanting like rappers, the residents gave their own incantation:

Keep coming back
'Cause it works if you work it
If you don't you die
So live it, everyday

One day at a time
Whoops, there it is!

"Man, I need this place."

From the stoop, Littell and I watched a few neighbors sipping beer, at dusk, at a foldout table they'd brought to the empty lot of gravel and patchy grass across the street. "If I wasn't here, I'd be under a fucking bridge. And you know something? I know I *could* go home. I finally called my mother the other day, and she asked me why I didn't call when I first got out. I wasn't expecting that. I haven't seen her in ten years. I figured I wasn't welcome." His voice faded away for a while, as if he wasn't satisfied with what he'd just said, but hesitated to say what he meant.

"Sometimes I feel guilty 'cause I think I should feel that love that's hard for me to feel. Even with my mother, even before prison, I didn't have that emotion for my family. It's nothing my parents did. They didn't beat me, they didn't abuse me. They tried to teach me all the right things. I just didn't develop that strong bond. It's like something missing in me. I've never had a real solid relationship with any woman. Just wayward types, ho's. That's who I always went for. Never that feeling. Never like we were on the same page. If I think about the fucking situation I'm in now, some way it's all tied together."

A gleaming red sports car drove onto the vacant lot. Its driver left the engine running and the door open and hip-hop music on low, and joined the beer drinkers.

"I want that type of relationship with a woman so bad, I know I could be bamboozled. I want to lean back—I mean, all the initial phases have to be over with, all that—and sit behind her on the couch, just talking. She's leaning back against me, right against my chest, with my arms around her like this." He demonstrated with arms held outward, encircling air, and added, "Whenever problems came up, I'd have the perspective and knowledge to deal with them. I'd stay calm and handle things."

One of the drinkers jumped onto the table and did an old break-dance move, spinning on his shoulders, somehow frictionless, whirling, whirling. He retook his seat as if he'd done nothing.

"But I got to establish myself first. I got to get out on my own. Some kind of apartment and a vehicle. You see, I don't know if I can get started getting those things here at O'Brien, 'cause you're not allowed to miss but so many meetings. I'm thirty-eight years old. I ain't no fucking teenybopper anymore. But you know what's worse? You're not allowed no fucking sex. They tell you none for six months. They suggest not for a year. When I heard that? At my first community meeting? When Miss Katherine said that about the Boss Applesauce and does someone want to tell the new residents the rules? She says it's because relationships is part of what got us in trouble in the first place, and we don't know how to choose the right ones yet, but she's not used to dealing with nobody who's spent fifteen fucking years in prison, fifteen years without even *looking* at a pussy. I wish I was in Lake Charles. I know some ladies there, I could take care of my business, take this pressure off. Baton Rouge is too clean. Where's the tenderloin, where's the stroll? The other day I went out, I told Miss Katherine I was looking for work, and I couldn't even find a store selling that porno. I wish I'd brought my shot magazines from Angola. I gave them all away when I got short. I need to get near some pussy. I need to smell it. It's a pressure on me. Fifteen years! *Fifteen years!* I'm looking for the dirt, man, I want to see the fucking dirt."

A month later, still having tried nothing to fight my way back inside Angola (as though the warden had depleted my will the way the geography of the prison affected many of the inmates'), I joined an audience of sixth and seventh graders. Littell, along with five current Angola convicts, sat before the church youth group. We were in a part of Baton Rouge far from O'Brien—those Episcopalian youth in that church basement wore short pants and the whitest, cleanest socks I had ever seen. I kept staring at those tube socks. It was as if their mothers bought them a new pair after every soccer game, every tennis lesson.

The church minister gave a monthly service at Angola, and Miss Katherine was fairy godmother to the CPR team, booking their classes around Baton Rouge. Tonight they had arranged for a group of five lifers—escorted by two guards—to give testimonials. The speeches had a theme: "Choices." The convicts were supposed to be warning these kids away from the wrong decisions, but given the cleanliness of their socks (and the bands and bows in the girls' glossy hair, the polo shirts on the boys' skinny bodies), it was hard to imagine their bad judgments could be too dire. It seemed the minister and Miss Katherine had scheduled this event so the inmates could have a few hours to convince these children—anyone outside Angola—that they were not evil. Littell was there because, amid his talk of "establishing" himself, he spoke vaguely of wanting to work with kids.

Behind the six speakers, the youth center's drip-painting project hung on the wall. Each kid's miniature experiment with Pollock-style scattering was taped up neatly, the pictures mounted squarely on blue construction paper.

"The choices you make today are going to determine who you are tomorrow," one convict said precisely, his blue work shirt tucked in tight and buttoned at the collar. He had been in Angola twenty-five years. After describing his progress from drug abuse to shooting a policeman, he walked along the rows of twelve- and thirteen-year-olds. In front of each child he stopped, bent over, opened his mouth wide so that he seemed to breathe emphatically on each milky face, and displayed the .357 bullet hole in the roof of his mouth, the result of a dispute somewhere between choice one and inevitability.

Another man recalled the bar fight that had ended in his murder charge. "I should never even have been in that bar to start with."

They seemed to explain the ruin of their lives by a single, not so terrible mistake—a first tab of LSD; a drink in a bar—perhaps because it was easier for themselves or because it kept even these kids a little worried: A few missed homeworks and the road led straight to Angola.

Littell stood last. His story had less focus, no single turn. "I'm staring at this little kid," he began, and the second-row boy must have been terrified. Littell wore a striped shirt as neatly ironed as the child's, but Littell's lips, with their tightness, their retraction at the corners, were all hostility, and his black eyes did nothing to work against his mouth. "I'm looking at this kid, and I was just like him, fishing, bike riding, that's all I cared about. That's who I was. And this is me now."

What came between was a list of detention centers. "I grew up in these places," he said, hands ungesturing, unmoving at his sides. "I'm talking about where eleven-year-old kids have to prove themselves with knives or be raped. That's what they call a cottage. They put all the younger kids together in their own cottages, and that's supposed to keep them safe. These places, that's where I went to school, that's where I went to sleep. That's where I ate my breakfast every morning." He recounted the months after every release, the time "with the fellas," and two years of angel dust in the Marines. It all led to his being stabbed at Angola, "with a knife the dude soaked in garlic, and garlic poisons," Littell informed. "It does something to your blood, and I had a fever and green pus leaking out of me, and I was laying on that bed in Earl K. Long Hospital where they brought me, and my father was dead, and my mother didn't know where I was, and my brothers didn't know, and my sisters didn't know, nobody knew. I was nobody."

And who knew what was running through the minds of those kids with their impeccable socks pulled up around their calves? The minister thought it might be time to switch directions. "Why don't you mention to these people what it is you want to do now."

"Well," Littell told them, "I'm almost a hundred and thirty-five years old, but I took my GED test while I was at a treatment center right after Angola, and just last week I found out I passed."

The middle-schoolers laughed at the joke about his age, and whether or not they even knew what a GED was, they applauded because he'd passed a test.

He laughed at his own joke, and found himself smiling with their applause.

"I'm getting ready to go to college," he added. "I'm an old man now, but I'm ready to get an education."

The clapping doubled in volume, and Littell sat down, nicking water with one knuckle from the corner of his eye.

The next morning I drove him to the Social Security office. There were jobs he could fit around O'Brien's schedule (the problem was his desire to combine a job *and* college, on top of O'Brien's meetings). A few residents worked for minimum wage with a trash-hauling company—but to get hired he needed something besides his prison I.D., which would not be a selling point with employers. With a Social Security card he could apply for state identification at the Department of Motor Vehicles and, as soon as he'd studied the booklet for the written test, for his driver's license.

The Social Security office was in a squat building with a shiny entry room, and there Littell confronted a machine that dispensed numbers to waiting customers. His mouth was in full disgust, full hatred, as he stared at the red plastic case. The numbered slip poked outward like a kid's tongue. If he'd seen anything like this in the Lake Charles of his childhood he couldn't remember it. He knew only what the sign said: PLEASE TAKE A NUMBER AND... Was there a button to press? Was he supposed to wait until someone did something, until the machine was activated? He didn't want to break anything. He didn't want any trouble with the security guard watching him from the back. He didn't want anything to hurt his chances of qualifying for a card right away, or at all. Besides the guard, an Arab family and two reedy, disheveled women watched the drama.

"Just pull," I said discreetly.

He did, barely stroking the paper.

"You have to pull."

It didn't tear.

"Let me get it," I said. "For my small part in your official identification process."

As we waited for him to be called, he read through a sheet of instructions. He read with his finger. It wasn't a belabored, word-by-word sort of reading, but there was his forefinger sliding steadily across each line.

His turn came. He went to the window, sat across from the clerk, a dwarfish blond woman whose head scarcely rose above the counter between them. She wore a formal blue dress with great puffy short sleeves. From the breast pocket of his shirt Littell took his proof of existence: three Angola I.D. cards, his most recent and two from years ago, and his Marine discharge papers. He removed the rubber band that bound them all together. The papers were torn at every fold, ready to disintegrate.

"I just got out of prison," he confessed when she reached for his credentials.

She didn't react. Her elaborate sleeves stretching up to the counter, she spread what he gave her and glanced over it. "Well," she said without irony, without aversion, in a tone of beautiful indifference, "you definitely have enough identification." And with that, though she did no more than pass him along to another clerk at the computers, the midget in the bridesmaid's dress became, for Littell, that day's figure of grace.

We celebrated at a Chinese restaurant. From our booth he gazed

in all directions at the ornate black-and-gold wallpaper, another won-
derment. We talked more of Camp J, mostly because I couldn't imagine the person across from me, eating his spring roll delicately, fearful
of mishap, with his knife and fork, existing for years in a cement cell
so narrow he could stand in the middle and touch both walls, existing for years seeing only two or three hours of daylight each week,
existing for years with the knowledge that he could make only one
phone call per month, a virtual end to the possibility of crying out to
someone who might listen, an end that seemed no less terrifying
because he already had no one to call, existing for parts of those
years eating the food loaf with his hands and for parts denied all
clothes except a paper gown and for parts spreading water on the
floor and sleeping in the puddle to lessen the heat and for parts not
having a mattress anyway, it too having been confiscated as punishment. I could not put this human being together with that life, and I
could not, here in the Chinese restaurant in a strip mall in Baton
Rouge, connect him with the things he had done to receive those
extra sanctions. When I imagined myself locked in at J, the bars clos-
ing and the guard walking away down the tier and the nightmare of
being buried alive turned real, my chest constricted—I didn't think
I'd be able to breathe.

"I just don't think I could make it," I said, a lie, because of course
I knew that despite the shrinking of my lungs I would take that first
breath, and that having done so I would take another, because the
only alternative was not breathing, and chances were I wouldn't kill
myself, wouldn't cut my wrists with a sliver of blade cracked from a
disposable razor or devise and carry out some method of hanging
myself with the bedsheet; chances were I would go on just as I had
after the judge sentenced me to life without parole, an idea that had
once, before my first trip to Angola, put me into that breath-
narrowing, thigh-weakening dread, made me think I would rather
die. We live for whatever it is possible to live for—that was the only

sure lesson I ever drew from my year, and since it's no lesson at all, I don't mind making the revelation here, well before the end.

But in Littell's reply there was something beyond this basic human resilience. There was something particularly his. There was an impregnable strength built by sheer will. "The first time I went to the detention center, when I was twelve, they shut me in a cell, in solitary. And when they slammed that metal door, I wanted to run at it. I wanted to ram my head against it. But I caught myself. Even at that age I knew I just couldn't let myself go crazy. I didn't even let myself scream. It was the same at Angola. If I let myself have that feeling of suffocating, I knew I wouldn't never get through."

He chewed a small section of spring roll and sipped his tea.

"And maybe one day out of the year, something nice might happen. I'm not talking about getting a new dude paying draft for protection, or a new shim for coming out of my cuffs in the bullpen—that was the game. That was regular. That's what they call it, 'He's in the game.' I'm talking about one time a few years ago I was in the blocks, not at J but over at Camp C, and this music, this guitar, starts flowing through the walls. It was that Jimi Hendrix song 'Wind Cries Mary.' It was that beginning, *doon doon drooon.* It was that sadness. I guess the music room at C was somewhere near those cells. 'Cause I could just hear that electric guitar. It was beautiful. And later I found out it was this dude named Myron Hodges. He was in my dorm one time. I never knew him. You can sleep two beds across from a dude at Angola and never speak. Not hello. But Myron was kind of famous. He was in the prison band. They used to travel all over the state. And he was a monster on that ax. Do you know those notes? *Doon doon drooon.* Man, I was so grateful for that. I wanted to thank him later."

The fortune cookies were set between us on the black plastic tray. I didn't want mine. Littell opened both. The first slip read, "You will pursue higher education, whether in academic or spiritual form."

The second was one-in-a-thousand, a fortune cookie mistake—no paper inside at all.

"Do you see this, Dan?" he asked, as we walked toward the car. "Yours didn't have nothing in it. It could have been mine. But it wasn't. I'm keeping this. 'You will pursue higher education.'"

He asked if he could drive.

"Have you driven since you've been out?"

"Nineteen eighty-two," he said.

"In the parking lot."

He sat behind the wheel, held it with hands at 10 and 2, and only then, after he had that feel, shifted into drive. He made a few 10 M.P.H. circles around an empty section of the strip-mall lot. I waited for him to ask if he could venture onto the road; I waited for him to go without asking.

He stopped, pushed the stick into park.

"That's it?" I asked.

"You're getting too nervous." He smiled again, as he had before the church youth group. "And that's all the driving I need for right now."

At the end of his fifth week at O'Brien, Littell told his life story to the residents. This was part of the program, a scheduled date. While the cigarette-lighter woman ran the flame along her forearm, and while Littell sat expressionless in his new turtleneck, Miss Katherine opened the meeting with a psalm read from her Life Recovery Bible.

> O give thanks to the Lord
> Sing to him; yes, sing his praises
> And tell of his marvelous works.

"You can't do this on your own," she said. "Without God helping me, giving me strength, I would have never made it this far. When I was in my own recovery, all that self-will and ego kept getting in the way. I didn't think I needed God, I didn't think I needed any community. I didn't think anyone else had anything to tell me. But I kept going back to those meetings, because I saw there were people who'd found another way to live. And now I know I went through all that pain and all that turmoil for a purpose, and my purpose is to be sitting here in front of you all today, working on alcohol and drug recovery, and helping you all to find that change."

Before she introduced Littell, she took care of some community business. People had been smoking in the dorms upstairs. "There will be no violating that rule, are we cool on that?" She became briefly stern. "Because I'm not going to let O'Brien House be closed down by the fire marshals. This is part of *my* recovery, and I will not jeopardize that. I said, Are we cool?"

"We cool" was the chorus.

"That's good. Because I am the Boss Applesauce," a shriek of laughter, "and don't you forget it. If you do, we will go outside, and I'm pumping iron. And what was that I'm going to learn?" She glanced around, waiting for help from someone she'd talked with earlier. "What was that thing?"

"Tai chi," a man called out.

"Tai chi," she said. "I'm going to get you with my tai chi."

She asked Littell if he was ready.

He asked her, "I want to know at the outset, can I use profanity? I don't know if I will, but I might have to. It might be what's inside me."

Given permission, he began.

"I was born in Lake Charles, Louisiana. I was the sixth child of Joy and Willie May Harris. I was born in the front room of their house, in the house my mother lives in to this day. I've got two brothers and four sisters. There wasn't much love in the way of hugging and all that. My daddy worked, and my parents went to church, I'm not saying that. But as far as that warmth? Maybe I just didn't feel it. My brothers and sisters I haven't seen in so long, and I care about them, but we're not close. I don't miss them."

The biography continued through a childhood in friendship with a boy named Ricky Coleman. "He was my Ace Boon Coon. In 1979 he went up to Angola for life. But when we were kids, we started out stealing hubcaps and eight-track tapes from cars while guys was inside the nightclubs. We would make a sweep of the whole night-club area, and we would sell our stuff to a fence, and some of the older dudes they started to admire our courage. They took us under wing, and they taught us the Murphy. For anyone who don't know what the Murphy is, it's like this. You see some horny dude, which Lake Charles had a lot of them from the military base over in Texas. And you tell him you have the number of a lady where he can go. He gives you cash, and you put him on the pay phone, and she talks sweet. So the dude drives off to meet her. Except there's no one at the address, and we're long gone when he comes looking."

Soon they robbed drug dealers. Soon they were doing drugs. But none of it was quite the heart of Littell's story, the heart that emerged as the wall clock wound down on his half hour, as he rushed through his years at Angola and reeled from chronology to outcry: "And sometimes I'm just filled with hate." His voice swelled and his back straightened in his chair and his hands clenched and his arms lifted, fists near his waist. "I got so much rage and hatred in me right now and I got to deal with that. I don't know. It's just there. And I either got to deal with it or it's going to deal with me. Sometimes I be rip-ping up inside. I just be wanting to *rip*. Destroy everything, *destroy it*. It's going to kill me. It's going to kill me."

When he was through, and when Miss Katherine had spoken, the residents joined arms and gave their chant.

Keep coming back
'Cause it works if you work it

If you don't you die
So live it, every day
One day at a time
Whoops, there it is!

Later Miss Katherine explained to me that the final line, adapted from a rap song, was the residents attempt to remind themselves that one day, after all their struggle, the change would take place as though by miracle, as though they had merely tripped into a new and easier life.

Three weeks later, at the end of May, I was ready to wage what attack I could on the warden. I flew down to Baton Rouge to begin.

One night, from my motel room, I called O'Brien House. Miss Katherine told me Littell was gone. He had decided to leave the program that past Sunday morning. He would give her no reason. He said only that his mind was made up.

In all, he had spent two months at the halfway house.

"The gates of Angola are opening up wide for you, Littell," Miss Katherine warned. "And the next time it's going to be forever."

He packed what he had in a cardboard box and crossed the vacant lot to the Greyhound station.

NINE

JUDGE POLOZOLA, CHERUBIC FACE TOPPED BY CURLY black hair, spoke pointedly to my attorneys: "I want you to read through the case law. All the decisions. I want you to make sure you do that. Because all this might be true," he touched the pages of my lawsuit, "but I'm still going to have a hard time ordering a reporter inside a prison."

He was the earthly power, the one who existed beyond the domain of the warden. The judge had never released Angola from his indirect supervision. He had never quite trusted in the permanence of its reforms. So when the inmates felt they had been wronged, abused by guards or denied treatment at the hospital, they could appeal to him. They sent their letters to his chambers, to the office of his court-appointed expert, to the pair of lawyers he had named to defend the inmates' civil rights. The letters started with propitiations. They wished well-being on the judge and his family; they prayed that Jesus or Allah—or both—would bless the judge or the expert or the pair of civil rights attorneys. And then came the stories. An inmate had been "stuck out bad" and was at Camp J "for dun nothing." Another had been switched from metal-shop clerk to the grass crew for conspiratorial reasons not even the most sympathetic reader could follow. Most of the letters were read and filed and forgotten. The judge and his appointees were overrun by petty grievances. Most of the complaints didn't deal with the prison at all but with claims of injustices at trial, of ineffective counsel, of innocence of everything. But sometimes the stories were relevant and troubling enough, and sounded true enough—a game of "Rambo" played amid the tall okra, where a group of guards arranged to look away while weaker inmates were raped—and a small, informal investigation began. The prison knew it couldn't stop the two lawyers from wandering the grounds. It knew it couldn't interfere with the expert's interviews. Polozola's authority helped guarantee that games of "Rambo" remained the exception.

With two expensive attorneys to make my supplications, I hoped the judge would improve my situation as well.

My lawsuit against Cain did not, technically, fall within Polozola's supervision of the prison. He was entrusted with the inmates' civil rights, not with any writer's. But there were only two federal judges in his district, and once my case was assigned, at random, to him, I let myself believe I had a chance. He had dealt with Cain. He, at least, would listen.

I knew before I started—and the lawyers I'd hired in Baton Rouge kept reminding me—that my chances weren't great. Cain's effort at extortion was secondary to my suit, which alleged that the warden had breached my First Amendment rights by barring me from Angola and which requested restored access. The attempted shakedown, as part of the story, was featured in the papers my lawyers filed. And it certainly seemed a problem for Warden Cain. But it could not, in itself, put me back on Angola's grounds. And my First Amendment rights to be there in the first place were basically nonexistent.

The United States Supreme Court, in a series of decisions going back to the 1970s, had helped to ensure that the nation's prisons stayed isolated and unknown, that criminals, once sent away, could be forgotten. They had to be kept without physical cruelty—yes, on that the court was firm—but beyond that their lives would be ignored. Law-abiding citizens wouldn't have to think of them.

This was not, of course, the explicit rationale behind the 1974 ruling in *Pell* v. *Procunier,* which set precedent against the media when it comes to entering prisons. The rationale was that the press had no First Amendment right to go anywhere that the public couldn't go. A journalist's right to express what he wished was protected by the Constitution; his ability to gather information was not. When a California state prison forbade reporters from interviewing specific inmates, the justices backed the state: The reporters weren't on the inmates' prison-approved visiting lists. That the reporters weren't legal counsel, family, spiritual advisers, or friends deemed by the warden to be rehabilitative—and therefore, by prison guidelines, *couldn't* be placed on the visiting lists—was judged irrelevant. The prison was merely enforcing a uniform set of standards on the public, and the reporters didn't meet those standards.

This and later decisions meant that wardens allow the press into their territory only when—and to whatever degree—they wish, and that the country knows almost nothing about the lives of 1.7 million of its citizens. What the Court failed to acknowledge, in writing that the constitution does not force "upon government the affirmative duty to make available to journalists sources of information not available to the public generally," is that most government officials feel that duty anyway, as a matter of survival. They need to retain the public's attention and its trust, and so they offer up a good deal of information. What they try to hide, other officials, also fighting for survival, help to expose. But with prisons the public doesn't much want to pay attention; it has already handed over its trust.

Wardens and state corrections departments have little motivation to share anything. Even the statistics they offer to prove what the Court *does* require, that their institutions be run safely, are useless for comparison and not necessarily reliable in themselves. The category of "significant injury" in a prison's annual report can mean almost anything, depending on the state's directives and the warden's own definition and his instructions, direct or subtle, to employees about what to write down and what to leave unrecorded. Except for inmate deaths, it is impossible for anyone to judge from prison statistics how safely an institution is run. It is impossible to judge without being there—and being there for extended periods. (Inmates can write to the media, but their mail to reporters is subject to review in many states. Even where court rulings have made such letters confidential, inmates risk reprisal if their criticisms are discovered, and their accounts are difficult to verify. They can write confidentially to lawyers, but interested attorneys are hard to find.) So by allowing prisons the authority to shut down press access, the Supreme Court has aided in the guarantee that the lives of our inmates occupy no place in our minds.

When I had arrived at Angola, back in September, I'd had no right to anything beyond what Cain had granted other reporters: a guided tour, and interviews with inmates while an escort stood nearby. I may not even have had a right to that. But as Cain had grown confident that my vision was sufficiently affected by his Gospel-infused proclamations, as he'd told his staff early on that I could "see it all," that I could have "carte blanche," and that no eaves-dropping was necessary, I gained a tenuous hold. My suit was based on the legal doctrine of unconstitutional conditions. Having entered into an unwritten contract with me, covering my access, he could not revoke what he had granted because I would not sign away what was indeed my fundamental right: to publish whatever I found to be accurate and true.

As my attorneys first explained this legal theory, I was ecstatic, almost giddy with hope. It was cut-and-dried. I couldn't possibly lose. There was no way the facts could be interpreted against me. He'd given me the access, then taken it away only because I wouldn't meet his unconstitutional demand. The doctrine of unconstitutional conditions. During the days before filing suit, I must have spoken those five words to friends and acquaintances two hundred times.

But even as I repeated the phrase, I knew the problems. Cain could deny he'd agreed to anything, or he could invent some security-related reason for my banishment. It didn't have to be much. He didn't have to say he'd found contraband in my car, or that I'd stood in the cotton fields and called for a riot. The Supreme Court had accepted wardens' arguments that interviews with the press built the egos of inmates, and in this way threatened the balance and peace of their institutions. Cain could say the inmates I'd been following had begun to seem too self-assured.

I tried to convince myself I had proof. I had the agreement he'd given me to sign the morning of my expulsion. But he could claim there were other issues. He could tell his first deputy and his press secretary, who'd been there at the galvanized fence, to lie about his reasons. He could tell the two assistant wardens, whom he'd called into our January meeting, to lie about his worries. Would they? Would they perjure themselves in federal court?

The two lawyers I'd hired were calm, conservative corporate types. The judge took them seriously enough to ask us into his chambers after reading through the suit. The four of us sat around a long conference table, well-burnished like the one in Cain's office, but of a far more expensive wood. Around us were dark shelves filled with law books, not the framed flattering clippings Cain hung on his walls. The room held a comforting power, but its elegance unsettled me. How much would the man who presided here want to involve himself in a fight over the warden's crass control? Yes, Polozola had invested himself in cleaning up Angola for twenty-five years, but he was known as a conservative thinker—wouldn't he suggest that my lawyers and I had no chance, suggest we reconsider?

His warning was not unkind—"All this might be true, but I'm still going to have a hard time ordering a reporter inside a prison"—it was only crushing.

He turned to me. "And even if I did, what makes you think any of those inmates are going to talk to you? What makes you think Cain hasn't warned them already? He doesn't have to threaten them physically. Those men are in a maximum-security prison. They have next to nothing. So a little crumb means a lot. They know if they cross Burl, they're going to get that little crumb taken away."

"Judge," I said, "if I may just answer that."

He nodded.

"I know you're right. I know that all he has to do is take away that crumb. Or let them know he will. But I don't think he has yet. I think—and I don't know how tactfully I can put this—that his ego is so big, and that he's used to such total authority, that he figured when he threw me out I'd just stay away. He didn't need to threaten anyone."

"But he's going to find out he was wrong this afternoon, as soon as this suit gets served. And the inmates are going to hear about it on the news, and it's going to be all over the paper, because your suit is going to be right there when the reporters check the court press box. He's not going to need to threaten anyone then, either. The inmates are just going to know. Don't talk to Bergner. Don't open your mouth to say hello. He sued the warden."

"That's why we hope you'll issue that restraining order, Judge," one of my lawyers broke in, referring to the preliminary step we asked for in the suit: that the judge prohibit Cain from communicating with the inmates in any way about the suit, and that he prohibit any reprisals against the inmates for talking with me.

"Even if I sign the order," Polozola said, "you know I can't stop every tiny thing. I'm sitting here and Angola is a long ways away. And a tiny thing is all it's going to take."

"We do understand that, Judge," my lawyer said. "But it would give our client something, in the event he does get back in."

Polozola stared at me. If he signed, it would be, at least, a show of sympathy, something I could cling to. I tried to demonstrate, through some minute adjustment of posture and expression, that I was no loose cannon, that the story I told was true, that I had given Cain no legitimate reason to throw me out, that if the judge took this initial step he would not wind up embarrassed. Perfectly motionless now at that table of venerable wood, I tried to believe he could tell that I had committed not a single transgression at Angola, that I had refused even to buy an inmate a Coke when he'd asked. But the judge may not have been sizing me up at all. He may have been thinking about everything he knew, as an insider, about the unproven crimes of Warden Cain.

He signed.

What happened next happened fast. The judge called us in for another conference later that day, this one including the Department of Corrections' chief counsel. "I want you to think about settling," Polozola told him. "You don't want a trial on this one."

As we talked about possible terms, one of my lawyers, trying to soften the opposition, mentioned that I had begun the year with a favorable impression of the warden. "Maybe Mr. Cain can get back to that."

"I wanted to write this book," I added, "because I was interested in his unique thinking about criminals and prisons."

"Unique," the judge said, exchanging a glance and raised eyebrows with the department's counsel.

"Yeah," their lawyer muttered, "Cain's unique all right."

■

The reporters were just then picking up their copies of the day's business from the clerk of the court downstairs. I flew back to New York, my attorneys betting the Department of Corrections would give me everything I needed, and me not so sure about the odds. Cain ran the show. It might not matter what the department's lawyer advised him.

I waited by the phone. At four the next day, my lawyers called. Cain had been persuaded to settle—he might succeed in keeping me out, but there was no way he wanted a trial that examined the shake down. I was given a kind of five-month visa, to complete my year. My interviews would be unmonitored.

Not wanting to spend my time inside a maximum-security penitentiary where the warden felt any angrier than he already was, I declined much comment when reporters called. But fortunately one of the writers, working from the public record, discussed the judge's order against reprisals. The story ran on the front page of the *Advocate*'s Metro section, so, once convict word got around, the inmates would know that they were—in theory, anyway—protected.

Right after the settlement became official, my phone rang.

"Hello?"

"Dan, this is Burl. How you doing?"

"All right, Warden Cain."

"That's good. Now, look. I figure we just got involved in a little game of poker. But instead of just going on playing, you stood up and shot me. I just hope you didn't kill me."

He waited for my laughter, and I tried to be polite.

"Listen," he hurried on, "we got this thing settled and we're going to get along good. You know that and I know that. There's not going to be any reprisals against any inmates. There's not going to be any obstruction. But I wish you *would* talk to the press. Tell 'em everything's fine and there's no war on between us. Tell 'em I didn't do anything wrong. I'm not talking about you doing the legal thing, I'm talking about the human thing. Would you do that for me? 'Cause my wife can't go to church. My son can't go out of the house. This is costing my family a lot of pain. Would you do me that favor? And it's taking a toll on the prison. They're all talking about it. You really ought to do it for the sake of the inmates. 'Cause I'm trying to run a Christian Walk, and this don't look good for that."

I apologized. I said that I couldn't give a statement of exoneration.

But within a few days, the press attention died out. And no state or federal prosecutor ever called to inquire about my charges of extortion.

Still, the warden didn't want any more trouble with Polozola. So when I arrived for my next visit he called a meeting. He put out word across the penitentiary that all the inmates I'd been working with be brought to the Main Prison visiting shed. "Right away."

Cain asked us to gather around him. We formed a semicircle. Attentive. He spoke quickly, and joked weakly with me about my minimal hair, but he wasn't overly uneasy. "I want you to know that everything they've got in the papers isn't true. Me and Mr. Bergner's not fighting. Are we?"

"No," I said. "I appreciate your cooperation."

"You see? We're getting along fine. 'Cause I want you to talk to him. Say whatever you like. Tell him the good things, but tell him the negative, too. Tell it all. Tell it like it is. 'Cause I bless this book."

T E N

"YOU LOOKED SAD WHILE HE WAS TALKING," ONE OF
the inmates said to me discreetly as the warden walked away after
giving his blessing. I cannot write which inmate. Despite Judge
Polozola's sympathy and the possibility of appealing to him about
any reprisal, I can, in fact, offer the convict little protection. The
same man soon explained that I was just starting to see what the
inmates had learned ahead of me, that Cain loved both glowing publicity and making money exactly as much as he *didn't* care about the
inmates, exactly as much as he wasn't the warden they'd longed for
when he first arrived. "Dumb to say," the man went on, "but what
we're always wanting with a warden is sort of like a caring god."

I denied my sadness to the inmate, denied it until the very last
day of my year, when we said goodbye outside the rodeo stadium.
Then, as he said, crying, that he wished he was leaving with me, I
allowed that he'd been right about my emotions. But for the meantime I shrugged, telling him my feelings were irrelevant. "I'm here
about you," I said.

And two days later another of the convicts shook me almost as
thoroughly as the warden had.

Donald Cook's surprises began when he opened his mouth to show me the sugar bags of marijuana between his teeth and tongue.

With his shirt off on that 90-degree June afternoon, sweat shone on his tattoos: the lion-monster, the helmeted woman, the spiderweb, the declaration LOUISIANA CRACKER. Sweat trickled below his short black hair. Facing the Main Yard, we sat on a concrete ledge outside the dorms. Two of his customers lingered separately at a distance, waiting for our talk to end. Occasionally one would circle close, then wander ten or twenty yards away, letting Cook know they were impatient. They wanted to make their buys.

"Be cool," he told them. "I'm having a conversation. I'll find you by the hobby shop. You'll get it before chow time."

"These guys are pathetic," he said to me, smiling with his bright, slightly overlapping front teeth, and indeed his customers seemed it. One, bearded and paunchy and slack-shouldered in his V-necked T-shirt, looked more like an old hobo than a dangerous convict, though undoubtedly he had destroyed someone, murdered or raped someone, sometime.

"Back last fall," he went on, "I told myself I was going to quit dealing, 'cause of my mom and all. I didn't want to get caught no more. I didn't want her thinking about me in the cells. It was killing her, thinking I was doing so much wrong. But I missed it. The thrill. That's really what it is. It's the money, that's part of it, but it's the thrill. It ain't having it to smoke. I see some dude coming down the Walk and I'm supposed to deliver? I drop the bag right there on the concrete when he's just that far in front of me? So he can pick it right up when we pass by? The timing's got to be just right. I got to watch him and the freeman, both. That last second? When I'm just about to drop? When I got to take my eyes off the freeman up ahead and I got no idea anymore whose eyes are in back?" Cook smiled with those overlapping teeth, then shook his head, exhaling through narrowed lips. It was clear what he meant without his saying anything: Always, at that moment, his heart was locked rather than beating, and he loved the fight to overcome that dread, loved hurling himself at chance, proving his will greater than his fear. This was his self-discipline, this was his strength, this was what made him the opposite of the slack men circling him now, just pining to stupefy themselves and, with their indiscretion, adding to his risk of getting caught, keeping his adrenaline high even as we sat there and he recounted his day.

That morning he had woken at about three A.M. This was from habit, the routine that had taken hold during the fall when he'd quit dealing and hated the dorm, wanted to put some distance between himself and the person everyone else expected him to be. He still liked to get out while almost everyone slept.

A few other men, having returned from their night shifts, moved like ghosts under the blue security lights. Their slippers scraped on the cement floor as they walked toward the showers. The industrial fans vibrated. Beneath these constant baseline sounds, it was easy for Cook to unlock his box, turning the key gingerly, and to dress and walk up the aisle, keeping his steps tight, without anyone hearing. His "bed partners," the men with cots on either side of him, always asked how he could get out so quietly; they were amazed that he never once disturbed them. He was amazed that they were impressed. There was enough noise to cover anyone. His care with his lock and footsteps wasn't even necessary. That was just something he did. "You just disappear," they said, as if they felt betrayed by his refusal to sleep as late as possible, to minimize the hours of consciousness.

Leaving the dorm that early morning, Cook had gone, as always, to the Toy Shop. Inside, just one man sat at a workbench, glueing blocks of wood to make flatbed trucks. He and Cook said hello, nothing more. Cook started painting the flatbeds a baby blue. He painted some pull-along rabbits the same shade. He was meticulous.

Any section designed to be a different color was left ungrazed by his slender brush. Every edge was sharp, all surfaces smoothly coated. He set the trucks and rabbits in evenly spaced rows to dry. The deaf toddlers who received these next Christmas would be thrilled.

He took a nap, curled on the vinyl couch. When it was time for work—he had been promoted again, from the kitchen paint crew to kitchen maintenance—he woke automatically. The job was often a matter of waiting for parts, which was why he considered it a promotion. That morning the crew was supposed to replace a drainage pipe. But they had no pipe, so after slouching outside the kitchen from 7:30 until 10:00, they were dismissed for the day. He walked out across the Yard, past the basketball court, where two inmates played a sluggish game of 21, past the weight pile and the little gazebo where one of the Main Prison barbers had set up shop. A guard in camouflage fatigues, one of the shakedown team, wandered the grass, waving a metal detector in front of him. Far off, at the other end of the complex, one of the field lines was being cleared back in for lunch, their boots checked for weapons.

A few scattered benches stood by the softball field, two farther out. Cook chose the one closest to the perimeter fence, absolutely by himself. He didn't mind baking in the sun (the Yard was without trees, to maximize surveillance). He was glad to sit with the nearest shade back at the gazebo hundreds of yards away, the price for both solitude and this particular view. He stared at the Tunica Hills.

Recently he'd done some maintenance work on one of the Main Prison roofs, and he'd had his first look at Angola's geography. He made it a very long look. Because the landscape was so flat, he could take in almost everything, from the river to the front gate. Behind the administration building, the hills rose up and the prison ended. He believed in Angola's buffer zone, but he, unlike many of the inmates, imagined an area of only a few thousand acres. Angola, to him, was not endless.

Today, from his bench, he gazed at the dark trees on the hills against the filmy, overheated sky. This had become a ritual, performed at least once each week. He considered those hills. He didn't doubt what everyone said, that pigweed and thorny vines grew everywhere. He didn't doubt what everyone said about the copperheads and rattlers. And he understood that what they said about the dog team was probably at least half true: that every week for practice they sent an inmate out with two hour's head start, that the dogs picked up his scent and just wouldn't stop, that they would track straight through brambles and even quicksand bogs, that those guards on the team were the craziest, meanest motherfuckers the penitentiary could find, that they didn't care if their partners got sucked under the mud and drowned as long as they got their inmate—and got to pistol-whip him if the chase was real—that every week the team caught the convict within a few hours.

In fact, Cook's understanding was closer to three-quarters true. The chase-team guards were extremely devoted. For their weekly practice they sent one of their own members along with one of the dog-tending trusties into the woods, and while this partnership tried to flee or hide, the guards did indeed charge through thickets and bogs, heedless of scratches and sinking and snakes. When I had gone out with them, they offered me the experience of taking the leash. I returned it quickly. I didn't want to plunge first through any of that terrain. One guard reassured me that he hadn't been bit by a snake in two years. I wasn't reassured. And I grew tired. My city exercise routines didn't seem to matter out here, where their bellies, tanked with the pecan pies they'd devoured before we left, kept them barreling forward. They found the two men in about ninety minutes, though sometimes the mock chases lasted into the night and they had to navigate these woods after dark. Once caught, the two men "loved up" the dog that found them, petting it and scratching it behind the ears. This, the guards said, was what the real escapees had to do. No more pistol-whipping, no more pummeling. That was the past. Now the trapped inmate was simply told, "Love up the dog, you better love him up," and made to stroke the bloodhound that had put an end to his flight.

As Cook sat on his bench, he thought of what he'd seen on the TV news yesterday morning. A convict had tried to escape the previous night. The tower guard had been asleep while the man had climbed two fences and pried apart the concertina wire. Word around the prison was, the man had been planning to swim a narrow part of the Mississippi. Sandbagging during the flood, he'd scoped out the river. But when he ran up the levee, razor-blood streaming along his arm, he saw that the flood hadn't gone down as much as he'd figured. There was too much swamp. And alligators lurking in it. He couldn't see a thing. After going a short ways, he couldn't make himself push his luck. He edged back toward the levee. He crouched down carefully in some bushes. He waited for the dogs.

When Cook had heard, yesterday evening, that the man had been caught, it hadn't affected him. He said it hadn't seemed to matter to anyone. Most of the inmates would never try to run; they dreamt of pardon hearings and appeals. And Cook knew he wouldn't try his escape the way that fool had. First of all, snakes were better than alligators. So you went to the hills instead of the river, especially since there were plenty of snakes in those woods across the water, anyway. And second of all, you had to plan. You had to maximize your chances. You couldn't just go without thinking things through. You had to find the right job that would take you to the right spot on the grounds, so you could reach those hills unseen before the next count. And then you couldn't freeze up as soon as you got scared. Which that stupid motherfucker had in the swamp. And which Cook knew he wouldn't.

Cook stayed on his solitary, sun-assaulted bench through lunch, remembering how he'd escaped once from a parish jail about eighty miles from his home in Alexandria, after an arrest for burglary. He'd begged a dollar from a Cuban in the pen with him, then yelled for the guard. "I need a col' drink." On his way to the soda machine in the front room, he made a quick survey. There were only the barred gate to the pen, the door into the front room, and the door out. The doors weren't locked.

He returned to the pen and shared his drink with the Cuban. Two hours later he asked for another dollar. The Cuban looked at him like he'd lost his mind. Cook whispered what he planned to do. The Cuban wanted the entertainment. Cook went with his money to the bars, yelled for the guard, whined about the heat. He needed another drink. He backed up as the guard unlocked the gate, and as the man tugged it open with his weight off balance, Cook drove at the bars. The guard reeled. Cook ran through the front room and down the street, gunshots behind him briefly. He cut down an alley, hid between shacks in the black section of town, stole a bicycle, rode through the rest of the night, lay flat beside the shoulder whenever a car passed by, slept the next day in a soy field, stole a truck, and almost made it home before he was caught.

That was all he wanted to do now, get home to Alexandria. To see his ex-wife.

He went back to his dorm for count, sat on his cot while the guard walked the aisles and made checks on a clipboard. Cook looked through his three-ringed photo album. A picture of his son— hair parted crisply on the side, cheeks fleshy in smiling, the boy around seven years old—had surfaced in his mother's trailer. She had mailed it along this week. She and Cook had no contact with his ex-wife, or with his son and daughter, who, he thought, might be in foster care. But sometimes relatives sent his mother snapshots. Next to this new one, photos of the children as toddlers, as infants, beamed up from the pages. He had cut them smaller than passport size, cut them tight around the puffy faces, because their mother had been in the pictures. The child faces were all the more otherworldly, all the more angelic, for their isolation.

"I want to take that chip off *him*," off God, I remembered him saying, as he told me about cropping his ex-wife from every photograph. The cropping was meticulous. No sign of her presence—not a fingernail—intruded on any of the pictures.

The count had to clear in every dorm before any door was opened. All it took to hold everything at a standstill was one innocent mistake in verifying the two thousand inmates at Main Prison. Twenty minutes, half an hour, forty-five minutes went by. Cook filled a few sugar bags while the guard sat at his corner table in the one o'clock heat, all his energy focused on keeping his eyelids from lolling shut.

"Count clear!" The words traveled, echoed by guards at gate after gate, up the Walk.

Later that afternoon, sitting with me on the concrete ledge and telling his drug customers he would deliver soon enough, Cook related that he had just called his mother. He saw her about twice each year; during the visits he would pull his chair beside hers, touching hers, and hold her hand for such long periods that other inmates occasionally mistook her for his wife. But making conversation could be hard, especially on the phone, especially because today there was information he needed to bury in case security was tapping in.

"Let's not both talk at the same time," he told her, their standard joke whenever the silences lasted.

She laughed. "You're my heart, Donald Lee."

"I just thought you might be getting sick, 'cause I caught them cramps again last night. But I guess not this time."

"No, not this time."

"I was right with them headaches, though."

"I'll probably feel it tonight."

"Mama, I'm sending you some money. I been selling some belts and things I made in the hobby shop. Dude's people are going to mail you a check."

"You been making some belts?"

"Yeah. Just a little money for you, is all."

"And I'm going to put it right back in your account."

"No. Don't you do that."

"Right back."

"It's for you."

"You need it worse."

"No, if I did I'd keep it. It's for you."

"You're my heart. You staying good?"

"Yeah, Mama."

"'Cause you know everything you do at that prison is wrote down."

"When you coming?" he asked, relieved to steer away from his drug money, which neither she nor the monitors could know about.

She said she had wanted to visit last weekend, but that her cousin wouldn't drive her, because they had just been to see Cook's brother at Winn Correctional.

The recorded voice came on to warn them: "You have one more minute for this call." Cook could phone her back for another fifteen, but he knew she couldn't afford it.

"All right," he said.

"I'm going to be there soon, I'm going to try."

"Write me something."

"I will, you know that."

"And thanks for sending that picture. I almost forgot that."

"You put it in your album?"

"I did. I love you, Mama."

"I love—"

The line went dead.

Then, after our talk and after delivering the sugar bags and borrowing a cassette from someone on his dorm, he would go running. The music on the cassette was unknown to him; he couldn't name the group. He paid no attention to the music. When he'd first asked his dorm-mate for a tape, Cook had said only, "Give me something loud." And that was all he knew about whatever he put into his Walkman and played twice over during his long run, that it was some kind of hard rock and that he kept it loud. "I really couldn't tell you," he said when I asked if the man gave him the same tape every day. He couldn't recite a single lyric or reproduce a line of chords. It was just a wall of sound, and he ran right through it.

In bare feet. Ten miles around and around the Yard, wearing cut-off jeans, no shirt, no sneakers. And he watched for the few stones, to come down on them. To toughen him. Not that he planned to take those hills without shoes. But he knew he would have to keep running, no matter where he was cut, no matter what bone he had broken, no matter if a snake bit into his leg. He needed to stay free only long enough to reach Alexandria. The last escape, before the murder, had been to be with all his family. This was to find his ex-wife and the friends who had turned him in. The music was nothing to him. The stones were nothing. Ten miles did not wind him. Every day for the rest of their lives, he wanted those people to think of him. "Because I'm going to be in Angola for the rest of mine." He would break into his friends' houses while they slept, and he would cut their right hands from their arms. He hadn't yet decided exactly how. He imagined a few options. But every time they reached for something, every time they went to open a door or pick up a cup of coffee, there would be Cook, remembered.

"I don't blame them for what I did," he said. "But I blame them for me being here."

And later that night, before the police caught up with him, he would pick the lock on his ex-wife's front door. He would climb the stairs quietly. He would stand over her bed while she slept. He would pour acid over her face. It would eat at her cheeks, her nose, her lips, her chin, her hair, her neck. He would be careful to avoid her eyes. Every time she looked in the mirror, there in her everlasting disfigurement, she would see him.

Part of me had believed, when I had found Cook in the Toy Shop back at Christmas, that his entire life was changing, and that the change would be solidified by the shop's charitable works. Now my hope—and the fact that I liked this man, despite what he seemed quite capable of doing—left me faintly sickened. I was sickened, too, by the immediate knowledge that I would write everything he told me, and that my words would probably cost him years at Camp J. But nothing ate at me quite so much, over the coming months, as my early ideas about Warden Cain.

Through June and July, I struggled to substantiate that my initial vision had been, at least partly, right. I tried to make the Huey Long version come true. I talked not only with inmates but with staff at all levels, asking again and again about Cain's role in the programs— Toastmasters, the Toy Shop, the CPR team, education—he advertised. The employees stared back at me quizzically, as though I might be demented.

They were happy enough to talk with me. I'd expected hostility when I returned after the lawsuit; instead, I received smiles and jokes, quietly spoken. Men who'd once told me Cain was the best warden in their long memories, now quoted to me from the newspaper's account: "'I love you like a brother,'" they mumbled or winked as I passed by. "'Just business, just business.'" When I ran into a group of guards in a bar down the road from the prison, they couldn't get enough of their favorite punch line: "Dan, listen," they leaned forward, breaking off from the topic of conversation, "I'm try-ing to build a barn for my wife...."

I began to feel like Dorothy, her house having just fallen on the Wicked Witch. The staff celebrated my victory. The only problem was, they were still besieged. The witch wasn't crushed, only bruised. Cain, worried that one of his staff might have the temerity to finger him for something that wouldn't dissolve, governed as he always had, warning his employees by flaunting his power, perpetu-ally demoting, shunting aside, and firing lifelong personnel. And the staff had no recourse. Cain held a seat on the civil service commis-sion and seemed able to influence a majority of its seven votes.

But now that the staff knew I wasn't his man, they were glad to answer my questions. So after searching my face for signs of demen-tia—how, after what I'd discovered firsthand, could I go on inquiring about his mission at the penitentiary?—they told me about Cain's commitment to Angola. Discounting for the fact that he didn't live on the grounds, he spent far less time at the prison than any warden they could remember. To facilitate this, he had commanded the gate guards never to log him in or out. Cain said that because he lived outside Angola, he needed to enter unrecorded so he could surprise employees who were up to no good. The staff found this wildly funny. If a criminal or abusive guard had a friend at the gate, he would be much more quickly alerted to the warden's presence by a call from the gate phone (or a message relayed) than by driving miles across the penitentiary to check the logbook. Cain's order, those at higher levels said, allowed him to spend his time starting up a private prison business in neighboring Mississippi.

"But what about something like the Toy Shop?" I asked. "Hasn't he accomplished something there?"

The shop was producing more toys now, yes, but only through the efforts of its convict founders and the assistant warden who was its sponsor.

"What about Toastmasters?"

Begun under John Whitley, it was the same size it had always been, twenty-five or thirty members.

"The CPR team?"

No different than when Whitley had started it.

"But overall, is it possible that more inmates are involved in those kinds of programs now than before Cain took over? Is it possible that there are more clubs, more organizations? Is it just possible?"

Maybe, I heard, Cain had played some role in the growth of the literacy program offered to the general prison population, from about one hundred to two hundred inmates. But the numbers themselves were suspect, and any expansion was due to the program's coordinator, who was tireless in finding convicts to serve as teachers, in scraping together materials and staking out classroom space. Cain was uninvested.

And no, there had been no overall increase in the number of inmate organizations. They were as scattered as they had always been, with no greater number of convicts involved.

I thought, as the staff asked me what else I wanted to know, of Danny Fabre somewhere among the 5,000 men on the 18,000-acre penitentiary. He had access to one of Angola's twenty or thirty student computers. He had his membership in Toastmasters and Captain Newsom's words of encouragement, given in passing once every two months. He was one of Angola's lucky few. He was on his own.

"You want to know what's grown?" one employee was asking. "It's Burl's lies."

The inmates, too, felt free to talk. One told me of a rumor that had circulated before the lawsuit: that I was Warden Cain's spy. Why else, the convicts had reasoned, would I be allowed to roam the prison and hold my interviews without anyone listening in? Warning

myself not to fall prey to the paranoid thinking that takes hold readily among lifers, I wondered nevertheless if Cain himself had been
the source of the rumor. I'd heard that he had tried to do this once
before, to one of Polozola's court-appointed team. It was a way to
make sure all comments were positive.

The comments, now, were not. The grumblings I'd heard—from
the abolished band and from others I'd dismissed, early on, as too
self-interested or too driven by a prisoner's flailing rage—grew louder
and much more frequent. "Be fair," I emphasized after the suit.
"Don't think I need to hear something critical. Wouldn't you have
said the same things about Whitley? Wouldn't you have said the
same things about Maggio?"

"Maggio was the Gestapo," one older inmate answered. "But he
had a prison to clean up. And Whitley? No, Whitley had some kind
of caring. I'm not trying to yeast things up, this complaining. I'm
telling you, when it comes to positive morale around Angola, Cain is
going to take whatever there is."

The changes Cain had actually brought to the prison, I learned,
were represented by his expansion of Angola's shoe-shining detail.
Shoe shiner had always been a semi-official inmate job at the penitentiary. But the bootblacks, provided for staff only, had been spread
thin. So Cain had told his classification officers that he wanted more
appointed. It wasn't necessarily hard to find volunteers. The job gave
the inmate an opportunity to joke and beg for a few cigarettes, or a
Coke, from the guard whose shoes he was polishing. And tradition
had it that the guard would sometimes humor the convict by paying
him in this way. I had assumed that the bootblacks had always been
prevalent. But only under Cain had the work become a thriving program. At any hour, at one of the gateposts along the Main Walk, you
might see a sergeant chatting with one of his colleagues, an inmate
with rag and polish crouched at his feet.

Or perhaps Cain's style of leadership—and his approach to the

humanity of the inmates—was best captured in his dealings with the
Angolite. The bimonthly magazine called itself the country's only
uncensored prison publication, and while this had always been
stretching the point (for the editors were kept by the men they might
criticize), it had, since the seventies, been instructed to include any
information it judged true. The result had been a number of national
awards and a place as a symbol of transformation.

Wilbert Rideau, the editor in chief, had arrived at Angola in
1962 with a ninth-grade education and a death sentence for murdering a bank teller. He had educated himself while on death row,
had begun working on the *Angolite* after capital punishment was
temporarily ruled unconstitutional in 1972, and had spent the last
quarter-century making a prominent contribution to journalism. In
addition to winning the George Polk Award and a National Magazine Award nomination, he had edited a collection of Angola writing
published by Times Books, and had narrated segments on the prison
for National Public Radio.

But Warden Cain did not hold Rideau's or the magazine's
accomplishment in much esteem. During the spring of my year
there, he shut off the phone line the writers had always used to
gather information from outside the prison. He prohibited the staff
from earning money by writing articles for outside publications, a
privilege the inmate journalists had always been granted. Given
Cain's many business dealings and his interaction with me, it made
good sense that he remind the staff who was in charge and whose
virtue they should never question. But he had difficulty with more
than the chance of critical reporting. He had trouble with the stature
of Rideau himself, with the way he was treated, by some, as a fully
rehabilitated citizen, someone worthy of respect and even honor.
That spring, Rideau got word of a decision Cain had made back in
January, when the Louisiana Bar Association had notified the warden that it was giving its Excellence in Legal Journalism prize to a

film on the death penalty Rideau had written. It would have been accepted procedure to let Rideau attend the awards dinner. (A previous warden had sent him with an escort to be honored at two press conventions in Washington, D.C.) Cain told Rideau nothing about the prize, sent his first deputy to the banquet, and kept the plaque in his office.

Yet what should I make of the contact visits and literacy classes the warden had instituted on death row? Or of Cain in the death chamber, holding the condemned man's hand and telling him the angels were coming? As I thought obsessively of the figure who dominated my life, the man who, though he avoided me through the summer, floated tauntingly before me like an image with one slender yet crucial fragment missing, I sometimes saw that he might possess a grand element of mercy. And then I would imagine him more clearly as he held the convict's hand and signaled for the lethal injection: Cain at the apogee, manifest as Lord, killing and forgiving and resurrecting in the same instant.

The final fragment wouldn't materialize until October. Then, at the rodeo, the figure became whole.

Meanwhile, I reckoned with the fact that Cain's emphasis on religion did help bring people—maybe only a few, maybe many more—a little bit closer to a life of peace.

Chaplain Holloway was assigned to Camp J. (Cain had hired extra ministers and put one at every camp.) Wearing a knit shirt with a pattern of tiny golfers, Holloway pushed a grocery cart full of inspirational literature. A grocery cart. Just like in the A&P. Just like the homeless on the street. This one had red chipping paint. He pushed it up the Walk at J, yelled out "Gate!" and waited for the guard to let him onto the dim tier. He pushed it past the cells, past the men who sometimes tried to pee on him through the bars, past the inmate who liked to flex in his own feces. "What's up, bro?" the chaplain asked at each set of bars. "What can I get for you, bro?" Built thick, a football player in college, he was a white hipster in a golfing shirt in the middle of the Inferno. I don't know what he was, but he was tireless. And kind.

"How'd you end up back on One, bro?" he asked an emaciated man, referring to the worst of J's levels, where you were let out of your cell—into a solitary dogrun—only two hours each week.

"I just told hello to a nurse on hospital call and told her she looked beautiful this morning."

"Well, you know, babe," the chaplain said, understanding what had probably happened, that the man had told her hello and started jerking off, "next time just say hi and skip the rest of the verbology."

He asked the man if he wanted to pray. They held hands and, leaning together, their foreheads almost touched. "In nine months you could be out of here, back in population," he encouraged afterward.

"All right."

"You want some reading?"

"All right."

He slipped through the bars a paperback of big-print advice and biblical quotations called *You Were Born a Champion, Don't Die a Loser.* They held hands once more, and the chaplain moved on to the next convict. This was his day, this was his life, cell after cell after cell.

I reckoned, too, with programs of Cain's that complemented the new opportunities in shoe shining. Before Cain, car washing had been enjoyed by staff informally, the way Johnny Brooks washed the trucks of the freemen on the range crew. It was Cain, I learned, who had created the official operation—covered carport; maroon and yellow sign reading ANGOLA CAR WASH—positioned beside the front gate. There he stationed two or three convicts full-time with a hose and buckets. (He appointed a car washer for himself as well, at the Ranch House.) Staff could tell the inmates exactly how they wanted their vehicles cleaned and waxed, and could expect the service to match their desires. Again, cigarettes were paid, so the car wash was, to some, a treasured assignment. The warden had no trouble locating convicts who would buff hoods and wipe headlights energetically.

But Cain's greatest flourish may have been the reintroduction of mule- and horse-drawn wagons to the vast farming operation of Angola for the first time since the 1950s. The long wooden carts joined and partly replaced tractors and trucks in transporting the peppers and corn and squash picked by the line crews. From late spring through the fall of my year, when I stared out across the cropland into the heat haze, I saw the ramshackle wagons inching up the rows, driven by inmates perched high in the sun.

"He likes it to look like slavery times," the inmates observed.

And so, that summer, the miraculous father figure, the improbable savior, was long gone from my vision. I could focus only on what was possible in a world where nothing wonderful was promised. On their own, what goals could the convicts cling to? What meaning could they build into their lives? How far could they rise?

E L E V E N

JOHNNY BROOKS HAD ASKED, DURING THE SPRING, to be transferred from the range crew to the car wash. The shorter hours allowed him time to run and work out, to devote himself to taking the all-around in this year's rodeo. In July I watched him on a rickety weight machine behind Camp F. His thigh muscles erupted as he straightened his legs. He'd always been the strongest of the riders, but last October he'd been slack in his training, hadn't capitalized on his edge. When he thought back to that failure, he felt it "right here, right here," he said, fist on his chest. His failure still hollowed it.

This time he was going to give those bulls everything he had. He was going to give an all-around and a bull-riding buckle to Belva's sons, who would be, officially, *his* sons by then. And he was going to give Belva what she'd only glimpsed in his five-second near-miss ride on last year's final Sunday, what had made her start to fall in love, what had made her write, in her first letter, that she couldn't believe how well he rode.

The quad machine rattled with his fifteenth rep. I tried not to stare at the jagged pronouncement of his muscles. The workout area was a concrete slab surrounded by mud. Nearby, beside the ancient, broken trunk of a fallen oak, a gospel quartet rehearsed its harmony:

Fix it, Jesus
Fix it like you said you would....

Standing and setting a barbell across his shoulders, Brooks told me
that if he got out of Angola he would try to compete on the pro circuit, no matter how old he was. "They going to look twice," he imi-
tated the double take of the rodeo world, "and say, 'Where'd this
nigger come from?'"

Brooks had been sentenced to the electric chair in 1975. That was
before Louisiana had devised a death penalty statute acceptable to
the United States Supreme Court. So he had wound up serving life
for a murder, he claimed to me, he did not commit.

I had been to the parish court clerk and read the "Statement of
Facts" signed by the judge after the trial:

> At about 11:00 A.M. on Saturday, September 21, 1974,
> Jimmy Boston left the small grocery store operated by his
> wife in the rural community of Gray, Louisiana. He was
> delivering some groceries to his sister who lived a short dis-
> tance away. While at his sister's residence, Jimmy engaged in
> a conversation with some other men about hunting dogs
> which delayed his return to the store until about 11:50 A.M.
>
> Initially upon reentering the store, Mr. Boston was unable
> to locate his wife. He walked around until he was in a posi-
> tion to see behind a four-foot-high counter. It was then that
> he saw his brutally beaten and bloodied wife lying on the
> floor.... The cash register was open and all that remained in
> it was two pennies.
>
> Shortly after the arrival of the Sheriff's Office personnel,
> Dr. Sidney Warren, Assistant Coroner, pronounced Mrs.

Genii Caraleta Boston dead. Later that same afternoon an autopsy was performed by Dr. Warren. A massive depressed fracture of the left side of the skull was determined to be the principal cause of death. There was other trauma present about the head and on the arms of the victim indicating that she had suffered multiple heavy blows with a blunt instrument.

The document went on to say that Brooks, eighteen at the time, had been dropped off near the store at about 11:15, and that, around noon, he had given an acquaintance a dollar bill showing traces of blood. This led the police to search Brooks's grandfather's house, where Brooks lived. They found bloodstained jeans and shoes and, in an overgrown lot behind the home, a blood-splattered shirt. The blood was type O, the same as Mrs. Boston's.

"No suh, I didn't do it," Johnny Brooks told me, at the car wash beside the front gate. "I just found the body." This, he said, was how the blood had streaked his clothes, and I did not have the heart to interrogate him. His flimsy denials, which I'd heard whenever I'd asked about the crime, made me quick to change the subject, partly because I would never know the truth for certain, but mostly because I felt I knew the truth already and wanted more from Johnny Brooks, at forty-one, than an eighteen-year-old's desperate defense.

Yet he was no less desperate now. After twenty-three years he still hoped the appeals court might overturn his conviction on grounds he could not explain. "I got an inmate counsel working on my case. I paid him some cigarettes and he's working on it," he said. "They got me bad." Around Angola, that was the expression for false charges. And that was about as explanatory as Johnny Brooks could get.

■

He wore a white straw cowboy hat while waiting for cars. When they pulled up, he set the hat delicately on his chair, tugged on rubber wading boots over his cowboy boots, and transformed from dapper rancher (dapper as could be, anyway, on his budget) to ready servant. The staff brought him cleaning fluids and leather revitalizers and hubcap polishes, and he heeded their instructions—"Yassuh," "All right, suh," "Oh, yassuh"—and went to work. He lavished their truck beds with soap, and cleaned and dried their windshields repeatedly to avoid streaking. He polished their fenders the way a butler would a set of silver, rubbing at every spot.

The job brought him tips, packs of cigarettes, from the employees. And it put him in contact with an array of administrators and ranking officers, people who might somehow, he could believe, help him win a commutation if he ever came before the pardon board. People who, he told me, cared for him.

"You know I got my wedding coming up now, Mr. Darrell," he said as, running out of rags, he used newspaper to blot Mr. Darrell's hubcaps. He stooped over and rubbed so hard, to prevent water marks, that he was out of breath.

The assistant warden, Mr. Mike's brother, a small, smiling leprechaun of a man who truly did seem as nice as Brooks thought, stood to the side. He waited for his truck to be finished and joked, "How you know she's showing up?"

"She better."

"You better put her in lock-down, from what I hear. Get her a cell till that date rolls around."

"Aw, Mr. Darrell." Brooks grinned but looked faintly worried: he was an inmate, she part of the free world; there was no telling what Mr. Darrell knew.

"How many dates has she missed for y'all to get your approval from the chaplain?"

"Her friend's car broke down."

"That's one."

"She works, Mr. Darrell. And she got four kids."

"Johnny Brooks. Family man!"

"Yassuh. You coming to the wedding, ain't you?"

"You let me know the date."

"September the fifth."

"You let me know *after* she makes it up here for that chaplain's approval."

"We already have the preacher. Mr. Rick LeDoux, Cowboys for Christ Ministry. He already set off that day."

"That'll make two of you waiting on her."

"Aw, Mr. Darrell."

"Johnny Brooks, *in* love!"

"Yes, I am. Yes, I am."

"Lost his heart."

"Ain't lost it."

"All right, Johnny." Mr. Darrell climbed into his truck.

"September the fifth. You can put that down."

The assistant warden put his truck into drive. "Only one Johnny Brooks!" he called out the window.

Late as the day had gone on the range crew, and demeaning as his relationship had been with Mr. Mike, I thought Brooks must regret his change in jobs. I remembered him galloping across the fields one dank evening. His long green rain slicker had been black in the dusk and had shuddered in the wind and looked as though it might tear open and fly out behind him like a cape. I remembered what the newest inmate on the crew, a man nicknamed Gumby because of his likeness to the tall, skinny, bendable children's toy, had told me with Brooks standing there: "One day I hope to be as good a cowboy as Johnny Brooks." And I recalled something that had happened the afternoon we went out tagging and castrating, the afternoon that ended with his playful whipping at the hands of Mr. Mike.

When Brooks flung his rope and leapt from his horse and sprinted toward a calf, the mother's instinct was to attack, sometimes viciously, sometimes in such anxiety and outrage she frothed at the mouth, and Mr. Mike and a convict named Bear had to keep Brooks safe. They positioned their horses like a wall; they shifted with the cow and urged Brooks to hurry; they never left him exposed. Mr. Mike was highly skilled in directing this interference. In a sense, to watch their three-man team at work was to see Mr. Mike saving Brooks's life, perpetually. That was touching enough. But that day they came across the rare mother with no protective inclinations. During the tagging she wandered off, hundreds of yards away, and when Brooks released the black calf it was lost.

"Maahh. Baahh," Mr. Mike called out, mimicking a calf's sound, trying to draw the mother back, for the calf seemed used to being abandoned and gave no cry of its own.

"Baahh," Brooks called.

"Maahh. Baahh," Bear, a giant of at least 275 pounds, gave out.

"Maahh. Baahh. Baahh," all three men tried together.

Meanwhile the calf, bewildered, had trotted away and slipped under some barbed wire into a separate field. Now the mother couldn't reach it, no matter how possessive she suddenly became.

"Go on out there and get him, Johnny. Put him in your saddle and take him to his mama."

So Brooks ducked through the barbed wire, roped the stray and passive calf from the ground, tied its legs, cradled it under his arm, and carried it back through the fence. Then he mounted his horse and, with the baby resting peacefully across the saddle, started slowly toward a gully where the herd had congregated.

"Maahh. Baahh," he lured. "Maahh." And at last he caught the mother's attention. Fifty yards away, to be sure he wouldn't be trampled, he swung himself down with the calf.

"Get on," he told it. "Get on."

And finally spotting its mother, the calf scooted forward. The mother didn't approach, only waited, as though nothing had gone wrong in the first place. Reunited, they ambled off. For the time being, anyway, Brooks had made their little family whole.

But he had no desire to reclaim his old position on the range crew. Besides paying for his legal work, the cigarettes he earned at the car wash allowed him to commission the belts and pocketbooks he had promised to send Belva's children. And recently, in the visiting shed, Belva had seen another convict give his girlfriend a wooden clock with a heart-shaped picture frame beside the face.

"Ooo, that's nice," Belva had said.

"You like that?"

"It's pretty." Her voice, even in this openness of want, stayed soft.

"You want a clock like that? All you had to do was say so. I can get you a clock like that. You just give me a few weeks, baby. I'll get you one no problem."

So he and a woodworker named Broomfield went through the patterns stacked under the workbench in the Camp F hobby shop. Around them, men began oil paintings by grid—they transferred and enlarged lakefront scenes or smiling clowns from art books onto their canvases. Others hammered patterns into belt buckles, and one inmate produced Chicago Bulls visors in leather, the lettering tooled in elaborate script. (The visor artist had perfected his handwriting on the cellblocks. Without access to a typewriter, he'd drafted a writ by hand, in painstaking letters that replicated typeface. He'd believed the appearance of type would help him in the court of appeals.) Some of these crafts would be sold at the rodeo; some, through relatives, in shops in the convicts' hometowns. Most would be mailed to family, an effort to be remembered.

Brooks found the pattern, and over the coming weeks Broomfield went to work with the hobby shop's jigsaw. Three days after sending the bedside clock, with their most recent visiting-shed Polaroid in the heart-shaped frame, Brooks waited for one of the dorm phones. He punched in his D.O.C. number and followed the computerized instructions, recording his name so that Belva would pick up and hear: "You have a collect call from"—pause—"Johnny"—pause—"at the Louisiana State Penitentiary. If you will pay, dial 3 now."

She hit 3. How sweet the sound of that touch-tone note!

"It's lovely, Johnny," she said.

"It's so the time passes for you. Just think about me and you."

"It's passing too slow."

"But listen here. Why didn't you make it up here last week? You said you was. Chaplain Comeaux said come find him and all. For our meeting."

With his forehead pressed against the cinder block and the noise of the nearest fan screening him in, he forgot everything in the dorm behind him as he listened for her answer, praying that if she had no explanation she would invent one, and dreading, in the instant before she spoke, that when she'd said "It's passing too slow" she'd meant something much more than the time between visits or the time before the wedding, that she'd reconsidered the years and years in front of them.

"I had to work a double shift."

"You tired?" He accepted the reason instantly, asking this question that made no sense—the double shift had been days ago.

"I'm worn down."

"You need to move to Baton Rouge, like I told you. Cut down on your ride."

"Then who would I ride up with?"

"You need to get you a car."

"And how am I doing that?"

"I don't know," he said, then added gallantly, "but I can get you a job. You can just let me handle that part. I'm about to talk to Gerry Lane. Next time he come through that gate. I'll be looking out for him. I'll wave him down. He'll get you a job right there in Baton Rouge."

"I'll think about it, Johnny."

"This call," came the periodic warning, "is from an inmate at a correctional facility."

"Think about it? I'm talking about Mr. Gerry Lane, Gerry Lane Chevrolet. Gerry Lane Enterprises. He's going to find you something. He liked how good I took care of Little Man. He's gonna do it. He's the one brought us those Chevrolet sweat shirts out on the range crew last Christmas."

"I'll be up to see you Tuesday."

"I'll handle getting you that job. You remember those sweat shirts I showed you? They was nice."

"I can ride up with Sandra on Tuesday."

"I'll tell Chaplain Comeaux."

"All right."

Hanging up when the fifteen minutes ran out (she, like so many at the other end of the inmates' calls, could barely afford this, let alone another fifteen; within weeks her phone would be shut off for overdue bills)—hanging up, he wished she'd sounded more certain. He wished she'd said yes about moving to Baton Rouge. He wished she'd said yes about that job. And that she hadn't already missed those two visits.

But she was the one paying for the rings, he reminded himself. She was already wearing hers. At least, she was the last time he'd seen her. She had been, hadn't she? Right there on her third finger. Hadn't he seen it when she put her hand down on the table in the visiting shed, put her hand down for him to hold? Hadn't he slipped it on his own pinky for a minute, the way he always did? Hadn't he?

He could still feel where it always pinched at his knuckle, where he always forced it down a little harder, twisting it, to remember the sensation. He could still feel that from last time, not the visit before, couldn't he?

She must have been wearing it. She had to be serious. She couldn't be backing out. If she was, she wouldn't have sounded so excited about that clock. If she was, she wouldn't have said, "It's passing too slow." She must have meant only about the time between now and September. She couldn't have meant anything else. She couldn't have, because they'd already talked about the years he might stay here. He'd already told her about that, been up front about that, told her it was no-parole and that he'd been denied the last time he'd applied for pardon. She'd known that all along. She'd known since their first visit.

She wouldn't back out now. She was a strong lady. She was going to fight with him. After that judge gave him the death sentence he'd said to himself, I'm going to give it right back. That's what he'd said. And he had, hadn't he? Well, he was about to do the same thing now. Give back these alphabets. Get some numbers. Or get the whole charge thrown out. That's what would happen, most likely. Pretty soon, he'd have it going in the courts. Pretty soon, he'd be working for Gerry Lane himself, raising Belva's kids like a regular father, straightening out her daughter and making sure the rest of them stayed on the right road. Pretty soon, he'd have a son of his own. Pretty soon he'd be lying in bed next to Belva with all their letters piled up between them, all their letters from when he was in Angola, to read over how they got started.

They would be a family. They were already. He hadn't met the two daughters, but the two boys had been to visit once, when there had been room in Sandra's car. He played Pac-Man with the boys. The four-year-old, Marcus, was crazy for it. He kept going back to Belva, saying, "Mama, give me some more money to put in there again." Brooks propped him on a chair so he could see the screen. Brooks stood behind him, bending down and holding him around the waist. The little Pac-Man munchers snapped their jaws, and Brooks urged, "Gobble 'em, son, gobble 'em, move that stick," and Marcus squealed, "Coon ass things! Coon ass things!" He seemed to think the Pac-Man prey were Cajun rednecks.

"Coon ass things?" Brooks laughed.

And Marcus saw that it was funny. "Coon ass things! Coon ass things!" He cracked himself up, and Brooks put his check next to Marcus's jittery, giggling head.

The boys had sent Brooks a Father's Day card, and after his phone call with Belva he took the card from his box, along with her letters. He lay back on his cot, head turned to the side so he could read with the ceiling light. Two bear cubs were pictured on the front of the card. Each read a newspaper, one called *Modern Grizzly* and the other *The Daily Growl*. Below this scene, the poem began:

No one chooses a Dad
From a magazine ad
Or a paper with classifieds in it....

But if we'd had the chance
For a choice in advance
You're the Dad we'd have picked in a minute.

Tight to the top of the inside page, the thirteen-year-old, Kenny, had drawn a smiley face and written, "You are the father we did not have."

Staring at the card reminded Brooks of another call he'd made to Belva's house. He'd dialed the number, and heard Marcus's faint hello. Then came the automated operator: "You have a collect call from"—pause—"Johnny"—pause—"at the Louisiana State Penitentiary.

If you will pay, dial 3 now." Marcus had no idea what to do. "Dad?" he said.

"Push 3, son," Brooks almost yelled, but remembered that the boy couldn't hear him; only at the inmate's end did everything come through. "Go get your mama," he said quietly, uselessly.

"If you will pay for the call, dial 3 now."

"Dad?" Marcus started hitting buttons. "Dad?"

"If you will pay..."

"Dad? Dad? Dad?"

In his dorm, with the 64 cots and 128 locker boxes behind him, Brooks held tight to the receiver and wished the boy would go on saying it forever. But the call was cut off.

T W E L V E

"WHEN I GOT LOCKED UP," BUCKKEY SAID, LAST year's runner-up buckle still in the box where his wife kept it for his son, in case he might decide he wanted it, "Chris was a little baby. And I thought that I didn't have to *gain* his respect or his love or his like, because I felt as though he didn't understand that anyway. You catch what I'm saying? So my main concern was holding on to my wife. And by doing that, I—I didn't *avoid* Chris, I just didn't pay as much attention to him as I should have. I guess the best way for me to explain what I thought was, If I keep the mother, I keep the child. That's what I felt. Because I was a kid too when I got locked up. I really didn't know any better. I was raised here. At Angola. All the things that I learned about my wife, I learned here. I never learned anything about Chris. I don't know Chris. I don't know what Chris likes, I don't know what he does. And that's my fault."

One July morning Buckkey taught me about horse feeders. They have two compartments, a trough for oats below and a slot for hay above. Preferring the oats, the horse always empties the trough first, then mouths the hay in sloppy bunches. Plenty of straw falls to the stable floor.

Buckkey had come up with a solution to the littered hay, and that morning he built a feeder of his own design. On the range crew, he spent much of his time as a welder, constructing trailer hitches or fencing in an open-sided shed at the crew's headquarters. Through the gnarled cypress trees he could see Lake Killarney and the narrow, white-railed fishing pier that stretched elegantly out onto the water. A transistor radio sat on a shelf amid his tools, set to a country station, volume low. When he shut off his torch to check his progress, the wispy, doleful music was the only sound. The other inmates on the crew, along with the bosses, were spread out over the farm.

He pulled down his welding mask and started again on the feeder, running the flame slowly along a joint, melting a perfect bond between the iron surfaces, a beading flawlessly even. He coaxed the bond partly by sight, mostly by habit and intuition. The darkened eye-protecting window in the mask distorted everything, made the flame small and far away and the metal almost invisible. Blindly, knowingly, he stroked with the slender jet of fire.

Hearing tires on the dirt road, he stopped, lifted his mask: Mr. Jimmy's D.O.C. pickup.

"Say, Buckkey, you got a visit."

"All right, boss."

While the convict stowed his equipment, Mr. Jimmy walked over from his truck. He had little in common with Mr. Mike. Mr. Jimmy took on the role of a reticent but kind father with his inmates, and in Buckkey's case he looked closely related as well. Mr. Jimmy's tan face had canyons for wrinkles above his blue eyes and dry rivulets below. Buckkey's leathery skin was collapsing the same way. At times he seemed to have aged five years during the months I'd known him. But at moments his hazel eyes still dominated his face with a child's need.

Mr. Jimmy inspected a feeder Buckkey had already finished. To me, its red iron seemed strangely animated, with the two arms that would hold the trough reaching outward in a shallow curve, and the spindles that formed the slot looking like giant teeth in a monster's mouth. It sat on the ground just outside the shed, solitary. It might have been a whimsical sculpture, the arms faintly supplicating, the face a child's rendering of some nightmarish creature, and the body without legs—the beast, if it ever moved at all, propelled itself only by wobbling.

The feeder would hang in one of the horse stalls.

"It's nice work," Mr. Jimmy said. If Buckkey's face hadn't been so worn, his boss would have looked like his grandfather instead of his father; Mr. Jimmy's silvery hair, when he took off his cowboy hat, picked up a scintillation in his eyes, the goodwill of a contented old man. "It's real nice."

"Yeah, hay's not going to fall all over the place, anyway," Buckkey said. "It's going to fall back in the trough. So after the oats get finished, the hay'll start filling up and—" Buckkey stopped himself. He twisted his lips to the side and rolled his eyes. "Pretty clever, huh? I'm a regular genius." He gave a grunt of self-mockery.

"It *is* smart. Can't think why no one's thought of this before."

"I've got a lot of time to think about feeders." Another grunt.

"We're gonna use 'em. Keep building 'em. We're gonna use 'em."

"Did I show you how the trough pops out?" Buckkey smiled. He knew he had. "So you can clean it? And so the whole thing's lighter?"

"Yeah, you showed me."

"Go ahead, Mr. Jimmy. Pick it up. Make my day before I go on my visit."

Mr. Jimmy grasped the top bar of the feeder and hoisted the contraption off the ground.

"It's lighter, all right, Buckkey. You ought to patent the thing."

"Yeah. Whatever. We'll just make 'em the special Angola horse feeders. My way of saying thanks for room and board."

"Well, you done good."

Two years ago, when Buckkey had lost his job after being accused of stealing wood from one of the range-crew sheds, Mr. Jimmy had lobbied to have him returned to the crew. "You home?" Mr. Jimmy had asked when Buckkey was back welding, and Buckkey had answered, "I'm home."

"Thanks, Mr. Jimmy," he said now.

"Let's go on that visit."

His back to the road, Chris sat on a picnic table as Mr. Jimmy dropped Buckkey off at the trusty visiting park. Buckkey had figured it would be his wife, Emily, with maybe his mother or one of his sisters. He spotted the boy right away. He knew the back of his son's neck below his short blond hair. Even from a distance, that was all he had to see.

Not that there was anything special about the neck, or the hairline or blue T-shirt that framed those two inches of skin. It was, simply, Chris's. After months and months of waiting, the runner-up buckle had worked—or hadn't made a bit of difference. But Buckkey's only child was here.

The father saw nothing else. Not his wife, who sat on a picnic bench facing him as he walked up the slight hill. Not the other trusties with their families at the dozen little pavilions with their tables and green roofs set on concrete slabs. He saw nothing else and said nothing at all, didn't call his son's name and wished, in fact, that the seventeen-year-old boy would never turn around, that he, Buckkey, could, that he could return immediately to his job while his son returned home, that there would be no chance of things getting worse than they already were.

Their relationship scarcely existed. Over sixteen years Buckkey had stayed bound with his wife, his mother, the rest of his family. His youngest sister had used the wedding invitation he had designed.

But with his son he merely hoped for change, afraid, when they spoke on the phone, to say much more than "I love you," afraid even to say that, afraid that if he asked Chris about school or gave anything that sounded like advice the boy would go mute and hand the phone back to his mother. She had practically forced Chris to talk in the first place. The boy's life was lurching out of control, Buckkey felt, and he worried Chris would wind up living the way he himself had between the end of high school and Angola—no direction except wildness. "And if I hadn't come to Angola," he told me, "I'd be dead." Lately Chris had bought a used truck, been pulled over going 90 in a 50 zone. His mother had pleaded with Buckkey to say something, pleaded that she was losing control, already had none, that Chris needed his father's discipline in any way Buckkey could give it. Buckkey couldn't bring himself to intervene. He felt he couldn't fix anything, couldn't risk everything.

On the tabletop, with his feet on the bench, Chris sat hunched over and didn't turn fully until his father stood at his shoulder. The blond hair was Buckkey's, but the face was closer to his mother's— the openness across his forehead, the softness of his jaw. Buckkey noted the difference from himself: It brought the same surprise and relief every time.

"Hey, Chris."

"Hey, Dad," the boy mumbled. He stood.

"Damn!" Buckkey said.

"What?"

"I can't even reach up that far to hug you anymore." It was a way of requesting permission. Chris granted it in silence. So the father wrapped his arms around the boy's shoulders, slapped once, and let go.

"I see you're getting a lot of use out of that buckle I sent you," Buckkey tried to joke, for Chris was not wearing it.

"I'm not a cowboy."

"I'm not much of one, either. Your mother saw me out there. She can testify to that." He smiled at his wife.

"She can tell you to quit that rodeo before you get killed," Emily said. She looked, already, drained by Buckkey's efforts to talk with their son, futility sapping color from her own blue irises—deeper blue, Buckkey usually thought, than anyone's he knew.

"You want to play some basketball?" Chris asked.

"All right."

Buckkey did not want to: it was what they always did. They stepped down toward the road, toward the court. A little girl in overalls and a gold LSU cap flew past them, up past their picnic table, arms pumping and legs churning as the incline got steeper near the trees at the crest of the hill. Her father chased and caught her, lifted her into the air.

"You can't go up there, Denise," the father said.

"Yes, I can. I can because I want to."

"Come on and play down here with me." He tickled her.

"But why can't I?"

"There's adult things on that hill."

Buckkey couldn't look at his son. If he were Chris, he wouldn't come more than twice a year, either.

The court was a patch of dirt with a steel backboard. Two jagged, sun-baked clefts, channeled by rainwater, ran outward at angles from the pole. Buckkey and Chris's one-on-one game was constricted by those gullies—trying to dribble over them usually meant losing the ball. Chris backed his way straight to the basket. In past years it had been his father who did this, Buckkey letting go of all restraint, all hesitance during their games, his wish for Chris's love turning inside out. He'd muscled the boy for rebounds, shouldered him aside for lay-ups. When Chris, trying to free himself for a jump shot, had dribbled off a rift and out of bounds, there had been no second chances.

If the boy managed to keep the score close Buckkey started blocking shots, stealing the ball, forcing him toward the clefts, to remind him who was stronger, in control, a father, to remind him he had no chance of winning.

Taller now, heavier, Chris leaned in. Buckkey set his legs, but the boy bent his father backward. Two-one, seven-four, eleven-seven, fourteen-eight, Chris pushed his lead wider, pried the game open as though with a wedge. Both players sweating through their shirts, they spoke only to mutter the score.

"Lasseigne!" The guard's yell saved them.

The food truck was here. On the road leading to Angola, Chris and his mother had stopped to order groceries at the store behind the gas station. There was a system, determined by the prison, for the park visitors. They turned in their lists at the register, were allowed to touch nothing themselves.

"I'll do the barbecue," Chris said.

Buckkey, picking up the sack of charcoal, glanced at him sidelong—the offer was a first. *You will?* he almost teased, but caught himself. "All right. That would be good."

Emily, loose blue turtleneck doing what it could to help her depleted eyes, short hair working to lighten her face, started on dessert. It had to be constructed at the park, from prepackaged and sealed ingredients, so no one could slip contraband into the filling of a pie. Emily sliced horizontally, twice, across a pound cake, then spread vanilla pudding and cream cheese on each layer. She fit the cake back together, dabbing the excess from the sides, scalloping white icing on top with the back of a spoon.

She had been eighteen when she married Buckkey. She had seen him for the first time water-skiing on the canal that ran behind his town, the town next to hers. He could ski on his hands, on his knees, on his butt with his legs in the air. Back on his feet he spun and swooped so his elbow almost scraped the water, and then he tipped the other way, rooster tail of spray as perfect as something painted before he righted himself and spun and spun and spun.

She couldn't ski at all, and months later, when he showed up at her job to ask for a date, she remembered him. She told him to call her at home that Friday night at six, that they would leave at seven. He forgot to call. "Oh, I'm ready anyway," she said when he appeared at the door, and he told her, "You know, you're just like a little paper doll—you just throw something on and you're ready to go." That had become her name between them, Paper Doll. It still was. Never Emily. Only Paper Doll.

It was the late seventies; he took her to a disco. "He was a good-looking guy and he could dance," she recalled, her voice as resigned as his wrinkles. On the floor he held both her hands, crossed them and turned her and pulled her toward him. Then he lifted her arm, guiding her away, guiding so she began to spin. She just kept going.

And found herself two years later with a drug-abusing husband and an infant boy and soon a barrage of headlines: SHERIFF'S OFFICE INVESTIGATING MAN'S DEATH...MURDER TRIAL SLATED...DEFEN-DANT TESTIFIES COMPANION KILLED STATION ATTENDANT...HEN-DERSON MAN GETS LIFE IN PRISON.

> Carey Lasseigne, 22, of Henderson was convicted here Thursday and the jury recommended life imprisonment for the first-degree murder of an 18-year-old service station attendant....
>
> Lasseigne took the stand Wednesday and claimed that it was a companion who shot Russell Landry, who worked at the Hungry Hobo restaurant and service station....
>
> Before he testified, the jury viewed a videotaped re-enactment of the crime....Lasseigne demonstrated in the videotape...how the victim was led behind the station where he was forced to kneel before he was shot from behind....

The jury Wednesday also heard Lasseigne's voice-recorded confession to the slaying....In both recordings, Lasseigne said he put gas in the car and then used the butt of a .22 caliber pistol to unsuccessfully try and knock Landry unconscious. He then showed how money was taken from the cash register and Landry was led behind the station...."He kept saying, 'Don't shoot me. Don't shoot me,'" Lasseigne was heard saying in the voice recording...."He just turned his head down and I shot him....He just kind of groaned, and... I shot him again. I don't even know why I shot him the first time. I just did it."...

The defendant testified that he confessed to the killing because he feared that his wife would not be willing to accept him again....

He was separated from his wife the month after the killing, and they have since divorced.

But they had been back together since his first year at Angola. When she and I had spoken about the crime, she was quiet about the innocence he still maintained, saying only, "I couldn't just leave him alone there" and "The Buckkey you know now is the real one." She recalled his crying over a dog they'd had to give up because the owner of the first house they rented wouldn't allow pets. His mother, a red-haired woman sitting with us that afternoon at the gas station restaurant they'd chosen, told me, "He didn't commit that murder. It's still like a dream. I'll never believe it."

Paper Doll let that go. "I'll always love him," she said.

"What kind of job you think I should get when I graduate?" Chris asked abruptly, forking the chicken on the barbecue pit. He prodded and flipped the pieces far too often.

"I don't know." Buckkey kept himself quiet, made himself wait. "I know your mother told you that I *suggested* you join an Armed Force."

"Yeah. But I can't leave Mom, can I?"

Buckkey absorbed the blow. The breeze had shifted; smoke billowed into his face. He didn't move, just let the cloud sting his eyes. "Well, what do *you* think?" he asked.

"I might want to—"

"You know," Buckkey cut in, edging away from the smoke, "if you did join you get to travel. You get to go all over the world. They put you through school and—"

"Be all you can be."

"Well, sometimes the ads say it best."

"I got enough school."

A year after his own graduation, Buckkey had signed up for the Air Force. He'd told me with his typical mix of self-deprecation and pride that he'd passed the test to get in, then another after boot camp to qualify for air traffic control training. He'd left with a dishonorable discharge when marijuana was found in his locker.

"I might want to learn to weld, though," Chris said. "I might want to go to trade school for that."

"Really?" It was not good news.

"I might want to."

"Give me that for a second." Buckkey took the fork, took over with the chicken. It gave him something to keep himself in check. Because all he knew about welding he'd learned in Angola, and the thought of his son in a welder's mask made him feel Chris's life would be crushed. "There's a lot more money you could make with an education."

"I told you I'm not—"

"And a lot easier and a lot cleaner jobs."

"I'm not—"

"It's just nothing. That's all welding is. Nothing. Over and over, back and forth with that little torch. Over and over and over, nothing, your whole life. Can you handle that?"

"I want to build things."

It made Buckkey stop. He heard his son describe watching some work done at his uncle's body and fender shop. It made Buckkey remember the feeling of joining surfaces together, of gliding the flame, of keeping his hand steady, knowing just which hydrogen rod to use for just which thickness of metal, leaving a uniform bead and a connection that could take any pressure. It made him think of the feeders he had invented.

"Well, I guess you know already it's not the best-paying job in the world," he said, as they sat down to eat.

"I just feel like it could be a good trade."

"It could be. You're right, Chris. It could be. As long as it's what you want."

"It might be."

" 'Cause you don't want to burn your life on something you don't want."

"I know."

" 'Cause your life would be burnt."

"That's why I might want to weld."

"Well, that's the right reason." Buckkey went on battling his own uneasiness, his own hope that Chris would enter the military, earn a degree, and leave the Navy or Army or Air Force in a way entirely different from Buckkey's exit. "You do something 'cause you enjoy it."

"That's what I've been thinking."

"All right."

"That's just what I've been thinking," Chris said.

It was, Buckkey knew as the pudding and cream cheese pie disappeared, and as the guard walked by to give Paper Doll and all the other visitors their passes to turn in at the gate, the best talk he could remember having with his son. They scraped the chicken bones into one of the blue barrels, fifty-gallon plastic drums that had held the prison's cleaning fluid. As they turned back toward the table Buckkey reached up and clung on. It didn't matter that Chris was taller. It didn't matter that he was heavier and stronger. Like a basketball center with arms that long, Buckkey wrapped him in, loosened his hold only slightly to kiss the boy on the side of his neck, then clutched again. Chris couldn't have gotten free had he tried. "Please," Buckkey groaned into the boy's neck. "Please. Please. Please. Please. Please."

"All right, Dad. It's all right." The boy's voice was half comforting, half crazed by his father's vise. Buckkey released him. Chris looked around for the basketball, found it on the grass, started shooting. Mr. Jimmy drove up before the bus arrived that would take the visitors to the gate.

"Take your time," he yelled.

Buckkey apologized to Paper Doll for not spending more of the day with her.

"I'm glad you didn't. That's how it was supposed to be. You know what he says now? 'I been visiting him for sixteen years. It's time *he* come.'"

Buckkey climbed into the cab of his boss's pickup. His arm dangling out the window, he lifted his hand almost casually toward his son. Then he leaned out, not only his head but his shoulders, like a dog, mouthing *Come back* silently as though to make it a subtle and pressureless message. Chris answered with a brief wave from the basketball court.

"You all right, Buck?" Mr. Jimmy asked as they drove beneath the great bank of sweet gum and oak trees at the edge of the prison and turned toward Camp F.

"Yeah. I'm all right."

THIRTEEN

SETTING OUT TO BE SAVED AFTER LAST YEAR'S rodeo, Terry Hawkins had believed that his new involvement with Rev and Sister Jackie, and with his Bible, would help him "stay out of wrong and make everything happen better for me."

He would rise from big-stripe to trusty, from fry cook to a job with the range crew. He would ride a horse that would be his own, learn to rope, meet Mr. Gerry Lane. With the promotion, he would be moved from his dorm at Camp D to one at F, where the compound had no barred gate and the men just wandered out their front door, strolled across the road, sat alone under the pecan trees on the banks of a pond. Terry had heard a family of ducks was living there. He had heard you could fish. He had heard it was a whole lot nicer. And the promotion and move had been sure to be given. Besides his commitment to religion, he had the guarantee of what he'd done at the rodeo, body catapulted and crumpled yet hand seizing the chip in the Guts & Glory—in front of Mr. Mike Vannoy and his brother, Darrell, and in front of Warden Cain.

But his effort at salvation had fallen apart. Since the day after his blowjob in the shower, he hadn't been back to Sister Jackie's church. It had been six months. And no assignment to the range crew or spot at Camp F had come his way.

Instead, by July, Terry lived in a dorm on the west side of Main Prison, the Wild Side. The dorms of the main complex bore the names of trees—the softer woods, Ash and Magnolia and Spruce, to the east, and the harder, Oak and Hickory and Walnut, at the other end. The west held younger, tougher inmates, men who hadn't yet hit bottom and had enough of J and begun to navigate some new approach to existing in prison. It held, too, older convicts who'd fallen back and been sent there, to begin working their way up again, after serving their terms in the punishment cells. In this, his twelfth year at Angola, Terry found himself living in Walnut.

There, at two A.M. one night, Terry woke to see a man sliding a pair of sneakers from beneath another's cot. While the second inmate slept under the soft blue of the security lights, the man pulled the high-tops onto his feet, laced them snugly, tied them, and, fully dressed now, walked up the aisle to his own bed. He removed the padlock from his box. Holding it, he returned to the sleeping inmate, knelt on top of him, and pinned his head to the pillow with one hand. Terry guessed he was about to deal out a whipping with the padlock, then saw he carried a razor in addition. Earlier in the day, Terry had overheard him complaining, in a high-pitched, half-whiny voice, about an unpaid debt, whether for drugs or gambling or the prostitution of his punk wasn't clear. Now he carved with the razor. He sliced deep from temple to jaw. *Then* he dealt out the lock-whipping. And *then* the guard's backup arrived.

Terry's route from Camp D to the Wild Side had begun one May afternoon when a shakedown team, in its military fatigues, had poured through D. The guards strip-searched the inmates, told them to dress, and sent them out onto the Yard while they tore through every box and turned over every garbage can. At a fence dividing the camp into sections, Terry watched a basketball game played on the other side. The shakedown team finished with the dorms and fanned out over the Yard. A sergeant, approaching the fence, saw Terry throw something—quickly—a few feet away into the grass. Terry insisted, to the sergeant and later to me, that it was a cigarette. With the sergeant, he pointed to a butt on the ground. The officer peered not far from that spot, bent down, and showed Terry a roach.

Right away, the lieutenant in charge of the search offered him a deal. For tips on stashes of drugs and weapons, the nub of marijuana would be forgotten.

"I don't know nothing about any of that," Terry said, abiding by the old code, though it was not so well abided or universally enforced anymore at Angola. The older convicts all said that with the safety that had come in the 1970s, the snitches had begun to proliferate. They didn't even have to ask to live in the protection dorms.

"I couldn't tell you about none of that," Terry insisted.

"Pack your toothbrush," the lieutenant said.

Angola's judicial system worked like this: The inmate was handed a white jumpsuit to change into; he was shackled and cuffed and taken to a cell; he was brought to trial within a week. The prison held hundreds of such trials every week, in out-of-the-way offices just big enough to fit a pair of gunmetal desks. The inmates, in the shackles and cuffs and the torn or half-buttonless jumpsuits and the slippers they'd been told to pack with their toothbrushes, lined up in a hallway. A guard called them in one at a time to stand before two judges, a senior officer from security and someone from classification. "Would you like the assistance of counsel?" they asked the defendant. They meant the inmate paralegal on duty that day, who stood sandwiched between wall and file cabinet, and who had won his job through recommendations from security and classification. Whether or not the defendant accepted, the hearing started right away and ended within two minutes. Charges were read; a rebuttal was put forth. "122173, Counsel Substitute Mark Hall, we ask you

to consider that those were prescription drugs the inmate had forgotten to take and was saving only because his prescription might
not be renewed. That, simply, is our defense." The paralegal tilted his
head at a mourner's angle as he spoke, though the reason seemed as
much shame that his client had provided him such a lame argument
as regret that his client was doomed.

After the paralegal's terse statement, or after the inmate himself
gave his account—"I didn't tell no guard no F-curse. I *explained* to the
man it was the other orderly's job, but I didn't tell him no F-curse.
Nah, I ain't about all that"—while gesturing despite the cuffs, which
were belted tight to his belly, so that his plaintive hands looked like
seal fins flapping from his stomach—immediately after the defense
fell mute, the senior officer told the two inmates, "Step outside." The
judges turned through the colored folder that held the defendant's
prior record at Angola, his "jacket." They conferred for thirty or
ninety seconds, called the accused and the paralegal back in, and
rendered a verdict grounded in past conduct, a necessity since the
present evidence consisted of a few sentences—or nonsentences—
scribbled on a pink slip by the arresting guard. But most of the
judges' assumptions were surely right. The same convicts appeared
in court again and again. Some shuffled in ten or fifteen times
a year.

Terry argued that he'd demanded a urine test from both the
sergeant and the lieutenant of the shakedown team, and that they
had refused. He requested a test again now, in court. The judges
replied that the charge was not for *smoking* marijuana but *possessing* it.
The test, they ruled immediately, would be irrelevant.

"Step outside."

Terry shuffled out.

His jacket showed more than fifty write-ups over his twelve
years. The violence seemed to have faded away—he hadn't blackened the eyes of any more guards—but he had a marijuana charge
only two years old.

And he'd told the same story then. He'd been denied a urine test that would have proven his innocence.

"Inmate!" one of the judges yelled, and the guard posted outside the door let Terry back in to receive his sentence.

So in May, he'd been put in the Camp D punishment cells. Double-bunked, the cells were about six feet across, eight feet deep, eight feet high. Between them, Terry and his cellmate weighed over four hundred pounds. Terry, the second to arrive, got the top bunk. The heat rose. He lay on his mattress, sweating, sheet "rain wet." Eventually he switched to the floor. His cellie allowed him the concrete. At Angola, the man with the bottom bunk always made this accommodation.

Other accommodations involved the toilet. You warned your cellmate when you had to squat; he sat on the floor with his face to the bars, closest to the corridor's air. And you kept flushing and flushing to cut down on the smell.

It was a working tier. Every morning, after sixteen hours of lockdown, the guard yelled, "Get it together! Work call! Get it straight!" and Terry lined up his rubber boots and shower slippers against the wall, dusted the bars of the cell to pass inspection, and pulled on his work boots. The guard opened the cells from the end of the tier; the locks released with a *thunk* and the bars slid back with a grinding and clanging like an old train getting started in a railway yard. Terry was grateful for the sounds, relieved to be marched to the camp gate, handed a hoe, marched a mile down the road, and ordered to hack at weeds in a drainage ditch. Work was better than the sixteen hours before and the sixteen hours after.

Through the early hours of the night on his top bunk, with the cracked concrete ceiling lowering close as the lid of a coffin to his face, he lived with his slaughterhouse boss, Mr. Denver Tarter. Terry had stood over him forever, it seemed now. So much returned to him so clearly, it was as if he had stared in order to memorize, not in disbelief. He saw the blood streaking parts of Mr. Denver Tarter's short, thinning brush of hair but not others. Focusing on the memory of the clean tufts, Terry could half convince himself for a second that the man had only passed out drunk, that nothing permanent had ever happened. Terry longed to bend and place his lips over the bloody, severed throat, to "blow air back inside him." That was what he longed to do *now*. But he couldn't forget what he had done then. Nothing. Just shaken his head finally at the monotone question running through his brain, *How did all of a sudden this happen?*—just shaken his head and walked away in a weird calm.

He stretched his hand toward the ceiling to assure himself it lay more than inches above him. There was no question of waking his cellmate to talk of what he heard and saw in his mind, though they got along well given the situation, played dominoes sometimes, even spoke of their children. Men at Angola just didn't talk of their crimes. Terry tried to think of anything—a pornographic picture that had once been his favorite; the Student of the Week certificate his daughter had sent months ago—to distract himself. He had flipped the ax to the sharp side and swung over and over and over and over.

He sat up off the drenched sheet and knelt facing the back of the cell, overlooking the steel sink and toilet. He shut his eyes. "Lord," he prayed, "Mr. Denver Tarter hunting me down tonight. I need you please to get him off my mind. He's on my conscience, Lord. Please do me this one thing, Lord. Please for tonight. Please put me sleep. Please take him off."

Terry told me he'd been put in the cell because he'd quit going to Sister Jackie's services. Whether he meant that God was punishing him for his absence with this false charge and unfair sentence, or that his lapse in worship had led to weakness, and to his getting high and getting caught, I was never sure. But I knew that his avoiding her Camp D church (because he was unforgivable) was a failure that, in itself, told him again how unforgivable he was.

Then, during the summer, he experienced a series of good turns—all because of the rodeo. First, an officer in charge of the field lines expressed dismay at the sight of Terry, with the others from his cellblock, swinging a hoe.

"Hey, crazy man," he yelled, stopping his truck. "Is that you, crazy man, crazy man from the rodeo? Come here. What are you doing out here with a ditch-bank blade?"

Terry stepped over. "Shakedown team got me bad. Said I was messing with marijuana. You know I don't mess with no marijuana."

"Crazy man, I can't have you sweating so bad out here. Got to save your energy for those bulls. How many times you grab that token last year?"

"Just once. Was the only one did it, though."

"I saw you that first Sunday. Bull had you up there, huh?"

"Won the Convict Poker last year, too."

"You're the one to watch, crazy man. Bull had you up there like a little girl on a trampoline. You hold on for today. Tomorrow I'll get you a layout."

"Thank you."

"Be out there in October, won't you?"

"Long as they got money between them horns."

"All right, crazy man. I'll get you that layout."

And the officer was true to his word. Starting the next morning, Terry filed tools. Or, rather, he sat at the roadside sharpening a hoe blade occasionally, as needed, and periodically, when the mounted guard beckoned him, Terry hauled water for the rifleman's horse.

Next, the rodeo freed him from his punishment cell. At the late June meeting Warden Cain had called to bless my book in front of the inmates I'd been following, Terry, in the cuffs and shackles required whenever he was out of his cell and not working, approached the warden. He informed Cain, in a deferential mumble, of his recent marijuana charge, of his innocence, and of the fact that if the review board didn't lift his sentence soon, he would be barred automatically from this year's rodeo. That, he said, would prevent me from finishing my book.

Terry's words surprised me. But I didn't interrupt to tell the warden that my project would survive whatever Terry's fate. Cain, nervous that any complaint from me might arouse Polozola's ire, turned to one of his assistant wardens and told him to look into the situation. By July the review board sent Terry back to the dorms, to Walnut. He was also promoted from filing tools in the fields to a job unloading and storing vegetables under the shade of a zinc roof.

A few times each day one of the warden's horse- or mule-drawn carts, piled with eggplants or squash, would plod away from the crops and approach the zinc shed. The wheel spokes revolved slowly and the horse shoes clomped deliberately along the road. At the driver's listless tug on the reins, the animal would veer along its own gentle, sleepy curve toward the shed and the vegetable crew. Divorced from what they symbolized to many of the inmates, the wagons were one of the most serene visions on Angola's soothing landscape. When I spent time with Terry, the sight of the long spokes turning and of the horses knowing, on their own, exactly where to park at the loading bay could slow and deepen my breath.

The vegetables were washed in metal vats. A vague assembly line sorted the produce and bagged it by size. Above, an air-conditioned guards' office stood on a platform. And soon the guards welcomed Terry from the shade into the air-conditioning.

"Hey, Terry! Terry Hawkins!"

He was hauling sacks of eggplant into a storage shed.

"You want to get yourself a layout?"

"What you need me to do?"

"Come get up here."

Terry stowed one last sack and climbed the wooden stairs.

"Get yourself some a.c., Terry," the guard said.

"Thank you."

"Major called yesterday. Said we should give you a new job."

"What you need?"

"Says you should stay cool and shine shoes."

Terry hesitated. "I don't know."

"What's the matter?"

"I don't know nothing about that."

"Major's orders. He's looking out for you."

"I never shined a pair of shoes in my life."

"Never shined a pair of shoes? We saw those cowboy boots you were wearing last week," a second guard encouraged. "Those were shined plenty. You trying to tell us you didn't shine those?" The two guards laughed. "It's a layout, Terry. We're not going to tell you to do ours but once in a while. Just set up here and relax. I got your wooden box right here. Your polish. Brush and rags. It's nothing but a layout."

And again, the staff carried out its promise. Terry spent a minimum of time squatting on the wooden box, polishing. They gave him a chair, allowed him to sit through the day in the office. With the guards' walkie-talkies crackling behind him, "TC1 to Camp J sallyport…Control center TC1," he watched as the crew below dunked and rolled the eggplants in the water so the dust disappeared and the skins glistened, then sent them along the line. The elevated view relaxed him: the tops of men's heads as they worked, their hands dipping in and out of the dark water. It was mesmerizing to watch the inmate who'd replaced him hauling sacks into storage. And from overhearing the guards, Terry knew the exact moment when count would be taken, and when precisely they would head in for lunch. It was faintly like controlling these things himself.

He worked mostly when other staff dropped by, either to check on production or just to pick up a few vegetables to take home for dinner.

"You need your shoes shined, Captain?" one of the guards asked.

"Is that Terry Hawkins you got here?"

"That's him. The bullfighter."

"Well, shoot yes, Terry. You gonna make my shoes look pretty?"

"All right."

"You seen his belt? Stand up and show him your belt."

Terry straightened his six-foot-three body off the eighteen-inch box.

"Turn around, Terry. Show the captain what you got tooled in back."

"Bullfighter," the captain read.

"You should see how careful he cleans it. Brushes it with corn-meal and water."

"*Cornmeal?*" the captain asked. "What's that for, crazy man?"

"That's the best thing for it," Terry answered, body refolded as he applied polish in quick circles to a shoe tip.

"You going to wear that in the rodeo?"

"I'll have it on."

"That's your good-luck belt?"

"That's it."

"Well, that's important information. 'Cause I'm putting ten on you in that Guts & Glory. Makes me feel better to know I'm going to win it."

"You'll win it."

"I figure you're getting rich I might as well make a little money, too. Right, crazy man?"

"You'll make it."

"How much you betting, Sarge?"

"I can't do but watch. You saw the first weekend last year? No telling what Terry's liable to do to get himself killed before he gets it. Thought he was going to get himself spiked clean through."

"He's out to win it, aren't you, crazy man?"

"I'm winning."

"Please take him off," Terry prayed late at night, in Walnut. "He's hunting me down again."

His bedtime ritual had been performed hours earlier. On his cot, he had read the verses he'd highlighted months ago during his Bible group back at D. He turned the thin pages to find the neat orange markings.

Lord, I cry unto Thee:
make haste unto me;
Give ear unto my voice,
when I cry unto Thee.
Let my prayer be set forth before Thee
    as incense....
Incline not my heart to any evil thing.

Then, twenty feet from where the man had lost his sneakers and gained a long, scythe-shaped scar on the left side of his face, Terry knelt beside his own cot and closed his eyes and lowered his head to his folded hands. Steam from the inmates' evening showers gathered dense in the air, almost a palpable substance around his shoulders. The huge fans hummed, dropping a kind of veil in front of the world, making it distant, creating something strangely like silence.

Our Father who art in heaven
Hallowed be Thy name,
Thy kingdom come
Thy will be done
On earth as it is in heaven.

"Lord Jesus," Terry went on, with a persistent hope that he was heard though he had failed to be saved, "thank You for looking over me; thank You for helping me be through this day safely; thank You for watching over my family; I love You, Lord; thank You for looking over Jamonica in school; thank You for looking over Quiana and her baby; thank You if you can put Mama in not so much sickness, Lord; I love You, Lord; I love You, Lord; please keep an eye on me, Lord; can You take some of this away, Lord?; can You forgive me, Lord?; I love You, Jesus; please lead me, Lord; can You help me a way out of this penitentiary, would You do that, Lord?; I love You, Jesus; could You do that, Lord?; keep an eye on me, Lord; look over me; look over me; thank You, Lord Jesus; thank You, Lord; amen."

But after midnight something had woken him, and now Mr. Denver Tarter wouldn't let him return to sleep. So Terry knelt again. The steam had cleared. The vibration of the fans was only that, a relentless noise.

"Please take him off. Please make him go away. Please just this one thing."

FOURTEEN

WE STEPPED AWAY FROM THE HOUSE, A SHABBY BOX of pale green wood, the house Littell had been born in, that his mother still lived in, that he had returned to. A corroded swing set stood in front, then a low, wilting cyclone fence, then a stack of four torn tires like a welcoming statue beside the fence gate. This was where I visited Littell, in the city of Lake Charles, a month after he had left O'Brien House. He hurried out front, his shirt still unbuttoned, when he heard my car. He never invited me inside, and I have always wondered what level of decrepitude or disarray he preferred not to show me. He led me away from the stack of tires.

Across from his house a vacant lot occupied half the block, a reminder of the property facing O'Brien, except that there the grass was cut low, while here saplings crowded one another amid shoulder-high reeds. An abandoned nightclub buckled behind the saplings. Within the tall grass were the charred boards of two houses leveled by arson while Littell had been at Angola. A pair of tremendous oak trees, draped with Spanish moss, had once shaded those houses. The trees still thrived, though now the effect was different, the dangling webs of moss no longer gentle but looking like an onslaught of chaotic growth spilling from the sky.

"This neighborhood was no Fifth Avenue," Littell said as we passed between the lot on one side and homes like his mother's on the other. "But it looked good. Fifteen years ago, a lot of these houses were still pretty new. Now it's like nature's taking back over. When people move into a community they build up on nature, and now it's like nature's coming back and the will of man is losing out."

At moments when he spoke like this, it was hard to believe Littell had read with his finger in the Social Security office.

His lips, as always, were in that slightly retracted position of disgust. He had shaved his head bald. He had lost weight—twenty pounds, he said, since Angola—and when he had come outside with his shirt unbuttoned I saw the bony plate of his chest. Will was most of what he was.

But he felt more threatened than I did, walking me around the neighborhood. Up ahead, three or four teenagers sat on the unrailed porch of a shack with boarded up windows. "They think you're here to buy drugs," he said, their eyes tracking us past the house. "They think I'm bringing the white dude around."

"I know," I said, and quietly laughed it off.

It was no joke to him. Problems with a 1978 speeding ticket had kept him from getting his driver's license, and, thinking he would clear this up any day, he hadn't applied for a state I.D. He had nothing to show the police if they stopped him for questioning. I assured him that I would explain, vouch for what we were doing together, but this did little to change the way he walked: a rigid and subtle strut that held an odd hesitance, his weight further forward on his feet than seemed normal, almost as though he were barefoot and didn't want to stab his heel on a piece of gravel.

"Every evening, I try to be back inside by eight o'clock," he said. "'Cause all I need is to be in the wrong place at the wrong time. They ask me for some I.D., they see I got none, they run a check, see I've been to Angola, that's it. Any unsolved robbery, they can pin it on me. You see, Dan, the new thing is that crack. And that's everybody. It's seldom you see anyone around here who's straight. Sometimes it makes me thankful for Angola—all the guys I grew up with are wasted on it. This block we're walking on right now is where I spent all my time as a little kid. I used to play basketball right over there." He pointed to an area unrecognizable as a basketball court, the fence and backboard long gone, torn down and sold for scrap by crackheads, and the pavement split apart by weeds and saplings.

"And the neighborhood's full of these little youngsters, they'll juke guys, they'll shoot guys, and if I'm with the wrong people, people I used to know that's buying those drugs?—I don't want to get in a situation where I'd be forced to do something crazy to somebody."

I told myself he was exaggerating, that trouble with the law would come only if he broke it, that nearly all these houses were filled with struggling, hardworking people. I told myself he spoke with an ex-convict's feelings of entrapment and self-pity: The world was worse than he was; the cops were out to get him; the world might cause him to do wrong again.

Then I listened to the neighborhood. At six-thirty in the evening it was silent, almost motionless. The dealers on their porch weren't speaking. Nor were the women in their dingy yellow or powder blue knee-length shorts, sitting on a stoop propped up on cinder blocks. They only stared. No cars drove by, so that Littell and I thought nothing of walking in the middle of the street. A few rickety bicycles drifted past, with grown men riding them. The supermarket where we went to buy sodas had steel mesh over every window and, inside, scarcely any light; the shriveling oranges in the fruit rack and the ice cream bars in the freezer lay in semi-darkness, and the cashier stood in a greenish gloom. The grocery seemed to be the only operating business around. Driving in, I'd passed a dilapidated store whose owner had advertised his best product by spray-painting in large, uneven letters across a side wall: TIGER ROACH SPRAY. Sometime later he had painted across the bare plyboard door: CLOSED.

The place was like a ghost town, still inhabited. Littell wanted me to meet one of his brothers, with whom he'd reestablished a relationship. We found him on the porch of another squat house with wood nailed over several windows. He sat with two men, drinking beer. Did someone actually live inside? Did his brother? Or was this merely a lost building where three middle-aged men came to pass the evenings? Littell and his brother were awkward with each other, almost wordless, at least with me there, and I didn't know how to start conversation. Suddenly I was thinking with relief that my year would be over soon, that I would be far away from this kind of life. Suddenly I didn't have the energy. Their poverty was so thorough.

And it became possible to think that Littell wasn't exaggerating much, that most of these homes held someone doing or dealing crack, that it was the only source of energy left in this corner of this small city. It certainly wasn't hard to think that in such a degraded place even the most fair-minded policeman would assume an ex-Angola inmate was guilty of any crime he was caught near.

Those bits of gravel I imagined him avoiding as he walked were land mines. One misstep and he would be back in prison forever.

"There's one other person I want you to meet," Littell said. "That's Mr. Cameron. He's a real positive influence, someone I can go to for advice."

Mr. Cameron's tiny front yard was decorated to excess, with flower beds and brightly painted bits of scrap metal cropping up from every inch of ground. The outside of his shotgun house stood undecaying, inasmuch as I could see it. Small, lush trees leaned against every wall, their leaves sprawling like thatch over the roof, but because of the tended yard the cushion of trees looked quaint, intentional, rather than beyond control.

"I'm very proud of Littell," the wiry man said. He was fifty, maybe sixty years old. "He's trying, truly trying." And then Mr. Cameron began a list of the community's problems, from his car that had been blown up last year by the drug dealers to the natural gas the oil companies had drained from under his land using secret pipelines back in the sixties. He rambled on and on about the pipelines, urging me to write my next book about them, until it seemed clear even to Littell, who relied on him, that he was something of a kook.

"Littell's going to make it," Mr. Cameron said, as we left.

Miss Katherine had told Littell the gates of Angola were opening wide, and a part of him had worried she was right. When the Greyhound bus heading from Baton Rouge to Lake Charles had climbed and descended the long, arching bridge that crossed the Mississippi, Littell was on the other side of the river for the first time since he'd been driven across that same bridge, in the opposite direction, on his way to prison. Once, while living at O'Brien, he had walked through downtown to the levee, sat on the bank, and stared across the water. Over there, 120 miles beyond the opposite shore from Baton Rouge, his past waited, everything he had done, as a teenager and in his early twenties, to destroy himself. He knew that. At the halfway house he was safe. "It was a hell of a step," he said, remembering the day he'd left O'Brien for the only other place he could live, his mother's house. "But it was a step I had to take."

During the month before he quit the program, he had begun sleeping with a young woman, an addict at O'Brien. This violation of Miss Katherine's rules, and the suspicion he felt constantly around him ("Everyone staring into my mouth whenever they saw me having a conversation, all the residents, thinking it was their business, just like rats at Angola"), reminded him of all the other house rules, from the schedule that would keep him from combining a full-time job with college, to the way the house held what little money he earned, to the sign on the pay phone that warned of a write-up for anyone who talked longer than ten minutes. A write-up! This was

exactly what he'd lived with in prison, exactly the words! Every little thing controlled, fifteen years of feeling like a child.

"I'm not going through those gates again," he told Miss Katherine during their last meeting. "That's the one thing I know."

And in Lake Charles, he had found work. His brother had a temporary job with the Conoco Oil Company, for $8.50 an hour, and
managed to get Littell on the crew. At first, Littell described the work
to me only as "construction," then as "laying pipe." Eventually, as we
drove at dusk to the fence of the Conoco plant, so he could show me
the site on a waterway leading to the Gulf of Mexico, he explained
more accurately. He cleaned sludge from under the pipes that ran
between the storage tanks and the docks, where the transport ships
came to have their holds filled with petroleum.

The tanks were gargantuan cylinders, and the hulls of the ships
swept outward and loomed above us. They made me faintly anx-
ious, made me direct my gaze unnaturally high, tipping my neck, to
be sure the darkening sky still existed, that the tanks and ships
weren't able to blot everything out. Beneath them, in a fire-retardant
suit, Littell dug with his gloved hands at the sludge. The pipes had
been leaking for years. Chemicals had been seeping into the soil, and
from there into the Gulf water. The sludge was like a cross between
black oatmeal and black Jell-o. Littell had been hired to clean away
the poisoned ground before the company laid concrete beds under
the pipes.

Soon he hoped to be working on an oil rig offshore, making a
thousand a week. Either that, or studying in business school. He'd
gone to the Delta School of Business to ask for information, and ever
since they'd been calling his mother's house, "recruiting me, almost
begging me," he said proudly.

He'd been to his first interview for an offshore job. He'd seen an
ad in the paper and reported to a conference room at a Best Western
motel wearing his fire-retardant suit, to let the interviewer know he
was already employed, that he was serious. He filled out the appli-

cation in an anteroom, waited to be called in, and told the man, "I've been in trouble."

"What kind of trouble?"

Littell spoke the words "armed robbery"; he said, "Angola."

"For how long?"

"Fifteen years."

The man glanced back and forth between the application and Littell in the blue jumpsuit. He said they were looking for dependable people. He said it was obvious that Littell worked hard. There was a chance he could be hired as a galley hand. He would be taking a cut in pay, to minimum wage, but the job would get him familiar with the rigs. Littell asked when he could start. The man told him ten days.

On the twelfth day Littell called. The interviewer apologized; they just couldn't take a chance with an ex-con on the rig.

As we stared at the hulls and tanks, Littell told me he would keep at it, stay with his job at Conoco, maybe lie at his next interview.

I asked if he was worried about the close quarters offshore, out in the middle of the Gulf, that would resemble Angola.

"Not really," he said. "And you know what? I *draw* on those years. I know what I've already gotten through. Offshore is nothing. You're getting paid. You're eating the best of food. I'll stay out on that rig six months if they'll let me. They'll have to call the Coast Guard to come make me take my break."

By October, he predicted, he would be able to buy his own car, maybe a '94, maybe even a '95. He would drive to Baton Rouge, to O'Brien, to see Miss Katherine. "I've got nothing to prove to her," he said, "but I just want her to know how I'm doing."

The week after I left Lake Charles, Littell broke his self-imposed curfew. One night at ten, a woman called him from a motel room. He went.

Two days earlier, he had noticed her at the edge of the overgrown lot, the shell of a nightclub, the cascade of Spanish moss, the chaos of saplings and charred boards beside her. Weaving, she made slow progress toward the corner, now leaning against a parked car, thoroughly drunk—that was what he noticed first; then, that despite her staggering she looked good: light brown skin, lush body in a blue-jean skirt. He watched her long enough to see a driver stop to run his chatter while she walked on, keeping her path a bit more straight. Littell left his yard and turned up the street, away from her.

He heard his name, unslurred, voice loud. Not a drunken woman's voice, though he knew there was no one else behind him it could be.

"Littell! Littell!"

She had crossed to his side of the street. She wore a jean vest—just that—to go with the skirt. She looked *very* good, but she was no one he knew. Two men he recognized huddled at the far end of the vacant lot; he figured they'd told her his name, put her up to this. *Get the drunk bitch to mess with Littell. He been so pussy-starved....* He kept going.

"Littell! You don't remember me? Littell Harris!"

He turned again, let her come close, checking down the street and waiting for the two men to bend with laughter. No matter how much the vest revealed, the sour breath and veiny eyes repelled him, and when she leaned forward, inches from his face, he had an urge to put his hand behind her neck and shove her to the pavement.

"It's Deborah. And you're Littell Harris. You can't say you're not. You know me. You *know* me. You do, you know me. You know me."

She started to laugh, as though *he* were playing an innocent trick on *her,* and when he still said nothing she doubled over, upper body almost parallel to the pavement, and took little mincing steps backward, shaking her head and making a sound that was part gurgle and part snicker: *"Kch, kch, kch, kch, kch."*

"I don't know who you are," he said.

She straightened, stared, doubled over again, and backpedaled farther from him, *"Kch, kch, kch."*

And then a man he did know emerged from a nearby house.

"You don't remember her?"

"Don't fuck with me, Mako," Littell said.

She leaned against another parked car, arms folded, looking almost sober, looking satisfied to be under discussion.

"That's Debbie Foster."

"Who?"

"Who's been drinking," Mako asked, "you or her?"

It clicked. Maybe because of what Mako had just said. Maybe because in high school she hadn't touched anything, no booze, no drugs, while Littell had barely *been* in high school between detention centers.

"You dated her, man."

Yes, Littell realized. No sex, just some sort of puppy love–holding hands in the halls–amid the unraveling of his life. And it was strange that he hadn't recognized her. He saw now that she didn't look much different. There was the pointy, turned-up nose, unmissable on a black woman's face. There were the wide caramel eyes, no matter how threaded, and the short Afro, same as ever. How could he have forgotten? He felt off-balance, as though he'd cut his own life in half, amputated everything before Angola. Since returning home he'd avoided everyone, suffered through the sodas they bought him when he refused their beer, suffered through the conversations they wanted when he'd run into each of them for the first time outside the grocery or on the street, hardly nodded hello when he'd passed them since. And now his brain had done something with Debbie Foster. He felt he had no past whatsoever, nothing to stand on except prison.

Cautiously, he stepped toward her, told her how pretty she still looked.

But she, without keeling, had fallen half-asleep, and murmured, "Thank you, Mako." Littell caught the rank breath again, saw the slack mouth, and any desire to reclaim some bit of his past dissolved. He asked the man to do him a favor, to walk her home.

She called late the next afternoon. She sounded sober, or at least he couldn't tell otherwise. They talked, not about where he'd been but about her. Married, divorced, drinking, losing custody of her kids, still keeping a job as an attendant at a convalescent home. She still had that.

"You know what I thought about all last night?" Littell asked. "How conservative you were in high school. Intelligent. And now I'm listening to you talk," he heard Miss Katherine's counseling as he spoke, "and you're covering up some tender places with that booze. Losing your kids and all."

He asked if she was "doing that other stuff."

"No. I used to. But not anymore."

Then, the following night, she phoned from the motel a few blocks from his mother's house—another functioning business besides the dim, mesh-windowed supermarket. A red-painted cement bunker, it held eight or ten rooms. Littell had stayed there once since returning home, paid the twenty dollars through the bulletproof Plexiglas just for the chance to be completely alone. Now Deborah said she needed someone to talk to.

And he had been daydreaming, since their first phone call, about getting her away from Lake Charles, getting her a job offshore. Littell still believed he himself would find one, and in the motel room, sitting on the grayish-white sheet (there was no bedspread), leaning against the headboard with her leaning against his chest and his arms gently around her waist and the two of them staring at the TV that was turned off and talking over the vibrations of the a.c. that was sealed with duct tape to the window, he laid out a plan, told her about seeing women at the Best Western interview, said she would have to clean herself up because the rigs were absolutely alcohol- and drug-free and they gave everyone breath and urine tests to make sure, promised to start taking her to substance-abuse meetings to put her on the right track, said he really ought to go himself, anyway, on account of his past, talked about the kind of money she could earn. "Out there," he said, "you can reestablish yourself."

They walked to the grocery to buy orange juice; they would toast their plan. Strolling back, he heard a car slow alongside them—the driver and the woman next to him knew Deborah, and they asked if she and Littell wanted a ride.

"I tried to keep her moving, not even stop," Littell explained to me over the phone. "'Cause I saw what make of car it was, and it was after midnight, and I was reading the signs. You know, I was getting to where I could see the signs out there. And I knew I didn't have no identification. I knew I shouldn't even be out there, and I knew there was drugs in that car. But I'm not lying to you, Dan. I was thinking about some pussy."

Deborah leaned down to the driver's window, chatted awhile. She turned toward Littell. "Don't you want a ride?"

"No. *Hunh*-unh. We was just out walking."

She leaned down again, elbows on the window, ass in the air. Littell backed to the pavement's edge, glanced toward the corner. If the police cruised by now, if they rounded the four of them up, there wouldn't be any distinction between who was outside the car and who was in.

"Can I get just one?" She stepped over to him.

"What the fuck?" He grabbed her arm. "What—? Just start walking."

"Come on, baby."

"Fuck no."

The woman in the car bent across the driver, called toward the curb, "Y'all sure you don't want a ride?"

"Nah," he said. "We don't need no ride."

Inside the motel room again he opened the two pint cartons of orange juice.

"You going to let me get one?"

"Look—"

"I'm only talking about just one."

"Deborah, I've known you since the second grade. The second grade!"

She looped her arms around his neck. She wore loose, billowy pants, but the same jean vest from when he'd first seen her. It snapped down the front. Three of the snaps were already undone. There was, between her pressed-together breasts, a line for his tongue to follow. She said, "I'm talking about 'cause we're making plans. A thousand a week!"

"You're a fucking waste."

"Please, Littell." She let go. "You *know* me. You know who I am."

"Would you cosign—"

"I'm not—"

"Would you cosign if I put a .44 Magnum next to my head?"

"I'm not talking about that."

"Would you?"

"You can't say you don't know me."

"So what? So I know you, I know you."

"So you know it's just one."

She stood with her back to the door now, framed there. The turned-up nose, the short Afro. The snaps would come apart with the softest tug. He could let her, first, go and make her buy. She could smoke it somewhere else. He could remind her not to bring it here. And she would come back, and they would get things going through the last few hours of the night, and they could work the rest out tomorrow, and soon she would be in a program anyway, getting ready to go on those rigs....

When the silence lasted too long, she started begging again.

"What do you want from me?" he asked. "You can go any second."

She remained still in the doorway.

"It's on you to make some kind of move," he added.

Right away, he understood how his words sounded: that all she needed to do was come toward him, kiss him, make love with him, and that then she could do what she wished, leave and take care of her business and still have him to return to. He let that possibility linger.

"You can't do that and come back here. This ain't about just you."

She looked bewildered, incapable of figuring out what he meant. He felt almost cruel for trying to wedge his own problems into her private fight. She seemed so terribly at a loss, so helplessly immersed in herself.

My main concern is me, he reminded himself, for he was about to comfort her, to put his arms around her, to force some other human life into her small, sealed universe, to seal himself to her. *My main concern is me. My main concern is me.* She slipped out the door. *My main concern...*

He lay back on the bed. He couldn't sleep, but forced himself to rest, to save his energy. Because in a few hours, it was time for work, time for Conoco.

F I F T E E N

Lynn Clark's granddaughter, Brittany, liked to play with rocks. The little girl was two and a half, and Lynn was fifty-one, and together they gathered rocks from around the yard, piled them, patterned them, stashed them like treasures. Lynn, a welfare caseworker, had just taken a new job, and lived alone, an hour and a half from her husband of thirty years and from the yard where she and Brittany sometimes did their collecting. One evening her neighbor, a young man named Danny Fabre, asked to use her telephone.... "She was always falling for a sad story," her husband, Jack, a retired newspaper editor, remembered....Later that week Danny stopped by for the same favor. And the following Monday night he asked if she could give him a ride to a nearby town.

Earlier on that Monday her husband had received a delivery of gravel—he planned to resurface the driveway. The small pyramid stood beside the house, and periodically throughout the afternoon he thought, I should call Lynn. I should tell her, "You and Brittany won't have to go looking for rocks anymore, 'cause I've got a whole mountain of 'em." He imagined their joy, playing with that mountain. He started to call, but something distracted him. And afterward, he thought that if he had, somehow it would have steered the day a degree or two to the right or left, onto a slightly different path, just different enough that the murder would never have happened. A mound of gravel—a miracle to a two-and-a-half-year-old child—would have saved his wife.

Instead she was beaten and choked to death, and rammed with a stick through the right eye, and burned, and left in the woods, and found two days later so badly charred and decomposed she had to be identified through dental records.

How much could it matter to that grandmother's husband that Danny Fabre was struggling to edge his reading grade level past a 7.3, that he was about to give his tenth Toastmasters speech, that he was, one September evening eleven years after the killing, sitting in the Angola chapel waiting for an Episcopal service to begin? What would Jack Clark have said about the three convict acolytes standing in a back corner in their albs, one of them holding a tall, sleek cross while they giggled and surveyed the five or six women among the group that always arrived with the visiting minister and that milled with the crowd of inmates, and what would he have said about the way every convict in the modern, white, octagonal chapel waited for his five-second hug, his five seconds of press-time with one of those women, and about the way Danny Fabre got up to get his, circled to the back to find a crystal-eyed, heavyset, bow-haired woman in her twenties who came monthly to the prison to have the inmates swarm around and claim their moments, to have them fall in love just that fast, to have their kisses miss her cheek and graze the corners of her lips, to have their ribs and bellies crush her breasts, to have their arms loosen so reluctantly, to have Danny enfold her, and what would he have said about the way his wife's killer, right after his allotted seconds, turned to me and pointed out how so many of the other convicts came to church only to be near the women, and how he didn't think that was right, didn't like that at all?

Exactly how moved would Lynn's husband have been as the service began and the inmates attending for the first time were asked to stand and introduce themselves and did so not only by name but by prison dorm, "Joseph Powell, Ash One," "Tyrone Michaels, Spruce Four," "Preston Causey, Mag One," the incantation of their Angola homes rising to the gently pitched ceiling? Exactly how moved by the cherubic minister's attempt to restore, in his optimistic tones, a sense of sanctuary after the guard took the count—how moved when the minister's reading from the Book of Common Prayer, "O mighty God, to You all hearts are known...," pandered so thoroughly to what these men wished to think of themselves, that their hearts, their invisible hearts, were as good as anyone's, maybe even better, that their crimes were things of the past, that it was only in blindness, non-heart-seeing blindness, that humanity could condemn them? And how moved would he have been when the congregation, fully attentive now (even those ten or twelve who'd won the chair jockeying and wound up sitting beside a female), gave their self-serving response, "Glory to God in the highest.... You take away the sin of the world." Exactly how moved?

Especially when the sermon illuminated the difference between the laws of man and the law of God, how the necessity of Moses' rules ("to reveal God to the world") had been distorted by the Pharisees who made themselves supreme judges and whose decrees divided humankind by mere earthly notions of good and wicked ("The laws of Moses had been to glorify God and wound up shaming men!"); especially when the minister told of the confrontations between the legalistic Pharisees and the loving Jesus. "Now when the Pharisees gathered unto Him, they saw that some of His disciples ate with hands unwashed. And they asked Him, 'Why do Your disciples not live according to the tradition of the elders, but eat with hands defiled?' And Jesus answered them, 'Well did Isaiah prophesy of you hypocrites. You worship in vain, with your lips but not your hearts! You teach as doctrines the precepts of men! You leave behind the commandments of God! And of those commandments, two reign above all! Love the Lord thy God with all thy heart! And love thy neighbor as thyself! Love above laws! What really matters is not what's on your hands! No! What matters is what's in your heart!'"

But there was blood on those hands! Those hands had punched and throttled her. They had taken that stick and driven it into her skull. They had scorched her body. Her life was on those hands. And she had been that neighbor, the one with a place in her heart for everyone, the one who had let him in to use the telephone and given him a ride when he needed it, and he had broken her, mutilated her, and now sat transfixed as the minister declared, "We must not think of salvation as something we in ourselves can accomplish. We are all the same in our helplessness. When we ask ourselves what, in our souls, can we lay before God that God wants, the answer, we all know, is nothing. So we turn to Jesus and say, 'I can't save myself, can You do it for me?'"

Nothing? Nothing? All the same? She the same as Danny Fabre? Did nothing we do matter? Nothing as long as you said 'Forgive me'? Didn't it matter what Danny Fabre had done? And didn't she have a thousand times more to lay before God than he did, a million times more—how could you measure the difference between them? And he sat there so riveted, so soothed.

And how much could it matter to Lynn's husband that Danny's efforts as a Toastmaster earned him, that summer, a red CTM tag to wear on his white T-shirt?

And how much could it matter that a few weeks after earning it he let his temper surge in a dispute with several other club members, an argument he described incoherently to me and that I never fully understood and that wound up involving a guard and that resulted in Danny's being suspended by the Forgotten Voices? He hadn't hit anyone, but his hands had been raised. How much could it matter that Captain Newsom, the taciturn and gawky officer who had allowed Danny into the organization a year ago, who Danny felt had "seen I was sincere," spurned him at a going-away gathering when he retired, wouldn't so much as make eye contact with him, because a glimmer of Danny's past, a sign that it was unpurged, had shown itself in the fight? And how much could it matter that the club president and his fellow Forgotten Voices executives later told Danny that they knew his heart was in the right place and that his commitment to self-improvement was strong, and assured him they would vote to lift the punishment soon?

For his tenth speech, the one that brought him his CTM pin, Danny had stood behind the lectern with the appointed ah-counter—pencil ready above his legal pad—sitting to his right and the pink cone hat beside the dictionary on the foldout table, and below the window to his left the razor-wired passageways. Danny gripped the edges of the lectern with his large hands and leaned slightly forward. He looked for a good while at the members in their school chairs—the man with the wounded, half-shriveled eye and the man whose hobby in a previous life had been sailing and who wore Top-Siders as a way to declare *that* life still present—and he began with such histrionic drama it would have been laughable anywhere else: "Hope."

He paused a long, long time. But no one in the room shifted and no one could possibly have felt that Danny was struggling to find his next thought or didn't have any next thought prepared and was on his way to another sputtering performance and no one could possibly have noticed the right-angle ears that sprung from below his short hair (the ears he seemed less and less needful of discussing with me now, though he had decided to ride in the upcoming rodeo), because everyone was focused on that single word which his sonorous voice and his explosive forward-leaning body and the prolonged gaze of his yellow-tinged green eyes had given a presence. He stepped out from behind the lectern. "Does anyone in this room know who the author is, of hope? Anybody? Raise your hand." He waited, as though he actually expected someone to answer. "God. God is the author of hope."

And God, too, between the cone hat and the traffic-light timer, had a short-lived presence, if only because Danny wished it.

"I want to tell you a little story.

"Last summer, exactly a year ago, right before I joined Toast-masters, I got up for breakfast one morning. And I said, I'm going to lay back. I'm not going to go. I don't feel like eating. But there was something pushing me out the dorm. There was something pushing me down the Walk.

"And there by Spruce was this little bitty kitten. And I reached down to pet it. But somebody said, 'Watch out.' And I turned like this. Sudden."

Danny twisted his neck abruptly, acting out his fast turn, staring back at the lectern he had left as though at the man who had warned him.

"He said it had a big gash on it. But I bent down. I picked it up, and I turned it over. The middle of its belly had a gap where something had done tore it wide open. So I took this little cat—it had maggots falling out of its belly—and I went to the freeman at the C.C. gate to get me some peroxide. I shampooed this cat. I washed him up real, real good. I got all the infection out of him. And that night I left him in a hobby-shop box. Closed him in with the tools. And next morning when I went to check on him, that cat was so weak—the way he wobbled out of that box? He made it across the hobby-shop floor, and out the back door and across the Walk, and onto the grass to use the bathroom.

"I picked him up again. I asked this ho, Patricia—y'all know him—I asked him, 'Pat, can you build a box on your drop, put some little steps on it so this pitiful kitten can get in and out?' And he did.

He built it. And that's where the kitten lived. But over the next few days, when it would wobble out and go curl up outside one of the dorms, I'd see people take it and shove it to the side with their foot, like this, and I almost got in fights behind that cat. I almost. But I never did.

"And do you know after a couple of weeks, it seemed like everybody on the East Yard, at one time or the other, stopped and gave this cat milk or something to eat. This cat had so much food in front of him. This cat was loved by everybody. And within a month's time this little cat was healing up. He was growing. You'd walk by and he'd just jump up on your leg. Just *jump up*. Because that cat had hope. Because I had hope.

"Mr. President, Mr. Master Evaluator, Mr. Sergeant at Arms, Captain Newsom, fellow Toastmasters, hope will heal your wounds. Hope will fill your heart. Hope will help you, someday, make it out of Angola. Hope will keep you moving ahead. Hope will make you live. Hope is your master key."

How much could any of it matter? When we spoke over the phone about Danny Fabre, Lynn's husband remembered that eleven years ago he had "literally wanted to tear him apart." He had hoped for a death sentence. In the middle of his trial, Danny had asked to plead out, and when the prosecutor came into the hallway behind the courtroom to seek the approval of the victim's family before he accepted the plea, Jack Clark went along only because he thought of the years and years of appeals the family would have to live through before the execution. He expected—because Fabre looked so wild in the courtroom, his long hair disheveled and his eyes strange in a way Clark recalled but could no longer describe and his feet chained to the floor—that Fabre would wind up killed by another convict soon enough.

"Now," Lynn's husband said, "the desire for retribution is a little bit less....Let him think about it for the rest of his life." So I mentioned, briefly, the changes Danny was trying to make, and asked if these could ever have any meaning, not necessarily in terms of his imprisonment or release, I struggled to explain, but in some sort of moral terms I couldn't find the words to express. To which Jack Clark said simply, quietly, "I want him to stay there forever for what he did."

It was, perhaps, the closest thing to a miracle at hand: the provision of time, the possibility of quietness, the difference between "tear him apart" and "stay there forever."

S I X T E E N

I ASKED MYRON HODGES—THE GUITARIST LITTELL
had once heard playing "The Wind Cries Mary," the guitarist *I* had
once heard playing the same wistful Hendrix song, the guitarist I
had hoped to hear at last year's rodeo, the guitarist whose band had
woken late for a rodeo rehearsal and been told by Warden Cain the
day before the event, "Y'all won't touch an instrument again as long
as I'm warden of this penitentiary!"—what advice he would give
Johnny Brooks about getting married in prison. I don't know why I
have waited so long to write about Myron Hodges. Sometimes I
think I have put it off, postponed it until so near the end, precisely
because Myron, of all the inmates I knew well at Angola, was the
man I imagined freeing. Johnny Brooks or Buckkey Lasseigne may
have been equally safe bets for a second chance. But for me, Myron
was the one. Despite the warnings I gave myself about fantasies of
pardon-board heroics, I often imagined helping him out of Angola,
helping him to a new life as a musician.

As my year wound to a close, Myron emptied trash cans and
mopped floors at Angola's hospital. When cellblock inmates were
brought to be examined, they waited their turns in one-man cages;
sometimes one masturbated to the sight of the nurses walking by.

Myron mopped up the semen. But he also helped to change the bed-sore dressings on a man who'd broken his neck in a prison football game two years ago and was now a quadriplegic. James, the quadri-plegic, often requested Myron's help. He liked Myron to shave him as well. Myron was careful, and Myron told him stories about his music and about his marriage.

"Get that yellow pan right there from under the cabinet, and rinse it out and fill it with water," James had instructed the first time the nurses sent Myron in to do the shaving. "Now get the lotion from out the top drawer."

These days James said only, "Run me another ep."

Another episode. Another installment of Myron's Angola story.

James didn't have to give any other instructions. Myron came into the room easily now, without hesitation or revulsion or fear, say-ing, "Well, looks like you're about ready for a nice tight shave," and going straight to the cabinet for the bowl and the lotion and the washcloths, and setting them on the bedside table. Myron knew to ask for two disposable razors at the nurses' station, not just one, and these he placed next to the other things. Then he sat on the edge of the bed. With wet fingertips, he painted the Vaseline Intensive Care, which James preferred to shaving gel, over the left side only of the paralytic's face, because the shaving was slow and otherwise the cream would dry before he reached the right side.

The face had plenty of movement. Between strokes of the razor, as Myron dipped the blade in the warm water, James smiled often, gold caps on his front teeth. Plaited hair, with balls of frizz at the ends of the braids, lay on the pillow.

Movement ended completely at the neck. A nursing home, to which James's care had been farmed out for a while, had failed to perform any therapy on his dead limbs, so the muscles in his arms had contracted irreversibly. His right forearm lay across his chest, the wrist bent beyond 90 degrees, as though the palm were trying to flatten itself to the arm. His left hand, half-fisted, lay permanently just below his throat.

His hands might have modeled for a dishwashing liquid, except that they far exceeded any woman's dream of elegance or delicacy or smoothness. The slender, atrophied fingers were a caricature of femininity, and the backs of the hands, contracted to the width of a child's, were barely wider than the wrists, adding to the effect of hallucinatory grace and uselessness. The atrophic skin glowed. It was like a dark and grainless wood, polished to a glassy extreme. And at his folded elbows, infant-size joints on arms that looked like toxic deformities, you could almost see a reflection of the room in his waxy flesh.

The rest stayed under the sheet as Myron edged carefully with the white plastic razor around the goatee—James's special pride, because one of the nurses had said she liked it—and told him about the beginnings of the traveling band. The group had been through other incarnations going back in prison history, but this one had received Warden Whitley's support, in 1991, after Myron taught himself an old Led Zeppelin song. He had grown up in the New Orleans projects; he had not grown up on Led Zeppelin, nor had any of the other musicians who hoped to get the traveling band off the ground. But they knew their warden had been a Zeppelin fan since his days in classification in the seventies, and when they got word that Whitley would show up at one of their rehearsals, Myron made sure to learn every progression, the nuance of every high-volume, high-necked note that lanced the air above the bass line. Zeppelin wasn't, in the end, all that far from Hendrix, and before turning to Funkadelic and George Benson, he had grown up on Hendrix.

Whitley called him aside. "If I make you trusty and then approve you to travel, are you going to run off on me?"

Myron was only twenty-six years old then, had been at Angola only five years, was serving life for killing a nightclub owner during a robbery. "I can't answer that question," he said.

"Why not?"

"Because if I say no, you'll think I'm just telling you what you want to hear. And if I say yes, I'm not going to be in that band."

"You've got a point," Whitley said, and approved him.

The Big River Band performed all over the state, pulling up in its mesh-windowed schoolbus, with one guard for an escort, at the Baton Rouge State Fair, at the Trade Days in Natchitoches, at the Rayne Frog Festival and the Four Rivers Raft Race, at schools and nursing homes (where the elderly clapped along to Michael Jackson tunes), playing five or six gigs every month. They recorded four original songs in a Baton Rouge studio, the first Angola inmates to record their work while serving time since 1934 when Leadbelly, discovered by a musicologist, had sent a blues song to the statehouse and won a pardon.

If I had you, Gov'nor O.K. Allen,
Like you got me,
I would wake up in the mornin'
Let you out on reprieve.

Myron dreamed he could play his way out of Angola, that someone powerful would someday hear him and be so moved by his talent he would convince the governor to give him clemency, but the song he chose for the studio was a different kind of plea. It went back to something that had happened when he first came to prison. His girlfriend, six years older than Myron, a singer he had grown up admiring and finally begun a relationship with four years before his arrest—the woman he had planned to marry—had tried to visit him, to keep things going. He had refused to put her on his visiting list. And then he had stopped calling.

The backup begged high:

Go on ahead

And the lead singer told her:

Get lost in the wings of another

The harmony begged:

Fly away

And the lead singer told her:

Along the way you are bound to discover

The saxophone climbed:

Another man

And left the lead singer beneath it:

You're going to need to be your lover

The harmony:

I understand.

Finished with the first phase of shaving James, Myron dabbed away the excess lotion with a washcloth. He emptied the plastic bowl and filled it again with fresh water. The room was quiet except for a few droplets falling back into the bowl when he wet his fingers to start again. A blurred and crackling voice, volume low, came from the walkie-talkie of a lieutenant passing by in the hall. "Can you give me a 21 at 2257?" Across the hall an open ward of twenty or thirty beds held the lifers dying of cancer, of AIDS, of other diseases and complications people die of anywhere. James's room was a lock-down cell for patients deemed violent or obscene. The heavy steel door had an eight-inch slot where food trays could be passed through. James's door stayed open. His prison record had been poor, but he was, oddly, somewhat upbeat now, and certainly he was no risk to expose himself or attack anyone.

Though Myron's life as a travel-approved trusty had been far from what James had known as a big-stripe, James had no trouble believing the scenes Myron described: crowds pressed to the stage; the manager of a Jordache factory and his wife half-adopting him and filling his locker box with jeans; a woman reporter from Channel 9 covering the studio session and predicting that he would, truly, play his way out of prison. Once, James had heard Mega Sound, the in-house version of Big River, perform at Camp C. The band played Prince and Maze and then Mardi Gras music that started the inmates second-lining, all the men dancing in frenzied New Orleans tradition (minus the umbrellas), shaking and fast-footing wildly, competitively, waving bandannas in the air. He knew what Myron was capable of, both the groove and the speed.

And on the road Myron's looks couldn't have hurt either: the perfectly molded features, the round wire-rimmed glasses that made him look thoughtful, the V-shaped torso.

Myron spread the lotion over both sides of James's face this time; the second, touch-up shave would go more quickly. With the new blade, he rounded the jawbone. A pinhead of blood appeared.

"Man, I'm gonna need minor surgery," James said.

Myron winced, blotted, twisted his lips in mock worry as though staring at a major wound. "Minor? I don't know about *minor*, but you're going to need some surgery."

"Run me another ep."

"All right."

"Wait. Take the edge of the sheet and rub my eyebrow. My eyebrow's itching."

Myron brushed across it.

"*Rub* it."

Myron pressed down.

"Rub it harder, man. Don't be scared to rub it. *Rub* it."

"Hey. I'm trying to be sure I don't break it."

"Man," James said, "you can't never break me."

Through his first six years in prison Myron had made himself numb. He had kept in contact with his mother, who visited every few months by taking the special Batiste Company bus, twenty dollars per ticket, that ran through the Seventh Ward of New Orleans and onto I-10 and 61 and 66 to Angola. And he arranged to speak occasionally with his older brother, Felton, who was in Angola for the same killing. But gradually his brother had grown incoherent and erratic—schizophrenic, Myron thought, and very, very paranoid—and he'd spent years at J and later been sent to the prison's mental-health unit. Often, Felton had no grasp on reality, scarcely knew where he was.

These were Myron's close relationships, until Natchitoches. There, a little girl who looked like an Eskimo yelled up to the stage, requesting a song by MC Hammer. Her mother wrote to Myron a week later. She had seen his picture in the newspaper the day after the gig; it was now taped to her daughter's wall between MC Hammer and Big Bird.

Marie, a thin, pretty white woman with light brown hair and a low, raspy voice, a medical technician soon to enroll in college, and LaShae, the chunky four-year-old with long black pigtails and puffy cheeks and yellow-toned skin, started visiting. In the trusty park, LaShae devised a game with sticks and paper cups: Run a stick through a cup and you had a sword with a handle. She and Myron dueled on a slab of concrete that was supposed to hold another picnic table. The table had never been built; the slab, LaShae announced, was the roof of a skyscraper. If she forced him off, he fell one thousand feet to his death. If he forced her, she turned instantly into Spider Woman.

They had plans, he and LaShae. A boy on her street had been to a farm in Canada, and reported seeing lots of animals. She wanted to move to Canada. He was going to take her. They would travel in an eighteen-wheeler, which he would teach her to drive. (He had no idea how to drive one himself.) At the picnic tables and in the visiting shed, he described to her how the lessons would go and how the journey would feel and how, after Canada, they would swing back into the States and stay on the road, he the star musician and she his manager. To seal the pact, she gave him an empty, torn-open plastic sack stenciled with Power Rangers—she decided to keep the fighting figures themselves.

He folded the sack and saved it in his locker box. He dreamed recurringly of their trip to Canada. He was driving the eighteen-wheeler, she in the cab next to him. Things were exactly as intended, except that they weren't on a highway; they were in an eighteen-wheeler *speedboat* on the Mississippi River. Other speedboats passed them by. He felt, in the dream, that something was terribly wrong, though he and LaShae were laughing, she bragging about how much better she could drive the truck than Myron and telling him to pull over so they could switch places, and he promising he would, just as soon as they were out of the river. The boats kept zooming by. He kept shifting gears. "You can't drive any faster than that?" she kept giggling.

During the visits, with LaShae persuaded to hunt bugs if they were outside or sent to the Pac-Man machine if they were in, Marie and Myron spoke of how inevitably he would be released, because

of either his music or the errors in his trial. Or both. No question the
errors were cause for reversal. It was open and shut. And once the
judge saw that he was a member of the Angola Big River Band, and
realized how talented he was and how much joy he'd brought to people all over the state, and noticed how good his conduct had been in
prison—never running off, never causing a bit of trouble despite all
the freedoms the administration had given him; *never breaking a trust*—
he would suggest to the prosecution that Myron be allowed a
manslaughter plea. And with the judge's discretion on resentencing,
Myron would be out in just a few more years. Marie's grainy voice
made this future seem full of substance, already almost real. And
whenever he doubted it, whenever he listed all the other inmates he
knew clinging to all their certainties, she told him, voice even lower
and raspier, "You're special. You're going to get out of here. You're
not the type to be in prison."

"Take care of my babies," he would tell her, meaning herself and
LaShae, when the prison bus came to end the visit.

"No," Marie would say, "you take care of *my* baby," meaning
Myron.

And soon, in a letter, she seemed to be proposing. The question
wasn't exactly straightforward, and the next time he called, after asking how she was, he mentioned the sentences and the suggestion
they seemed to contain.

"Oh God," she said, with a spurt of girlish laughter. "I didn't
think you'd actually pick up on that."

"Marie, let me get some numbers. Right now I got these alphabets. With numbers I can see some daylight. With alphabets I can't
see nothing."

The laughter ceased, replaced by the raspiness. "I'll do the seeing. Even if nothing else works, you'll get your pardon as soon as
you get in enough years to apply. So how far away is that?"

"About six years."

"Well, there's a number."

They met with a prison chaplain for approval. A black man in a meek-looking, textured white sweater, he was hard as armor. In an office alongside the chapel's sanctuary, behind a sliding glass door, he sat them down and stared cruelly at Marie. "You can't possibly love this man enough to marry him. You cannot. His sentence is life. L-I-F-E. How can you love him that much? Tell him you love him that much."

"I love you that much."

"Tell him again. Can you do it twice?"

"I love you that much."

"'Cause you're going to have to keep doing it. Right here in Angola."

"I love you that much."

"But do you hear what he's saying now, Marie?" Myron cut in. "The law of Louisiana doesn't feel like I'm so special. They feel like I'm a murderer. I'm an outcast from society and I'm right where I'm supposed to be."

"Next Christmas."

"Marie."

"It's not going to be all that long."

"L-I-F-E," the chaplain spelled again.

"Yeah, I understand." Marie turned on him. "Myron Hodges has a life sentence. He may never get out of Angola. And I never thought, never ever, that I'd fall in love with a man in prison, and I never thought I'd marry a man in prison, I never imagined it in my wildest dreams. But I did always say that if I ever marry a man I would love that man, and that my marriage would be for better or for worse, and that I would love that man for the rest of my life. No such thing as divorce or separation. Not if I can do anything about it."

"And you," the chaplain fixed on Myron.

"Yes, sir."

"You've got all the time in the world to sit down and figure out what this woman wants to hear."

"No, sir."

"Don't tell me no. You can say it just right. I've seen inmates, they can say it better than Shakespeare. And what you're really saying is you love her so much you want to use her. You want her to be your errand person now. You want her to be the go-between, between Angola and your freedom. You're not serious about this woman, you don't love this woman, and if you ever get out you're going to walk off and leave her."

"No, sir, that's—"

"And when you get her putting money in your account, and when she's all used up and she comes complaining, they're going to put state charges against you. Add a few more years to that life. And they're going to put you in J so you can't ever do it again."

"No, sir."

"Then share with us why exactly you proposed to this woman."

"Sir, I didn't propose. She proposed to marry me."

The chaplain coughed, chuckled. "Well, that's something new. Well. All right, *she* proposed. But what is your motive to *marry* her?"

Suddenly, with the chaplain's cross-examination slamming around in his head, Myron had no doubt at all about going forward with the wedding. He didn't hurry to answer. "I don't have a motive," he said finally. "The way Marie and I met, it was a way that seemed actually meant to be. Because up to then I made myself feel nothing. Nothing. That was my way. And my thoughts about marriage in prison were, It's totally ridiculous. It's out of the question. But in this particular case it's like we're already married. And a marriage is much bigger than a contract. It's stating that we love one another and we're going to love one another and that's just the way it's going to be. I need Marie to be there for me forever, whether I'm in this prison or not. So I really don't have a motive, so to say. But I more or less have a reason. My reason is that I love her, and I realize I need her more than I knew at one time."

■

James liked to have his face rubbed down with the Vaseline lotion afterward. Myron spread it over his own hands, and massaged James's cheeks and the rise of his cheekbones, his chin and his temples. The guitar-trained fingers moved in forceful, rhythmic circles. They crossed the forehead and smoothed over the bridge of the nose. James kept his eyes closed. Myron worked back toward his ears, followed the channels of the lobes, then with the third finger of each hand grazed over the eyelids. Though that was always the end of the massage, James kept his eyes shut. Myron dampened a washcloth, and slowly dissolved and cleaned the crusted mucus from the edges of James's nostrils.

Two members of the band serenaded the wedding in the Main Prison chapel, the keyboard player and the lead singer doing a soft "You and I" before the service. Marie wore a white, knee-length dress with a hairpiece and a short veil. She'd highlighted her shoulder-length hair a half-shade toward blond. The chaplain who'd interrogated them now made them both cry with his sermon, his talk of compassion and his calling down of blessings. The keyboard screamed Mendelssohn as they walked back down the aisle.

Regulations kept children from the interior of Main Prison. LaShae waited with a friend of Marie's in the visiting shed. The girl never wore a dress—she liked shorts or leggings or sweat pants so she could run, liked her hair in braids, off her face, so she could see where she was headed. Today she charged over in polka-dotted leggings and a red leotard top. "Mommy and Daddy is husband and wife!" she announced, the slivers of her black eyes glowing. "We're one big family now!"

Myron gave LaShae a wedding gift: a snakeskin belt with a

snakehead buckle. It was the second or third such belt he'd commissioned for her, along with a snakeskin pocketbook—not that she was
fond of pocketbooks or in much need of belts to hold up the elastic
waist of her pants, but she liked anything having to do with snakes,
and she loved popping up and trying to scare people with the buckles. In the park she would even rush at the guards, waving her fangs.

She thanked him, but put the cobra aside on the table.

"Daddy," she said, "you sit right here, and I'll sit here, and,
Mommy, you stay where you're at." She arranged herself between
them and turned toward Myron.

"Daddy, I need to talk to you."

"Oh, okay, baby. Let's talk."

"You're going to have to sit still."

"Okay, baby, I'm still."

"From now on," she wrinkled her forehead sternly, "and I want
you to listen real good, from now on you're going to be my real
daddy."

"I know, baby, I—"

"I'm not finished. I had a daddy, but…" She seemed to lose track
of her thoughts. She turned toward Marie. It was clear LaShae
couldn't remember what had happened with her father, what she'd
been told about his drifting off, but before her mother could supply
an explanation LaShae peered again at Myron. "Well, we lost him.
So from now on you're going to be my real daddy." After which she
became a five-year-old again, bounced out of her chair, attacked with
the cobra, and struck a deal that if she let Myron and Marie have a
few minutes of quiet he would, at their next park visit, spend two
nonstop hours dueling with her on the thousand-foot rooftop.…

"Take care of my babies."

"No, you take care of *my* baby."

…When the band was abolished by Warden Cain's decree (and
its members forbidden to play a note), Marie convinced Myron that
the band had been a danger anyway. Its freedoms brought too much

resentment, from inmates and staff, that in prison could lead quickly to trouble, fights you were goaded into and charges that were trumped up. Myron's chances with the pardon board could be ruined. It was lucky the band was finished, she said. Now he could fill his prison folder with more signs that he should be let go. He would play guitar again someday.

He joined the CPR team, took the training, carried his three-ringed manual constantly, kept a calendar of the team's teaching schedule as meticulously as he had the band's gigs. Not only did he give instruction to school bus drivers and church congregations and, once, to the residents of O'Brien House, blowing air into his plastic dummy and demonstrating chest compressions and the Heimlich maneuver and quizzing his students, "Are you supposed to roll a conscious or an unconscious person into the recovery position?"—he also took over a course for inmates. He corrected their mistakes carefully, without riding them too hard, and had thirty showing up to study in A Building where there had been only ten.

"Do you know how the CPR team got started?" he asked, keeping them inspired. "It was 'cause of a convict named Big E. He had a heart attack in his dorm, in the TV room. And do you know what the inmates did? The very same ones that went and started this program afterward? They did everything they knew how to do. They opened a few buttons of Big E's work shirt and turned the fan in his direction."

And he enrolled in GED school. When he called to check on LaShae's grades, he told her that now he, too, was a student. "And Mommy's in college, and LaShae's in third grade—what do you think about all that?"

"Well," she said, "it means we're all smart cookies."

"Yeah, and it means if you keep your grades up, Daddy's going to have to get you another snakeskin something."

He brought his own grades up and, after two setbacks in math on the qualifying test, studied all night and made it to the GED exam. On the phone, when his exam scores came in, he told Marie, "I blew that little simple test to the moon."

"That's great. That's just so great, baby."

"I got my degree."

"I knew you would."

"Yeah. I'm a smart cookie, aren't I?"

"Yes, you are."

And she put LaShae on to say, "I'm so proud of you."

A nurse came in after making her rounds on the ward. Myron pulled on a pair of surgical gloves. The nurse drew the sheet away. She checked James's diaper for urine and for any discharge that hadn't reached the colostomy bag. She opened the front of the diaper like a flap—it was never fastened, as he could never shift to disturb it. His penis looked strangely normal, dangling senseless but unwasted.

The knees were irrevocably contorted. A rolled blanket divided them, to keep them from gravitating yet further toward each other, to keep his legs from twisting inward, for his body was trying to close in on itself as though to eliminate limbs altogether, as though to become a single ball. And like his arms, his legs appeared polished, polyurethaned.

Myron lifted one of James's legs off the mattress while the nurse unwound the gauze wrap from his calf. The gauze secured medicated pads to his bedsores. Myron took care to hold the old pads in place as she unwrapped, a precaution against their fingers grazing the fluid from infectious sores and spreading the bacteria. Their hands weaved around each other, he all the while keeping the bent leg in the air. James's calves were not glassy. In patches the sores were as dense and raw as a rash abraded by a metal file. In places you could see straight to the muscle. Otherwise the sores were shaped like stars, a whitish red, moist like the inside of a lip.

"Run me another ep."

"You want another?"

"Yeah. Give me an ep."

"All right. I'll give you one."

Back in February, after three and a half years of marriage, Marie had quit visiting.

It was August now.

"But you said your family was doing good," James protested. "You been telling me that for months."

"That's all you're getting of that ep. I'll have to run you another."

In June, he had quit the CPR team. One of its leaders, jealous, it seemed, over Myron's success with his class, had begun correcting him at every opportunity—during presentations outside the prison, in front of free world people, and during team meetings—and Myron, counting the months and weeks and days since he'd last seen his wife and daughter, could barely endure it. One morning the man leaned his shaved, bullet-shaped head into Myron's A Building classroom, then stepped inside to observe. He signaled Myron out to the hallway while his students waited at their desks.

"You're telling them wrong information."

"How am I doing that?"

"You told them: Look for the sternum notch. That's misguiding."

"How's that?"

"There ain't no sternum notch."

"What the"—Myron edited himself with James's nurse in the room—"do you call this right here?"

"That's the xiphoid process."

"It's the sternum notch. Go get your book while I teach my class."

"I don't need no book. Xiphoid process. Ain't no such thing as a sternum notch. The sternal notch is up by your neck. You ain't teaching according to American Heart Association standards."

"No such thing as a sternum notch?"

"No such thing."

"You a sorry excuse for a team leader."

"You want to do me something?"

"I want you to keep your hard head out my classroom and let me do my job."

"You ain't *doing* your job. You risking lives."

"Motherf— You need to look up 'sternum notch.' And you *need* to learn about communication before you go calling yourself rehabilitated."

"I'm not rehabilitated? You calling the xiphoid process the sternum notch and I'm not rehabilitated?"

Things had grown louder—and much less elevated—from there. Until Myron had walked off, announcing his resignation.

"You want another ep?"

He had received his GED diploma a few weeks ago. It looked like nothing more than the 127 other certificates he'd earned since coming to Angola—the certificates of gratitude for every Big River concert ("We, Cavalier Festivals, Inc., hereby offer our sincere appreciation to your band for the performance you held on…") and for every CPR class he'd taught outside the prison ("On behalf of the Girt Town Community Resource Center…") and the "attendance certificates" he'd earned for a dozen two-day prison programs (the "Success Leadership Series" and the "Conference of HIV Prevention") sponsored over the years by Angola clubs—these proofs nothing more than sheets of white paper printed with frilly borders and fancy script and a line where his name could be typed in. He'd saved them all, but he'd thought his high school diploma would look different. He'd thought it would come inside a leather folder. He'd thought, at least, it would be printed on a nicer kind of paper.

"You want another ep?"

Just about the only song he'd played in the past year, since last October, when Cain had shut the band from the music room, was

"Chestnuts Roasting on an Open Fire." He'd been allowed to plunk that out on the electric piano, behind the mock singing of an inmate comedian at the Toastmasters Christmas Banquet.

"With Marie and without music, I was okay," he told James, whose spirits he had tried, until lately, to bolster with his stories. "And without Marie but with music I would be too. But without both..."

The nurse squeezed fresh ointment onto clean pads, and these, as well, Myron held in place while she circled the lower leg with a new roll of gauze. They treated the other calf and ministered to the sores on James's heels. He asked for Myron's help in coughing. Setting two fingers against the gauze covering James's tracheostomy, Myron jabbed the heel of his palm below the ribs, until James said, "Good. Good." Myron held a Styrofoam cup for James to spit his phlegm into. The nurse changed the colostomy bag and left for another patient.

"Let me tell you that other ep."

Myron didn't know why Marie had stopped visiting. He didn't know why she had quit writing. He didn't know why she told him, whenever he called, that her phone bill was too high. No. He did know. It was because her car had broken down and because her mother was in the hospital and because she'd been studying for exams and because LaShae had poison ivy. And it was all true. But none of these things had ever stopped her before. She'd found a way to visit two, three times a month for years. And when she'd talked about the phone it was sometimes despair but never "Try not to call." And she'd written. That was what the chaplain had told them: Communicate. "No matter what else is happening, no matter how bad things get, no matter when MCI cuts off your long distance, put something on paper. Keep that line of communication." And now it had been six months. Not one letter in response to his own. And when he called to ask why, she pressed 3 and told him he just couldn't call again for a while and assured him nothing was wrong, that it was only because she'd been busy and because LaShae had been wearing her ragged and that if he put in for a park visit they would come next month. They didn't. Which was all right, he told himself, because it was a long drive and you never knew what could happen on the road these days and he didn't want her to exhaust herself, especially when she had to take care of LaShae, who honestly was a handful—it was better that she didn't visit. Really, he was glad. But he wished she'd write. Just that. And he wished that on Mother's Day he didn't feel so timid about calling that when the automated operator told him to record his name he said, "Happy Mother's Day," instead, so Marie would know she didn't have to press 3 at all. And he wished that the few times he'd had the courage to supply her with explanations for what was happening, that either she'd found someone else or was simply beaten down by a marriage to someone who couldn't provide for her in any way—he wished she'd had the courage to answer yes.

"Between you and me," he asked LaShae during one phone call, when Marie had handed her the receiver quickly, "do you think Mommy still loves me?"

"Of course she do, Daddy. She's been grouchy with me, too. *All day.*"

How shitty he had felt for asking, for putting LaShae in that position. And did he really not know enough of the truth? That it was those alphabets, L-I-F-E; that it was a governor who still, twenty months and counting, hadn't signed a pardon, a governor who had two and a half years and then another term remaining; a state that wasn't going to elect anyone less conservative; a pardon board that had just decreed a six-year waiting period between applications, so that if you were rejected once you could forget about the future for a good long while; a parole board dominated by a victim's rights advocate so that if you did, somehow, get what was impossible—the governor's gold seal on a commutation to fixed years—you were going to serve *all* those years, all twenty or thirty or forty of them, which meant that even with the impossible, he, Myron Hodges, would be fifty or sixty or seventy before he got out.

He knew perfectly well what was happening with Marie, and he spent his hours, when he wasn't at the hospital, lying on his cot. Not sleeping. Sleep wasn't all that easy to accomplish. But reading. Romance novels. A cardboard box of used Silhouette and Harlequin paperbacks had somehow found its way to his dorm, a detoured donation to the library. The stories always began with an unexpected, magical love he couldn't quit following, then swooped into misery and back out into a happy ending that left him angry but eager to start another.

He imagined a final scene with Marie, if she ever showed up again at the park. He would pick her a handful of roses from around Main Prison, and these he would present to her along with his GED diploma and all her letters from the years before this one and the first picture they'd ever taken in the visiting shed in front of the streaking light—Marie in a pink sweater and LaShae in a darker pink top, Marie and Myron with their arms around each other, and LaShae in front holding their free hands—and his wedding ring.

In the meantime, on his cot, he took off the band and placed it in his locker box, inside LaShae's empty sack printed with Power Rangers. It stayed there for two days. But knowing he might never see Marie or LaShae again, that they might already have vanished permanently from his life, he needed the ring back on. He unburied it.

They were still married, weren't they?

And he sent LaShae a homemade card for her birthday, an eight-frame comic strip drawn in stick figures: Myron baking a birthday cake and burning it; Marie taking over, placing nine candles in a perfect creation of angel food; Daddy charring the ribs in the yard behind Marie's trailer; Mommy bopping him with a spatula to chase him away again; she and LaShae cooking, warding off Daddy's help; Daddy and LaShae sword-fighting with sticks and paper cups; Daddy knocked off the skyscraper and falling a thousand feet; Daddy climbing back up.

Myron had two answers to my question about advice for Johnny Brooks. "I would tell him not to," he said emphatically, at first. And then: "I used to be numb. I used to not feel anything."

He left the room sometime after the dressings were changed, returned to mopping floors and emptying trash. But before the end of his shift he tried to stop back in, to make sure James didn't need anything, and to massage his face one last time: chin; cheekbones; eyelids; forehead; temples.

S E V E N T E E N

JOHNNY BROOKS CHECKED HIS WATCH. IT WAS 8:14 in the morning, the chapel quiet except for the scattered words spoken by Brooks and the two convicts in his wedding party. Their special clothes were as carefully planned as any set of tuxedos, as any ensemble of blue blazers and white flannels. The groomsmen wore identical light blue short-sleeved dress shirts to go with their sharply pressed jeans. And the groom, whose jeans matched theirs perfectly for shade and ironing, was distinguished by a simple gray western shirt with faux-pearl snaps, by his white straw cowboy hat adorned with a black band, and by a 1992 "All-Around Cowboy" belt buckle.

They compared watches. 8:14. 8:15. 8:20.

"Eight-twenty? You got eight-twenty?" Brooks looked wide-eyed at the groomsman with the fastest watch.

"Call it eight-sixteen, Johnny," the other one said.

A few weeks ago, Belva had finally made it for the chaplain's conference. They'd finally gotten approval. But she and her bridesmaids weren't here now, and the wedding was set for eight o'clock.

Brooks pried a pack of Wrigley's Spearmint from his tight jeans pocket. "My heart's beating a hundred miles an hour waiting for my fiancée to walk in that door."

"You sure they had a car?"

"They had one."

The talk died out. Sitting on one of the red-cushioned chairs, Brooks leaned far forward with his elbows on his knees, all but doubled over.

It was 8:30. Or 8:31. Or 8:36.

"You want me to ask the chaplain will he call and see if they're at the front gate?"

"Yeah. See can he call."

The chaplain picked up the phone. The three men watched him in his side office, behind the half-open sliding glass door.

No, Belva wasn't at the front gate.

A cake with flowered icing, made by one of the inmates at Camp F, sat on a table at the back of the sanctuary, next to a yellow-and-maroon water cooler. Brooks, jamming more gum in his mouth and leaning forward again, spoke toward the floor: "I was up all night just staring at the ceiling."

No one answered.

Eventually one of the groomsmen exclaimed, "I'm going to get to kiss the bride!"

Brooks straightened, gave a playful glance, smacked his fist into his palm. "You giving her away," he reminded.

"To who? I'm gonna say, 'I can't. She loves *me*.'"

"She'll say that's not true."

The others listened to this literal-minded fear dangling in the air, not diminishing.

"Nah," the joking one assured. "I'm glad for you. I'm glad you got somebody in your life."

8:50.

"It's hot," the groom declared, sweat beading below his hat, though the sanctuary was air-conditioned, comfortable. "After the ceremony I'll take off this undershirt I bought—you can take it back to the camp when me and Belva go on to the visiting shed."

8:55. 8:56. 9:01.

He stood, paced, went outside for a cigarette, stepped back in, cowboy boots clicking on the tile. "Wow!" he announced, laughing, not quite believing she wouldn't come but nowhere close to believing how sick he felt.

9:08.

The chaplain hung up the phone.

They'd just come through.

September the fifth, 1997. That was Johnny Brooks's wedding day. In exactly one month, on Sunday, the fifth of October, the rodeo would begin. And this inmate so determined to look special, to look *right,* for anyone from the outside world, whether for his bride or for the entire rodeo crowd, whether with his wedding clothes or with the turquoise and black suede vest he'd sported in the stadium last year— this rider, Johnny Brooks, would be required to wear a shirt of thick, coarse cloth with black-and-white stripes two inches wide. He would be forced to wear this replica of the old-fashioned convict uniform. He would be made to wear what hadn't been worn at Angola in almost half a century, what had been abolished during the reforms that followed the heel slashings of 1951. He would put on the stripes that had been a symbolic flogging, that had been a reminder to the inmates of their abject powerlessness, and a reminder to the public, whenever it saw photographs of the convicts, that those men were different, were scarcely men at all, were something closer to animals.

At 7:30, the morning of the wedding, Mr. Darrell had stopped by Camp F for Brooks and his groomsmen. He had driven them, in the cab of his pickup, to the front of Main Prison. It was an honor to ride with an assistant warden. Brooks was pleased. He never complained to me that neither Mr. Darrell nor Mr. Mike attended the wedding. He never complained that Warden Cain didn't show. Perhaps it didn't matter at all once Belva arrived. Perhaps I was the only one waiting to see whether the people who insisted that they saw Brooks as a human being first, and a prisoner second, would make the gesture of standing at the back of the sanctuary. Perhaps I was the only one waiting to see whether the man who called himself Daddy would make an appearance to offer congratulations. (Brooks was, presently, Cain's own car washer at the Ranch House.) In the idiosyncratic world of Angola, such personal gestures on this one day wouldn't have broken any unbreachable codes. But perhaps Brooks had known all along that they wouldn't come, even as he'd spoken—all eager expectation—of their presence. Perhaps, at some level, he didn't want them anywhere near his wedding.

One of Belva's bridesmaids, wearing a long black lace dress and a choker of pearls, pinned a white boutonniere near the collar of Brooks's shirt. The second member of her party, also in black, also in pearls, fixed the same white rose to each of the groomsmen. Below a spray of baby's breath in her short hair, below pearl post earrings and her pearl necklace, Belva wore a white satin suit, its high neck trimmed in brocade. Over the rest of her large, forgiving body, the suit was shimmering yet simple, resplendent but dignified.

"How you doing?" Brooks asked, slipping between the other women to stand cautiously beside his bride in the sanctuary's entryway.

"I'm all right, Johnny," she said slowly. She looked drained by the two-and-a-half-hour drive and by a delay while the women lined up, in the hut outside the gate, to be scanned with a metal detector and patted down by hand, and she looked dazed by the fact of this moment in this place, deeper inside the prison than she had ever been, down the Walk on this cloudless, dry-aired, gorgeous morning, through internal gate after gate after gate, past the disciplinary cases in their jumpsuits dusting the cement walls and the yard orderlies slapping listlessly with their hoes at the already-tilled ground and the library man tugging his crate of old law dictionaries toward the cell-blocks, casters squeaking as he pulled the fraying rope. There was, between bride and groom in the chapel, a prolonged hush. There was nothing.

"Hi, Johnny," she said for a second time since arriving. And then her smile materialized—a smile that remained almost without interruption for the next half hour—heightened by the flowers and the earrings and the necklace and the dress against her brown and smooth and glowing skin.

The stripes—for Johnny Brooks, for Buckkey Lasseigne, for all the riders—were Cain's idea. Before the rodeo he put out word that he wanted the previous year's participants brought to the Main Prison visiting shed. "Right away." There he told his audience of his vision, what an improvement he thought it would be, how well the riders would stand out. "But we're not going to force y'all to wear them. We're going to put it to a vote. How many of y'all want to wear those uniforms? Raise your hands."

Everyone did.

The warden's move had particular significance. He had encouraged an ABC news program—one of the shows that had portrayed him so favorably in the past—to film the rodeo. And the cameras were coming. Were the stripes some involuntary gesture of self-exposure on Cain's part? An unconscious effort to announce to the world who he really was? Or was his message much more conspiratorial, was he seizing his chance to whisper—to a TV audience of millions—that he could fulfill some of our most fundamental wishes? For as the rodeo began, and the inmates started flying and crashing for the fans in the stadium and for the cameras that would broadcast their catapulted bodies all over the nation, the stripes served us in two ways. They helped to tell us that those bodies belonged to convicts, that the natural desire to see a man bloodied or demolished could be indulged, in this case, without much guilt. And then, too, the uniforms helped to gratify another longing just as basic: that murderers and rapists and armed robbers—the worst of sinners—be not at all like us, that they be largely inhuman. So we could indulge our violent instincts and purge them at the same time. *We* weren't the animals; along with the rodeo stock, the animals were out there, in the stripes, in the ring.

The Cowboys for Christ minister arrived at the chapel around the same time as Belva, but no one had worried that he wouldn't show. Rick LeDoux, with his own oversize belt buckle (embossed with a Bible and a dove), belonged to an organization of three hundred preachers devoted to missionary work among cowboys worldwide. LeDoux proselytized at horse shows and led evangelical trail rides and came to Camp F twice each month to hold services. A horse trainer by profession, today he wore a black neckerchief and gray Wrangler jeans. He touched the couple's shoulders and asked if they wanted their ceremony to include anything special.

Brooks and Belva looked at each other, laughing shyly. "Just getting married," Brooks replied.

So in the quiet, nearly empty sanctuary the groomsmen offered their arms and led the bridesmaids up the aisle. One of the men returned for the bride. The procession moved as deliberately as if a wedding march resounded to the ceiling, as if two hundred guests filled the red chairs.

A bridesmaid started to sing a cappella, got through one verse before choking up.

I believe that every night
A candle glows....

Then LeDoux, tall and reedy, unzipped his little black Bible case and began. "Well, I'm not your traditional preacher. But Johnny's a cowboy and I guess it's right that he have a cowboy to marry him."

How fine that must have sounded to Johnny Brooks!

"I guess it's right that he have something a little different."

Yet what has stayed with me, in the time since, is how much of the wedding was like countless others, once it came down to those three people—minister facing the attentive couple—with the groomsmen smiling and the bridesmaids snuffling in the background. LeDoux read the standard passages: the creation of male and female; the path of man from parents to wife; the warning, "What God hath joined together, let not man put asunder." And half deaf with nervousness, the bride and groom heard what few words they absorbed as if those phrases had never before been spoken in quite this way.

Look therefore carefully how ye walk, not as unwise, but as wise; redeeming the time, for the days are evil....Be filled with the Spirit, speaking to one another in psalms and hymns.

Johnny and Belva turned to each other and held hands, his cradling hers. They repeated, "I pledge my heart and my love to serve you all of my days."

They exchanged rings, repeating, "As you wear it, let it continue to remind you of the vows you have said to me."

Johnny's gaze was steady and Belva's voice was cracking and the bridesmaids' snuffling had become open weeping. The bride and groom kissed. The groom hugged the groomsmen, the groomsmen hugged the bridesmaids, and the minister kissed Belva and hugged

Brooks. It was over. Everyone filed to the back and no one knew what to say. The women giggled over something—or nothing—and the men stared at their cowboy boots. There was the distraction of signing the marriage license at a chaplain's desk, and of having me find the right angle to memorialize the moment with my small camera. "*Missus* Brooks!" a bridesmaid announced, and there was the distraction of thin laughter.

Then someone remembered:

"You got to cut the cake!"

"We want to eat that cake!"

"You got to feed each other!"

Hands overlapping on the knife handle, the newlyweds sliced into the pale green icing. Pretzling their arms, they stuffed each other's mouths and left dabs of green on each other's lips and chins. The minister cut more pieces and the groom passed out Dixie cups of water from the yellow-and-maroon cooler and after everyone ate I lined them up for a photograph in which Brooks smiles and tips his head back. He is blissful.

In stripes they mounted their bulls, their broncos. In stripes they waved to their families in the stands, those whose families had come. Buckkey waved to his wife. His son was not there. He had not visited since that time at the park months ago. "The little—" Buckkey cut himself off, aborted his own bitterness, as we spoke near the chutes. "He'll come. He's going to start coming," Buckkey decided. "I know he will. He'll take pity on his old man." He laughed.

"But you know what, Dan? I'm not doing this for him anymore. And I'm not doing it to prove anything to them." He gestured with the back of his hand in the direction of the range crew staff. "I don't know why I'm doing it. I guess it's just something for me. I guess I want to do better than runner-up. I guess I want to win it for me."

Then he walked into the ring for the Wild Horse Race. As teams
of three struggled to hold their broncos by a single rope while one
man tried to mount and ride, Buckkey, in stripes, was kicked in the
thigh and knocked to the ground. But he kept his hold on the rope.
He pulled himself up and edged forward. He maneuvered again to
throw one leg over. The animal snapped a kick like a black belt's,
driving its hoof into his stomach. Buckkey was on all fours. He
couldn't stand up. Other horses thrashed nearby. No one wanted to
get too close. Someone opened a chute gate, and he crawled ten or
twenty feet across the arena. He crawled inside. The gate was pulled
shut. From above, I stared down into the wooden well that was
horse-size, bull-size, and that made Buckkey look tiny. He waited for
the event to end, curled on his side like a fetus on the dirt.

Shucked, hurled, strewn. Danny Fabre, in stripes, somersaulted off a
bull, and in stripes, on the second Sunday, he got his hand caught
the wrong way in his rigging, cracking the bones along the back of
his palm.

He had been thinking, still, that the warden might authorize the
remaking of his ears. But in the days following his injury, his hand
and lower arm in a cast, he came to a decision. He'd had enough.
Other inmates, he knew, would have gone on competing.

"I'm not going out there to get killed for these people," he said.
"I'm not going to give them what they want."

Alone among the riders, Donald Cook—who went on biding his
time, planning for escape, and dreaming of destroying his ex-wife's
face with acid—didn't mind the stripes. He was in favor of them. "I
was thinking about how we should do this myself, even before Cain
brought it up."

He was kicked in the forehead—half an inch from his eye—as he

crept up on a bronco in one Wild Horse Race. With blood streaming into the eye, he collected himself, approached again, took another
kick to the head, blacked out, came to, pushed himself off the dirt,
and began yet another attempt before collapsing unconscious and
being dragged away. At the hospital he received thirty-odd stitches in
an arc from eyebrow to temple, and then lobbied a lieutenant to over-
rule his duty status so he could go on riding. On the final Sunday, in
the Bust-Out, a bull trampled over him, shattering his ankle and foot.
Still, before he allowed himself to be driven off by the EMS truck
and casted at the hospital, he hobbled toward yet another wild horse
as his teammates held a rope that could do nothing to keep the animal from planting a hoof that would pulverize him.

Besides the stripes, Cain had brought another innovation to the
rodeo: He redesigned the competition. Always, every Sunday, twelve
inmates were given places in the bareback and the bull riding. Traditionally, many of the slots had gone to the marginally experienced
men, the convicts on the range crew and those who worked the few
other livestock jobs at the prison. This year, Cain ordered that the
regulars not be favored over the completely inexperienced. The new
system, he said, made the rodeo more fair. It gave everyone a chance.
But it also reduced the minimal aspect of skill within the spectacle—
and increased the chances of injury. It made more likely what happened to one rider, in stripes, who sailed from a bronco and landed
directly on his back, breaking a vertebra, and what happened to
another, whose inner-tube belly and chunky, flaccid thighs marked
him as so clearly unqualified to ride. His horse reared and rocked
forward as it left the chute, flipping the heavyset man into a kind of
backward pike. He landed on his head. His neck folded under him.
He lay unconscious, motionless but for one quivering leg. Indepen-
dent of his limp body, the leg went on twitching, as though attached

to its own electric cable, until the EMS team strapped him down and carted him off.

Johnny Brooks, on the first Sunday, drew a piebald bull that vaulted off its hind hooves right out of the chute. Then it yanked Brooks forward, almost clapping his forehead into the top of its skull. Belva was in the crowd. Kenny and Marcus, Brooks's new stepsons, were at home, awaiting the bull-riding and all-around buckles he had pledged to win them. But for these seconds of riding, even the yearning to impress his bride and children was driven from his mind. Everything was driven from it. Brain useless with fear, body owned by reflex, Brooks was excellent and helpless, free. With his left arm held high in classic rodeo position, he sliced the air and regained his balance. The bull leapt and Brooks's ass floated off the hide. Two feet of atmosphere divided him from the animal. Yet, even airborne, he kept control of his body. Landing on the animal's spine, he stayed with the bull as it lunged and twisted. He kept spurring, fighting the spin. He sliced and sliced with his left arm against the pull of centrifugal force. He lasted.

Under Cain's system, Brooks was given only one more bull ride for the rest of the month. By that second ride, on the final Sunday, he had broken his wrist in another event and was competing in a cast. Belva had signed the plaster, and printed the names of his children and her parents, his new family. Brooks's second bull dispatched him within two seconds.

But he had accumulated enough points to win the all-around. The prize was awarded without much ceremony. Just before the Guts & Glory, the emcee announced Brooks's name. Quickly, almost covertly, Cain handed him the buckle at one end of the ring, near the chutes. The crowd applauded indifferently. They didn't know Johnny Brooks from any other Angola convict. They wanted to get to the Guts & Glory. But before the hurried presentation ended, and the bull with the red chip was sent into the ring, Johnny Brooks, in stripes, spoke to the warden. "Warden Cain," he said, as he had two years ago, "this is for you. To show my appreciation." And Brooks gave him the all-around buckle.

A short while earlier, Cain had been standing with the judges in their crow's nest. He liked to gaze down on the rodeo from there. During a break between events, he stepped toward the back of the perch and leaned against the railing. "Now listen up!" he called down to the convict riders in their section of the bleachers. "Y'all put on such a good show, made this such a successful rodeo all month, that I'm going to put an extra hundred dollars on the bull's horns today. Give y'all some added incentive in that Guts & Glory."

As I stood with the inmates, I lifted my eyes toward the bloated body, the small hands spread confidently on the railing, the luxuriant white hair swept elegantly across the forehead. My eyes met Cain's. For months he had been avoiding my attempts to interview him, scheduling and then breaking appointments. I could seize this moment, yell up to him. With the inmates all listening, he might have to ask me up to the crow's nest for a quick round of questions. I averted my gaze.

"And we thank you, Lord, for Warden Burl Cain," the chaplain had spoken during the rodeo's opening prayer. What did I really need to ask the warden? Two things, I suppose: What is in your mind? And what is in your heart? And given that these questions were, ultimately, unanswerable, I could let myself off easy. I could tell myself that my understanding of him, as he sweetened the bait for his striped men, was complete. Because I really didn't want to talk with him. Indeed, I really didn't want to watch the rodeo anymore. I wanted to go home.

Then Terry Hawkins went out to grab that Guts & Glory chip. During the month, he had used both of his strategies: He had taunted the bull and run away along a tight curve; he had stood and taken the direct hit. The bull had run over him, hoof cutting his cheek and grazing his throat. It had sent him into an airborne cartwheel. And now Terry found himself too close to the fence. He *knew* he was too close, that if he didn't flee he would be isolated and trapped, with nothing to distract the animal once it came for him. He stayed. He held the fence with one hand, thinking maybe he could force himself between the steel cords, escape that way. With his other hand he reached out toward the bull. It charged.

Swinging low with its horns, the huge animal struck Terry behind the thighs, upending him and flinging him into the air. His body spun on every axis. He gyrated and wound up falling with his belly facing the ground. It was almost the equal of last year's flight, but it didn't last as long. The bull didn't launch him over and over. Terry came down on a horn.

And of course, at times, I had thought that this was exactly what he wanted: to offer himself up to Mr. Denver Tarter, the slaughterhouse owner he had murdered. I had thought that this explained his devotion to an event no one else approached so recklessly. No matter. He discovered himself indestructible. The point of the horn met with the center of his chest, but he bounced off, the wind knocked out of him, and was left, after a week's healing, with only a bruise to the bone and a ragged, silver-dollar-size scab.

What would I have glimpsed had the horn somehow exposed the workings of his heart? What vision?

Unseeing, unknowing, I had, instead, only a list of reasons why he kept doing this to himself, a list I struggled to arrange in order, as though by weighing the importance of his motives, by assigning a rough percentage to each, I could understand him at his core.

Two hundred dollars.

The range crew.

Self-punishment and purging.

And then, too, another kind of cleansing, a momentary washing away of everything about his existence, in a thrill of fear and adrenaline.

How could I know what drove him most? And how, in the end, could it matter?

For one thing was clear, that in these desires he wanted what anyone, anywhere, did: money, a better life, a clear conscience, and oblivion.

And like anyone who climbs to some high, public precipice, ready to jump, like anyone who takes a handful of sleeping pills and leaves the bottle by the bedside, knowing that someone will come home, like anyone who has ever so much as imagined the wording of his own suicide note, Terry, beckoning the horns in front of five thousand people, wanted to be saved, whether he deserved it or not.

This was his way of asking.

A F T E R W O R D

"THE DEVIL'S GOING TO GET HIM," WARDEN CAIN set forth my destiny for Louisiana's state senate judiciary committee.

The *Harper's* magazine article—about the rodeo—that had first brought me to Angola had just been published in the February 1998 issue. But the article, in its final form, included more than the rodeo. It included Warden Cain. It included Amherst. And the chairman of the judiciary committee had called hearings, wanting to know more about my allegations, and wanting to find out exactly what was going on up at the prison.

So the warden and I sat side by side below the senators, answering their questions. When a microphone broke, we were forced to lean toward the same mike, our shoulders all but touching. The scene was intimate and, with the state's TV news teams in full attendance, very public.

Cain testified, at first, that he'd never demanded payment from me, only asked my opinion about what sort of advance he might expect were he to write an autobiography. Then he allowed that he had requested money, but only because he'd believed my book was to be a personal portrait of him and his family, unrelated to his position at Angola. He elaborated that in pursuing his biography I had met with his wife and family, and that, early on, I had spent time at his home. How easy it had been, he told the committee, for him to misunderstand the focus of my book. And how surely the devil would seize me for my lies.

And yet more important than the contradictions and comedy of Warden Cain's alibis (I have never met his wife, never been to his home) was his success at silencing any testimony that might corroborate my own about his approach to the inmates and his standing with the staff at the prison. The committee chairman, having heard through his own sources that my portrayal in the article was accurate, had tried to line up supporting witnesses. No employee would testify against Cain. Nor would any of the inmates whose long records of good conduct lent them credibility. They all believed their statements would be futile, that the hearings would amount to nothing, that their lives would remain, as ever, his.

They were almost certainly right.

As it was, the cameras rolled and the hearings led the evening news and made the front pages of the Louisiana papers, and eight months later Cain retains all his power and looks forward to more. A recent federal law, the Prison Litigation Reform Act, driven through Congress to ensure that incarceration not be too costly to the taxpayers or too joyful for the convicts, will likely free Angola from federal oversight within the coming months. Judge Polozola and his court-appointed investigators will be removed as the only check on Warden Cain's rule.

The warden's kingdom will soon be sealed.

It is a place I think back on with despair, a place I left with no soothing affirmation of God's presence. But I did see men struggling to rise, men whose efforts made me wonder constantly: What do we owe them?

A thousand times I repeated to myself all the reasons one could answer: Nothing. We owe them nothing. They have destroyed other lives; what obligates us to help in reconstructing theirs? What is our duty beyond protecting ourselves, our society, by putting them away?

Yet we are their keepers. They may need or deserve to be kept, but it is precisely in making this decision that we take on responsibility. We take control of their lives. And so, unavoidably, we are obligated. We owe them something more than a perverse rodeo as a vehicle for self-improvement and a way to make themselves known. We owe them our help and our attention. We cannot both claim and forget them.

For within them, there is possibility. Look, one last time, at Littell. Imagine stirring your own shit to douse your neighbor as he leaves his house. Imagine your life revolving around that. And measure the distance between that and the life Littell is now making for himself. He is working for a small trucking company, driving a route between Oregon and Georgia. He calls me every so often from truck stops. In his need to "establish" himself, he drives at least the legal limit of ten hours per day. He earns twenty-three cents per mile. He pays his expenses on the road. It is not much of a living, but it *is* a living, and when he calls he says he is doing great, that the job is excellent, that his boss is fair and prizes him for the relentless effort he puts in. And he reports that this country, all the land he passes, is "fucking beautiful." Try to measure the distance between what Littell was and who he is now. It is impossible. The distance is infinite. Or nonexistent. For both then and now are contained in one person.

And in that, there may be a sign for all of us.

ACKNOWLEDGMENTS

Endless thanks to my agent, Suzanne Gluck, and, for their faith and excellent guidance, to my editors, Steve Ross and Ayesha Pande. Huge gratitude also to Colin Harrison, Lewis Lapham, and *Harper's* magazine. And to Cynthia Fox, William Hogeland, Roland Kelts, and Laura Marmor, great appreciation for readings and criticism that, at various stages, helped to shape this story.

Beyond the literary part of this project, I owe a debt to more people than I can name. But without the perfect counsel of two lawyers, William D'Armond and Bradley Meyers, this book might not exist. Saul B. Shapiro also gave invaluable legal advice in moments of panic. And were it not for the late Alvin B. Rubin, esteemed judge of the U.S. Court of Appeals for the Fifth Circuit, I would never have come to know Louisiana and the Angola rodeo in the first place.

Jane Praeger, Brian Belfiglio, Alexia Brue, and Elissa Wald all gave vital support in seeing the book through.

My coverage of Angola's history relies heavily on several sources: Ann Butler and C. Murray Henderson's *Angola: A Half-Century of Rage and Reform* (Lafayette, Louisiana: The Center for Louisiana Studies, 1990); Mark Carleton's *Politics and Punishment: The History of the Louisiana State Penal System* (Baton Rouge: Louisiana State

University Press, 1980); *The Wall Is Strong: Corrections in Louisiana,* edited by Burk Foster, Wilbert Rideau, and Douglas Dennis (Lafayette, Louisiana: The Center for Louisiana Studies, 1995); *Life Sentences: Rage and Survival Behind Bars,* edited by Wilbert Rideau and Ron Wilkberg (New York: Times Books, 1992); the generously shared and prodigious unpublished research of former Angola assistant warden Roger Thomas; and the work of the *Angolite,* whose modern editors have been Michael Glover, Tommy Mason, Wilbert Rideau, Billy Sinclair, and Ron Wilkberg.

But how to thank all the people who put up with my hours and hours, days and days, months and months of questioning? In the cases of many inmates and employees, I cannot thank them; they would rather not be named. Yet I can express my gratitude to Keith Nordyke, civil rights attorney long involved with the prison, for returning my relentless calls and providing indispensable analysis on a wide range of issues. I am indebted as well to former warden C. Murray Henderson, who is, unfairly, scarcely mentioned in the book but whose unflagging belief in rehabilitation is an inspiration. I want to thank Hayes Williams, lead plaintiff in the 1971 lawsuit, for his recollections. And I think it is safe to print my gratitude to two inmates with whom I spent a great deal of time but who were not, finally, part of this narrative, Leotis Webster and Tyrone Jack. To them, to the men who form the core of this book, and to all the others: Your patience and honesty were crucial to me and, I hope in the end, important to everyone's understanding.

Finally, I want to thank my father: a moral guide.